EUROPE KNOWS NOTHING ABOUT THE ORIENT

A CRITICAL DISCOURSE FROM THE EAST (1872–1932)

Koç University Press: 238

HISTORY | CULTURAL STUDIES

Europe Knows Nothing about the Orient: A Critical Discourse from the East (1872–1932)
Zeynep Çelik

Translations: Gregory Key, Nergis Perçinel, Micah A. Hughes, İlker Hepkaner, Aron Aji
Translation editor: Aron Aji
Originally published in Turkish, *Avrupa Şark'ı Bilmez: Eleştirel Bir Söylem (1872–1932)* by Koç University Press.
Editor and coordinator: Sibel Doğru
Index: John Stonor
Book design: Gökçen Ergüven, Emre Çıkınoğlu
Cover design: Emre Çıkınoğlu

Print: A4 Ofset
Otosanayi Sitesi, Donanma Sk. No: 16 Seyrantepe/İstanbul

Sertifika No: 44739
+90 212 281 64 48

Koç University Press
Rumelifeneri Yolu 34450 Sarıyer/İstanbul
kup@ku.edu.tr • www.kocuniversitypress.com • www.kocuniversitesiyayinlari.com

Certificate no: 18318
+90 212 338 1000

Koç University Suna Kıraç Library Cataloging-in-Publication Data
  Çelik, Zeynep
    Europe Knows Nothing about the Orient: A Critical Discourse from the East (1872–1932) = Avrupa Şark'ı Bilmez: Eleştirel Bir Söylem (1872–1932) / Zeynep Çelik; translations Gregory Key, Nergis Perçinel, Micah A. Hughes, İlker Hepkaner, Aron Aji; editor and coordinator Sibel Doğru; book design Gökçen Ergüven, Emre Çıkınoğlu. -First Edition- Istanbul: Koç University Press, 2021.
    280 pages; 16,5 x 24 cm. Koç University Press 238; History / Cultural Studies
    Includes index.
    ISBN 9786057685353
    1. Orientalism. I. Çelik, Zeynep. II. Key, Gregory. III. Perçinel, Nergis. IV. Hughes, Micah A. V. Hepkaner, İlker. VI. Aji, Aron. VII. Doğru, Sibel. VIII. Ergüven, Gökçen. VIII. Çıkınoğlu, Emre.
    DS61.85.C4413 2021

Europe Knows Nothing about the Orient

A Critical Discourse from the East (1872–1932)

ZEYNEP ÇELİK

Translations: Gregory Key, Nergis Perçinel, Micah A. Hughes, İlker Hepkaner, Aron Aji

KUP

Table of Contents

Acknowledgments

Europe Knows Nothing about the Orient is the outcome of a collaborative effort and an intricate process. It would not have been possible to undertake this complicated production without the unequivocal commitment of Koç University Press. I cannot think of any other publishing house that would commit to such an adventure. I am very grateful to the editorial board for trusting me and for believing in the project. Rana Alpöz, the executive director, was engaged in every step, from our preliminary discussions to the printing. Her expertise, rigor and reliability, accompanied by her gentle demeanor, make her the ideal working companion. I would also like to thank Umran İnan, the president of Koç University, Buket Coşkuner and Christopher Roosevelt, respectively the manager and the director of Koç University Research Center for Anatolian Civilizations (ANAMED), whose support was indispensable.

I benefitted from Sibel Doğru's contribution on many fronts. As the managing editor, she coordinated difficult transactions, going back and forth between our many collaborators. She kept a diligent schedule, was prompt, professional, energetic, and always in a good mood. Sibel's engagement extended to the entire process. She helped me locate the relevant texts, choose the visual materials, and retrieve them from the archives. Her attention to detail was essential in the copy-editing and proofreading phases in both Turkish and English.

Looking back, I am overwhelmed at the scale of the labor involved and profoundly grateful to everybody who took part in it. There is a lot of teamwork in every book, but I believe we hit a record with this one, stemming from the heterogeneous nature of the original texts included. A trajectory of the history of its making may help explain its complexity. Let me begin with the Turkish version, published several months earlier than the English version: identifying the texts, selecting the relevant excerpts, transliterating many from Arabic to Latin alphabet, and updating the language for contemporary readers. Knowledgeable and talented individuals contributed with their intellectual labor. Fatma Damak and Esra Derya Gönen transliterated the Ottoman texts and updated their language. Sibel Doğru undertook the copy-editing of the package, followed by Nihal Boztekin's fine-tooth combing of the entire volume for linguistic flow, a particularly arduous task that requires keen sensibility.

Translating into English the Ottoman and the early Republic Turkish in which the historical documents were originally written is a notoriously challenging task, compounded by the differences in the voices included in the volume, as well as the shifts in the language over the period covered. The collection was divided up among several translators, the translations were then copy-edited, and finally revised by a translation editor. A dedicated team consisting of İlker Hepkaner, Micah A. Hughes, Gregory Key, and Nergis Perçinel translated the different sections. Using his top-notch linguistic skills in Ottoman Turkish, Gregory Key bravely copy-edited the majority of the entries in "A Reader." Aron Aji joined us in the final stage as translation editor. With his impeccable command of both languages, elegant use of English, and his concern and ability to preserve the multiple voices in the collection, he was able to capture the rich linguistic range of the original texts for English readers.

Bahattin Öztuncay took time from his busy schedule to select provocative photographs with me, and Ömer Koç opened his archives in his typically courteous manner. The cover and book designs were done by Emre Çıkınoğlu and Gökçen Ergüven respectively, with an aesthetic integrity in accord with the contents. I greatly appreciated the intellectual generosity of Ayşen Gür, translator from English and French into Turkish, and Aron Aji. They both provided substantial and relentless critical feedback. I am deeply grateful to them for their belief in *Europe Knows Nothing about the Orient* and for being terrific comrades. Aron Aji turned into a good Zoom friend, peppering our long conversations with his sense of humor. My communications with Ayşen were dotted with much laughter—and some family stories.

My thanks go also to İnci Enginün, who kindly went over my choice of texts, and to Rüya Pamuk, who read my first draft with great attention and made wise suggestions. My dear friends Zainab Bahrani and Jerrilynn Dodds convinced me of the book's value and gave me their enthusiastic support. A seminar I taught with Tunç Şen on methodologies in Ottoman historiography at Columbia University in Fall 2019 provoked my thoughts on the topic when I was writing the Introduction. I learned a great deal from our class discussions, and from Professor Şen. My last public lecture before Covid-19 hit New York City was on this topic at the Heyman Humanities Center of Columbia University, in March 2020. The questions and comments by the attendees helped me refine my text. Finally, I am indebted to my son Ali Winston. As always, I cherish his alert and unreserved critical perspective.

Note on Spelling, Transliteration, and Dates

Words and names in Ottoman Turkish have been transliterated without using the complicated system of diacritics. However, we remained close to Ottoman spelling as opposed to modern Turkish spelling, especially with respect to words ending in "b" and "d." For example, we opted for Ahmed over Ahmet and Edib over Edip. For words which have entered the English language, such as "pasha," we followed the standard English spelling.

Prior to the surname law, passed on June 21, 1934, and put into effect in January 1935, Turkish names constituted a person's given name, sometimes followed by his or her father's name. While all the texts included in "A Reader" date from the pre-surname law, their authors acquired surnames after 1935. These are indicated in brackets in the Authors' Biographies section.

The Ottoman dating system is based on the Hegira (AD 622). When the dates are converted to the Gregorian calendar, the Hegirian date is given first, followed by the Gregorian one.

"Europe Knows Nothing about the Orient":
A Critical Discourse from the East (1872–1932)

The Formation of a Discourse

"Europe Knows Nothing about the Orient" (Avrupa Şark'ı Bilmcz) is the *cri de coeur* of Ottoman intellectual Namık Kemal and the title of his famous article, published in the periodical *İbret* in 1872.[1] Namık Kemal's short essay marked the beginning of a passionate Ottoman discourse that targeted the misrepresentations, distortions, and factual errors of European authors who wrote about the history of the Ottoman Empire and about Islam. Namık Kemal's fiery rhetoric caught on. Worldly, cosmopolitan, and engaged in projects of modernity, late nineteenth- and early twentieth-century intellectuals in Istanbul did not remain passive to European representations of the "Orient." Dispersed throughout the pages of scholarly and popular periodicals and books, similar reactions surfaced in all genres of writing, from political commentary to literary criticism, novels, satires, and even poetry. The critique of European misconceptions focused on a wide range of social and cultural issues, among them religion, social norms, everyday life, gender, and fine arts. Many opposing voices attempted to "correct" the images that had been, and were being, drawn by Europeans. Charged with their own ideological agendas, the late Ottoman and early Republican intellectuals may have turned and twisted the cultural debates to serve their own ends, but their opinions coalesced into a discontented ensemble, albeit one heard only locally. Their discourse was disjointed, it surfaced in unexpected places, and it was expressed in powerful and often inflammatory language. But it remained unknown to audiences beyond the Turkish-speaking world.

This book listens to the tirades and the dialogues among the late Ottoman and early Republican intellectuals over the span of more than a century, hoping to widen the geography and historiography of contra-Orientalist criticism. The decades from the 1870s to the 1930s, the period covered in the current volume, were marked by

---

1   Namık Kemal, "Avrupa Şark'ı Bilmez," *İbret*, no. 7 (16 Rebiulahir 1289/June 23, 1872): 2.

several wars with disastrous consequences for the Ottoman Empire as well as major political and ideological shifts. The wars with Russia (1877–78) and Italy (1911), the Balkan Wars (1912–13), World War I (1914–18), and the War of Independence (1919–22) each ended with significant losses of land, the last two sealing the empire's demise. Politically, the state underwent two constitutional regimes: the first one was short-lived and lasted from December 23, 1876 to February 14, 1878, while the second one was led by the Young Turks from July 23, 1908 to April 11, 1920. The intervening years witnessed the long and controversial reign of Abdülhamid II (August 31, 1876 to April 27, 1909). Then came the foundation of the Grand National Assembly of Turkey (April 23, 1920) and the Turkish Republic (October 29, 1923), followed by the Lausanne Treaty that acknowledged it (July 23, 1924).

Dominant ideological positions moved back and forth between Ottomanism, Turkism, Turanism,[2] Islamism, nationalism, secularism, modernism, statism, and liberalism, and their myriad interpretations, with significant overlaps between them. It is not easy to imagine the mindsets of the individuals caught up in this storm. In *Suyu Arayan Adam* (A Man in Search of Water), Şevket Süreyya Aydemir offered some insights through his own life experience. As a young man, he wrote, he listened to "the fairy tale of an empire," then found himself in a short-lived state of "intoxication with freedom," imagined a "legendary Turkey" through Turanism, flirted with Bolshevism, and ended up at peace with the Turkish Republican ideology—all the while searching for water, his metaphor for an ideal.[3] His contemporaries must have all confronted such intellectual upheavals. Were there common threads that united them? Could they gather around a discrete, albeit broad identity? Is identity the wrong concept to use in this climate? Looking at such a diverse group of men and women from my distance in the second decade of the twenty-first century, I would like to suggest (cautiously) one common thread running through their diverse rebuttals: reaction to being misrepresented and "othered" by the European Orientalist discourse—arguably a shaky foundation to consolidate an alternative collective identity.

The insularity of the late Ottoman-early Turkish Republican discourse forms a dramatic contrast to the torrential reception of Edward Said's *Orientalism* a cen-

---

2 Turanism is a nineteenth-century nationalist ideological movement that claimed common roots to Ural-Altaic people, whose languages were deemed to share "Turanian" (Central Asian) origins. They included Turkic, Magyar, Mongol, and Finnish people. The Turkish version limited Turanism uniquely to Turkic people in an attempt to create a Turkish ethnic identity.

3 Şevket Süreyya Aydemir, *Suyu Arayan Adam* (Ankara: Öz Yayınları, 1959), passim.

tury later, even though the literature in Turkish shared *Orientalism*'s essential position. There are many obvious reasons for the dissimilar reception of the two bodies of work, including *Orientalism*'s methodological integrity, its depth of scholarly research, the political and socio-cultural climate surrounding its production, and the wide reach of the English language in which it appeared. Uncovering an early criticism of Orientalism, which came from the Orient, does not reduce the importance of Said's work. On the contrary, it is largely thanks to the dynamic discourse Said's book fueled that the importance of the earlier works surfaces at all. They can now be understood better historically as a collective body, even in their fragmentary and precarious state.

Said did not claim that he was the first to approach Orientalism in a critical manner. He referred his readers to key twentieth-century (and mostly Western) texts containing the arguments that had inspired his own thinking. For example, in chronological order, John P. Naish's short article (1930) on eighteenth- and nineteenth-century relations between Europe and India, Egypt, and Africa raised scathing questions about the connection between "commerce and scholarship" and about the "penetration of the East."[4] In reference to Norman Daniel's *Islam and the West: The Making of an Image* (1960), Said stated that Daniel showed how "Islam became an image." The book had had "remarkable implications for Orientalism in general," and although its focused examination of the representation of the Orient was limited to the Middle Ages, its arguments encompassed later eras. In his own words, Daniel aimed to bring forth Latin Christians' "representations and misrepresentations of Islam" during this time.[5] If his admitted primary goal was to establish facts, his secondary one sought to reveal "what is implied by [the] unpleasantness and ignorance in men's attitudes towards those they suppose to be their enemies."[6] Daniel's focus was religion, but he dealt with other related issues: violence, power, and sexual mores.[7] He thus coined the three overarching themes of Orientalist representations. Said also acknowledged the works of Anouar Abdel-Malek and Maxime Rodinson. Abdel-Malek had questioned the assumptions of

---

4   John P. Naish, "The Connection of Oriental Studies with Commerce, Art, and Literature during the 18th-19th Centuries," *Journal of the Manchester Egyptian and Oriental Society*, no. XV (1930): 33–39.

5   Norman Daniel, *Islam and the West: The Making of an Image* (Edinburgh: Edinburgh University Press, 1960; second edition: Oxford: Oneworld, 1993), 24.

6   Daniel, *Islam and the West*, 9.

7   Daniel, *Islam and the West*, chapters IV and V.

European scholarship on the Orient.[8] Fifteen years before Said, he had argued that the Orient was considered as an "'object' stamped with an otherness." It was "passive, non-participating, characterized by a 'historical' subjectivity, above all, non-active, non-autonomous, non-sovereign with regard to itself."[9] For his part, Rodinson had studied the "image of Islam" from the early Middle Ages to later anti-colonial struggles. Despite its shifting positions between admiring the Orient as "a cradle of civilizations" to perceiving it as a collection of "strange and exotic tales," and extending to it a "romantic exoticism ... [infused by] the magic delusion of local color," Rodinson's arguments inspired Said's *Orientalism*.[10]

The late Ottoman-early Turkish Republican criticism of Orientalism pursued multiple paths. In addition to being the main topic of entire texts centered on Orientalist constructions and misunderstandings, it appeared in a few punch lines in publications dealing with other subject matters. Nevertheless, this early discourse constituted a common denominator that brought together different fields and different ideologies, displaying a unified front, albeit unintended and organic, that extended across political and historical discourses.

For example, Ahmed Rıza, a leader of the Young Turk movement living in exile in Paris (and later a senator in the Ottoman Chamber of Deputies), wrote a political treatise on the "moral failure" of Europeans toward the Ottoman Empire. He declared that Europe had obliged him to raise his voice by insulting his country and his nation and by treating Turks as "savages" who belonged to "inferior races." He did not deny the "terrible" bloody pages of his own country's history, but reminded Europeans that their history was no "song of virtue and elation" either. Appealing to the "Europe of free thought and social peace, hidden behind imperialist Europe," Ahmed Rıza widened his argument to cover other geographies. He concluded that Europe's disrespect of nations simply because they were "Arab or Hindu" was in effect the "most certain sign of [its own] intellectual and moral decadence."[11]

Historians played a notable part in this reactive movement, although their criticism showed up only here and there and in-between the lines of their writings

---

8   Said, *Orientalism*, 261.

9   Anouar Abdel-Malek, "Orientalism in Crisis," *Diogenes* 44 (Winter 1963): 107–8.

10   Maxime Rodinson, "The Western Image and Western Studies of Islam," in *The Legacy of Islam*, eds. Joseph Schacht and C.E. Bosworth (Oxford, UK: Oxford University Press, 1974), 9–62.

11   Ahmed Riza, *La faillite morale de la politique occidentale en Orient* (Paris: Librairie Picard, 1922), 32–34.

on other topics. An important booklet by the leading members of the Council of Turkish History (Türk Tarihi Tedkik Heyeti), titled "Principal Outlines of Turkish History" (*Türk Tarihinin Ana Hatları*), was put together in 1930 to "remind the Turkish nation [of] its honorable past, based on historic facts"—especially its contributions to earlier civilizations—and to re-think the "roles played by Turks in world history." This was a collective endeavor to review "synthetic" books on the history of the Turks written in the West (specifically in France) and to rectify their errors. While the call was geared toward Turks, who ironically had learned their own history from books published in French, the implicit message was to a broader readership.[12]

An alternative search for new methodologies, based on Ottoman archival sources, was already in the making before either Ahmed Rıza or the Council of Turkish History put pen to paper. A good indication of this direction is a 1910 article by Abdurrahman Şeref, the last chronicler of the Ottoman Empire and the chair of the Council of Ottoman History. Opening with an envious paragraph on the state of European archives and the monumental buildings they were housed in, Abdurrahman Şeref detailed the impressive contents of the Ottoman archives and emphasized their tremendous significance for all aspects of the empire, ranging from law and ownership to military and diplomatic affairs. He then moved on to the poor physical state of the Ottoman archives, lamenting their dispersed storage in different buildings, their lack of organization, and the poor environmental and preservation conditions. All of this culminated in an appeal to valorize them in a manner comparable to their counterparts in Paris and Vienna.[13] This did not happen for decades and stretched into a slow, gradual process, but the writing of Ottoman history did eventually shift to archive-based research. The move stemmed, in part, from a reaction to the way the Ottoman past was formulated by European historians. In the words of historian Halil İnalcık, who was admittedly influenced by Atatürk's efforts to define the nation, one of the foundation stones of his intellectual formation was "the need to challenge Western literature on the Ottoman Empire." His commitment to study Ottoman history from "original Turkish doc-

---

12   *Türk Tarihinin Ana Hatları* (Istanbul: Devlet Matbaası, 1930), 2–3, 68. Curiously, Turkish historians corrected the French errors by "scholarly data and evidence" (*ilmi mu'talar ve deliller*) from other French sources (see p. 3).

13   Abdurrahman Şeref, "Evrak-i Atika ve Vesaik-i Tarihiyemiz," *Tarih-i Osmani Encümeni Mecmuası* 1, no. 1 (1910): 9–19.

uments" was a deliberate counter-position to Western historians who did not (and could not) work with Ottoman primary documents.[14]

Süheyl Ünver, whose prolific scholarship extended from medical science to art history, addressed the same issue in the introduction to his monograph on the seventeenth-century artist Nakşi. Defying Adolphe Thalasso's erroneous argument in *L'art ottoman, les peintres turcs* (1910) that there existed "no painting and no painters from the rise of the Ottoman Empire to 1874," Ünver charged that "unfortunately, foreign aficionados did not write anything accurate on the history of our art." The reason was obvious: scholarship depended on patient research conducted with modesty. Subjective observations could fill pages, but they remained speckled with "meaningless judgments." The repetition of unfounded ideas had further detrimental effects, as illustrated in the case of Ernst Diez, who was appointed to chair the Department of Turkish Art in Istanbul University's Faculty of Letters. Randomly picking up references from sixteenth- to eighteenth-century Western literature, and without doing any research with original sources, Diez had concluded that Turks had no national talent in the art of painting. Ünver countered that those who work on Turkish painting and ornamental arts should be proficient in reading their unique visual language. Secondary sources, from the East and the West, were not sufficient: original research was needed to understand Turkish art. Ünver cited his own monographs on Nigâri (written in specific reaction to Thalasso), Levni (written in specific reaction to Diez), and then Nakşi, to argue that unless and until a solid collection of such well-researched works was produced, it was inappropriate to make conclusive statements about Turkish art. Along the way he identified a methodological trap that continues to scar interpretations of illustrated manuscripts even today, namely, isolating the images from the text: without reading the text, it was not possible to understand the paintings.[15]

Against the broad canvas of this cross-sectional criticism, the current volume brings together texts that are particularly focused on criticizing Orientalism. While they share Said's positions in a multitude of ways, they barely intersect with *Orientalism*'s case studies. In fact, only two overlaps appear. The first, Ernest Renan, is one of Said's main subjects. Said examines his manipulations of philology, his essentialist views of Islam, his racial ideas, and his understanding of sci-

---

14 Nancy E. Gallagher, "Interview with Halil Inalcik," in *Approaches to the History of the Middle East: Interviews with Leading Middle East Historians*, ed. Nancy E. Gallagher (Reading, UK: Ithaca Press, 1994), 164, 155.

15 A. Süheyl Ünver, *Ressam Nakşi: Hayatı ve Eserleri* (Istanbul: Kemal Matbaası, 1949), 13–15, 28.

ence, making reference to his many publications. Curiously, "L'islamisme et la science," the text of a lecture Renan delivered at the Sorbonne on March 27, 1883, is not among them. "L'islamisme et la science," by contrast, is the object of Namık Kemal's attack in his pamphlet titled *Refutation of Renan*. The second, Pierre Loti, gets two quick and dismissive mentions in Said, but provokes a vast field of responses from the Ottoman-Turkish front, culminating in young Nâzım Hikmet's acrimonious poem, "Pierre Loti." The obsession with Loti is so extensive that it merits an entire section in this volume. Despite the scarcity of shared case studies, criticism from the "Orient" nonetheless covers a familiar Saidian list of issues: representations of religion and society, cultural ignorance, Eurocentrism, cultural hierarchy, colonialism, imperialism, exoticism, sensationalism, imagination, and an overarching essentialism.

A Reader

The shared attitude of the texts included in this volume unsettles the sharp rupture theories that separate the Ottoman and Republican eras. They display a smooth continuity between the two political regimes through the unlikely angle of a united front against European representations of the East. Together, they deconstruct the overarching claims of Orientalist discourse, that is, the flattened, uninformed, and distorted readings of religion, artistic and cultural productions, as well as public and private life. Derived from repetition, enriched by imagination, and frozen in time, Orientalist paradigms were begging for response from an Ottoman intelligentsia that was in contact with and highly knowledgeable of the European intellectual scene by the late nineteenth century. The texts belong to different genres: scholarly treatises, journal and newspaper articles of all kinds, novels, short stories, poems, and even a couple of photo essays. Likewise, their authors represent a wide ideological spectrum. Tevfik Fikret, the outspoken poet of the Edebiyat-ı Cedide (The New Literature) movement known for his opposition to the Hamidian regime, was joined by Halid Ziya, a legendary novelist from the same literary movement but with a quieter political voice. "That battered, single-toothed monster you call civilization," perhaps the best known lines of the Turkish National Anthem attacking the western powers, were penned by poet Mehmed Akif, whose Islamicist politics clashed with Tevfik Fikret's secularism.[16] Ismayıl Hakkı and Ömer Seyfeddin

---

16　The Turkish National Anthem was adopted on March 12, 1922. Tevfik Fikret and Mehmed Akif had engaged in a public battle, attacking each other in poems. For the controversy between the two poets, see Fahrettin Gün, *Mehmed Akif-Tevfik Fikret Çatışması* (Istanbul: Beyan Yayınları, 2014).

shared some general ideals about Turkism, and Şevket Süreyya, a government officer responsible for economic development during the early Republican era, was a spokesman for statism. Famously remembered for their political attacks on each other, poets Nâzım Hikmet and Ahmed Haşim stood on the opposite poles of the political spectrum: the former a devoted communist and the latter an individualist symbolist with a firm belief in capitalism.[17] Male voices are in the majority, but there are two prominent women writers in the group, Halide Edib and Fatma Aliye, both well-known novelists and essayists; the latter's book *Nisvan-ı İslam* (The Women of Islam), one of the two longest texts in this collection, centers on clichés about women in Islamic societies.

The texts organically yielded themselves to classification into five categories: Grand Battles, Art as Measure of Civilization, "Oriental" Women and Life at Home, The Unique Case of Pierre Loti, and Sarcasm as Vengeance. Nevertheless, these sections are not independent of each other and their boundaries are porous. It should be obvious, for example, that "'Oriental' Women and Life at Home" have much in common with "The Unique Case of Pierre Loti." Pierre Loti has an entire section to himself, but he surfaces elsewhere as well, for example in Tevfik Fikret's discussion of "Foreigners and Our Turkish" in Grand Battles and Ahmed Haşim's "The Hospice for Storks" (*Gurebahane-i Laklakan*) in Sarcasm as Vengeance. The chronological organization within each subgroup intends to point to some obvious referential links between the essays. Continuities commence with the title of Namık Kemal's 1872 essay, which opens the collection. The short and simple sentence, "Avrupa Şark'ı Bilmez" echoed not only in subsequent essays, but also made its way into the Turkish vernacular; it is commonly repeated today, mostly without any awareness or memory of its origin. In some cases, the authors respond to each other—and not necessarily in polite acknowledgment. Ahmed Haşim's "The Hospice for Storks" is a relentless piece of satire that not only shreds to pieces the French romanticization of Eastern ways, but also mocks art historians at home for their new obsession with creating an origin for Turkish art in Bursa's fourteenth- to fifteenth-century architecture.

---

17 The controversy between the two poets is long and convoluted. Ahmed Haşim's early admiration of Nâzım Hikmet's poems for their stylistic mastery dates from 1924. Their later quarrel is centered on the contents of poetry and ideological differences, culminating in Nâzım Hikmet's poem "Cevap, No. 2" (Response, No. 2), a virulent attack on Ahmed Haşim published in 1931 in *Sesini Kaybeden Şehir*. For an analysis on this topic see Mehmet Can Doğan, "Ahmet Hâşim ve Yakup Kadri'nin Nâzım Hikmet'in Şiiri Karşısındaki Tutumları" ("Ahmet Hâşim and Yakup Kadri's Attitudes towards Nâzım Hikmet's Poetry"), *Gazi Türkiyat*, no. 22 (Spring 2018): 55–67.

Grand Battles

Two pieces by Namık Kemal, one short, the other much longer, chart the larger, general topics that early Orientalist criticism embodied. The first, "Avrupa Şark'ı Bilmez," made an overarching statement about the stories invented by learned men from "eminent nations." These included depictions of Turks as a "savage tribe" that wanted to turn the world upside down, and of the harem as a place of pleasure and entertainment crowded with odalisques and concubines. According to Namık Kemal, there existed no serious books on the Ottoman Empire in European languages, and the works of the two most-acclaimed authors, Ignatius Mouradgea D'Ohsson and Joseph von Hammer-Purgstall, were marred by tales born out of ignorance.[18] D'Ohsson claimed, for example, that there was no Islamic law, while Hammer filled the history of Ottomans with bloody battles, attributing all their victories to historic accidents. Namık Kemal argued that it would be unrealistic to rely on Europeans to correct their errors; the solution thus was for Turks to excel in European languages and to re-write their own history.

Due to its emphasis on history, "Avrupa Şark'ı Bilmez" occupies an important place in Namık Kemal's work and hence in the history of modern Ottoman literature. Ahmet Hamdi Tanpınar, novelist and literary critic, identified the essay as the starting point for Namık Kemal's subsequent writings on history, namely, biographies of Salahaddin Ayyubı, Mehmed II, and Sultan Selim I, as well as *Kanije Muhasarası* (The Siege of Kanije), all written between 1872 and 1874. Tanpınar situated these four texts in the framework of "Avrupa Şark'ı Bilmez" and explained Namık Kemal's position in world literature. All nations drew inspiration from the important events and important personages of their history; Namık Kemal was simply the first to do so in modern Turkish literature.[19]

Namık Kemal unpacked the opinions he introduced in this article in a longer essay, his refutation of Ernest Renan's "L'islamisme et la science," written in the summer of 1883, but published in 1910—twelve years after his death.[20] Renan's reductive arguments had attributed an apparent inability to engage in scientific thinking in the Muslim world to the nature of Islam as a religion and to the racial

---

18 D'Ohsson was the author of the seven-volume *Tableau Général de l'Empire Othoman* (Paris: Firmin Didot, 1788–1824) and Hammer was the author of *Geschichte des Os manischen reiches* (Pest: C.A. Hartleben's Verlage, 1828).

19 Ahmet Hamdi Tanpınar, *XIX. Asır Türk Edebiyatı Tarihi* (Istanbul: Yapı Kredi Yayınları, 2006; original publication: 1949), 372–73.

20 Dücane Cündioğlu, "Ernest Renan ve 'Reddiyeler' Bağlamında İslam-Bilim Tartışmalarına Bibliyografik Bir Katkı," *Divan*, no. 2 (1996): 42–43.

characteristics of Muslims. This provoked retribution. Before Namık Kemal, Jamal ad-Din Afghani (1837–97), an influential Muslim modernist, had already penned his own "Réponse de Jamal ad-Din al-Afghani à Renan" on May 18, 1883, in the *Journal des Débats*.[21] Written in Arabic and translated into French, this polite treatise paid respect to humanistic philosophy and scientific reform and acknowledged Islam's hostility to them. However, Afghani maintained a distance from Renan's racial claims and offered instead an evolutionary process, arguing that acceptance of science and philosophy needed time. In his view, Muslim societies could be modernized if training in science was taken seriously. He hoped that "Muhammedan society [would] succeed some day [in] breaking its bonds and marching resolutely in the path of civilization in the manner of Western society."[22] Afghani's response was geared toward a European audience and was meant to complement Renan's polemic rather than to deny it.

There were further counter-voices to Renan's lecture in the following decades— among them that of Ahund Ataullah Beyazidov, the grand mufti of Saint Petersburg, who published a booklet in 1883, in Russian. Translated into Turkish as *Redd-i Renan: İslamiyet ve Fünun* (Refutation of Renan: Islam and Sciences) the same year, Beyazidov's essay criticized above all Renan's methodology, which, instead of following deductive reasoning, had made its conclusion the starting point. Based on a prejudice about Islam and constructed from a position of ignorance, Renan's theses had exposed his short-sightedness that associated science with a certain civilization or a nation. By contrast, Beyazidov argued, the origins of science and scholarship were both Greek and Arabic: the father may have been Greek, but the mother who "raised and educated" them was Arab.[23] Further reactions to Renan's lecture came from Ali Ferruh writing from Paris (*Teşhir-i Ebatıl*, Istanbul, 1306/1889),

---

21 For Renan's original text, see Ernest Renan, *L'Islamisme et la science conférence faite à la Sorbonne, le 29 mars 1883* (Paris: Calmann-Lévy, 1883). For Afghani's response, see "Réponse de Jamal ad-Din al-Afghani à Renan," *Réfutation des matérialistes,* trans. A.M. Goichon (Paris: P. Geuthner, 1942), 174–79; Nikki R. Keddie, *An Islamic Response to Imperialism: Political and Religious Writings of Jamal ad-Din "al Afghani"* (Berkeley and Los Angeles: University of California Press), 181–87. For a comparison with Namık Kemal, see York A. Norman, "Disputing the 'Iron Circle': Renan, Afghani, and Kemal on Islam, Science, and Modernity," *Journal of World History* 22, no. 4 (2011): 693–714. For reactions in a broader context, see Osman Cilacı, "Ernest Renan'a Karşı Türk-İslam Dünyasında Reaksiyonlar," *Süleyman Demirel Üniversitesi İlahiyat Fakültesi Dergisi,* no. 2 (1995): 181–91.

22 Quoted in Keddie, 95.

23 Ahund Ataullah Beyazidov, *Redd-i Renan: İslamiyet ve Fünun,* trans. Gülnar Olga Lebedev and Ahmed Cevdet (Istanbul: Tercüman-ı Hakikat Matbaası, 1308/1893), 21, 53. Ramazan Yıldırım, "İslam-Bilim İlişkileri Bağlamında Ataullah Bayezidof'un Renan

Seyyid Emir Ali writing from India (*Spirit of Islam*, 1891), and Celal Nuri writing from Istanbul (*Edebiyat-ı Umumiye Mecmuası*, 1918). In his comprehensive review of this literature, Dücane Cündioğlu summed up their collective rebuttals with a quotation from Celal Nuri: "İslam mâni-i terakki değildir" (Islam is not an obstacle to progress).[24]

Namık Kemal formulated his own rebuttal independently and in a more critical manner. Aligning Renan with Hammer, who had displayed an ignorance of Muslim religion despite his knowledge of Arabic, Farsi, and Turkish, Namık Kemal wondered whether the glaring misstatements made by the two Europeans stemmed from their reliance on other European texts of equally dubious scholarly quality. Reacting to Renan's vision of the people of the East and Africa, Namık Kemal expressed outrage: "How strange! Because we are Muslim, it seems, we have an iron ring clamped around our heads, and that ring keeps our intellect closed off to all forms of knowledge, all forms of learning, all forms of new ideas—and we still do not even know it!" Namık Kemal's deconstruction of Renan's speech stretched from the latter's peculiar explanation that the time of the noon prayer referred to an invented hadith about Satan who had placed the sun between its horns as a crown at noon, to the absurd claim that Muslims had lacked education in philosophy after 1200—a glaring contradiction to the curricula of the great Ottoman madrasas. He concluded that Renan's lecture stemmed from a combination of ignorance, anxiety, hatred, anger, and intolerance.

In the "Conversations in Literature" column of the Ottoman popular periodical *Servet-i Fünun* (Wealth of Sciences), Tevfik Fikret cited Namık Kemal's first article in his attack on European ignorance about the East in 1898. He reiterated that Europe had no knowledge about the East ("Avrupa Şark'ı tanımaz!"/"Europe does not understand the Orient!") or about the Turkish language. Citing a letter writer from London, Tevfik Fikret argued that Europeans, from ministers to village priests, who liberally expressed their opinions on the affairs of the Orient, froze the exterior appearance of the Turk as a dark-skinned individual complete with a turban on his head and a long, curved sword attached to his hip. The stereotype could be so obstinate that Tevfik Fikret alternately found himself bursting out in laughter or on the verge of crying in anger about European society. He lamented the self-entitlement of Europeans to represent the East—as illustrated, for example, in a book series by

---

Reddiyesi," *Yakın Doğu İlahiyat Fakültesi Dergisi* 3, no. 1 (Spring 2017): 75–88. See 80, 82–83, 86.

24   Cündioğlu, "Ernest Renan ve 'Reddiyeler' Bağlamında İslam-Bilim Tartışmalarına Bibliyografik Bir Katkı," 1–94. For his summary of the collective rebuttal, see p. 8.

Hachette on Western capital cities in which every entry was written by an insider, except for the one about Istanbul, which was commissioned to Pierre Loti. The grave consequences of such misrepresentations led Tevfik Fikret to distrust European literature on the Far East, for example, on India, China, and Japan. He admitted bitterly that European ignorance of the Orient did not translate into European disinterest in the Orient. Europeans knew well their economic interests.

Prominent journalist Ebüzziya had titled an earlier essay (1886) in direct reference to Namık Kemal's "important article." In his own "Avrupa Şark'ı Bilmez," the focus was again the ignorance of European learned men, albeit an ignorance that he insisted was not always due to naiveté and exaggeration. He ridiculed an article in a French journal, which reported on an alleged network across the Islamic world that was managed by a publication based in Istanbul.[25] Ebüzziya teased this entirely fictional information, linked it to dark intentions, and attributed its sources to dubious guides (siserons).[26] On his part, Ahmed Haşim turned his gaze homeward and censured the publishing scene and its misplaced fascination with foreign languages purportedly associated with knowledge and civilization. He mocked the translation of many silly books, which did not have any merit other than having been written in a European language.

As a counterpoint to the angry tone of these writers, novelist Halid Ziya expressed a fatigue; his upper-class, well-educated, and westernized protagonists reflect the lagging pain that the cliché-ridden European literature imposed on the East. Halid Ziya's fictional characters appreciated and respected the poetic beauty of such writings, but they rejected the "philosophical" thought behind them, without even bothering to correct the factual details. Two short sections bring Orientalist discourse into the *Nesl-i Ahir* (The Last Generation, 1908), a novel of more than 500 pages, likewise illustrating the critical mindset that characterized the educated Ottoman circles, as well as the unexpected places it emerged at the *fin de siècle*. Simultaneously, these episodes highlight the depth to which Orientalist denunciation penetrated all literary genres.

During the first decade after the foundation of the Turkish Republic in 1923, the battles with Orientalism continued, sometimes following the earlier tone, sometimes taking new directions. Halide Edib's *Turkey Faces West* (1930) did not offer fresh arguments, but briefly pointed out the Europeans' persistent and con-

---

25   The journal's title, given in Ottoman Turkish, is *Tabaat*. This is most likely *La presse*, published between 1836 and 1935.

26   The word *siseron* is derived from Italian cicerone (Latin ciceronem), after the Roman orator Cicero. It refers humorously to local guides, known for their loquaciousness.

tradictory interpretations of the "religious nature of the Turk," either equating it with fanaticism or accepting it with indifference, seeing no virtue in it either way. Around the same time, a fresh voice from the left-wing intelligentsia paired colonialism with Orientalism. *Resimli Ay*, a magazine edited by Zekeriya and Sabiha Sertel, published a short anonymous article on French movies screened in Turkey (1929). Addressing French "dramas" that denigrated Asian and African patriots while celebrating French imperialism, the article described the latter as "a rabid monster right on our Syrian border" and called for a stop to the screening of such films that were offensive to a Turkish nation that had saved its own country with its "blood" not long ago.

Şevket Süreyya, one of the founders of the monthly *Kadro* and arguably its "theorist," explained that the journal's mission was to crystallize "the content and the principles of the Turkish revolution." To promote a "conscientious and calculated statism" during its two-year history (1932–1934), *Kadro* discussed thorny issues related to economic, social, and cultural matters.[27] Approaching Europeanization attempts with great caution, the authors remained highly critical of the kind of history writing that placed Europe at the center. To this end, Şevket Süreyya penned a scathing article, "Europacentrisme'in Tasfiyesi" (Bankruptcy of Europacentrisme), in which he questioned a mode of historiography based on events that happened in a small place on the world scale, both geographically and historically. The division of world history into Antiquity, Middle Age, Early Modern Age, and Contemporary Times assumed that everything outside Europe was linked to Europe, that other civilizations were not autonomouos. He questioned the premises of "this saga," according to which any entity outside Europe or against Europe was destructive and barbarian. Şevket Süreyya claimed in reality the situation was the opposite: it was Europe itself that had become "aggressive and violent" in its colonialist stance.

Periodization, fixed by European scholarship, continues to be at the core of the way that history is conceptualized. In his masterful study, Jack Goody recently argued that "Europe had stolen the history of the East by imposing its own versions of time (largely Christian) and of space on the rest of the Eurasian world." The division of the past into Antiquity, Feudalism, the Renaissance, and Capitalism in a neat linearity translated into a "theft of history" intertwined with Europe's agenda for world domination, recalling Şevket Süreyya's claims about European colonialism.[28] Yet, there are other forms of periodization in other historiographic

27   Aydemir, *Suyu Arayan Adam*, 492, 498.

28   Jack Goody, *The Theft of History* (Cambridge, UK: Cambridge University Press, 2006), 1–9, 286. Like Said's *Orientalism*, Goody's book is "not so much about world history as

traditions, such as in Ottoman historiography that have enjoyed some scholarly attention.[29] Recent attempts to "reform the Parochial Western historical scheme" of "ancient, medieval, modern periods revolving around Western Europe" propose "a global Islamic explanation of world history" based on the writings of Muslim historians.[30] Şevket Süreyya's article, although confined to a relatively unknown journal in Turkish, is a precursor to this line of thinking.[31]

Art as Measure of Civilization

Ever since its publication, Said's *Orientalism* provoked the academic discourse in many disciplines, reached widespread audiences through popular publications, and sparked intense debates in everyday politics. Its unpredictable and transnational impact elicited many questions beyond the discussions found within its pages, sharpening contemporary approaches to cultural constructions and opening new windows to unlikely places. Visual culture is among these. Art and architectural historians—and not only those working on "non-Western" topics—found a fertile field of inspiration in Said's work. Despite the fact that Said himself did not engage in these topics, even the cover of *Orientalism*, which featured Jean-Léon Gérôme's *Snake Charmer* (late 1860s) and served as a straightforward short-hand to the book's contents, raised charged questions about the power of visual representations. In her now classic article, "The Imaginary Orient," Linda Nochlin argued that Gérôme's painting may be "considered as a visual document of 19th century colonialist ideology, an iconic distillation of the Westerners' notion of the Orient couched in the language of a would-be transparent naturalism."[32] It summarized the main assumptions of the discourse in titillating clarity, enhanced by minute attention to space, "the ferociously detailed tiled wall" (again Nochlin's words), an assurance of the conveyed story's authenticity. The image was not used in the

---

about the way that European scholars have perceived it" (p. 305).

29   Hakan Karateke, "The Challenge of Periodization," in *Writing History at the Ottoman Court: Editing the Past, Fashioning the Future*, eds. H. Erden Çıpa and Emine Fetvacı (Bloomington and Indianapolis: Indiana University Press, 2013), 129–54.

30   Khalid Blankinship, "Islam and World History: Toward a New Periodization," *American Journal of Islamic Social Science* 18, no. 3 (1991): 423–39.

31   Aydemir studied economics and social theory at the Communist University of the Workers of the East in Moscow, an institution founded in 1921 to train leaders for colonial and dependent countries. He attended the Congress of the Peoples of the East in 1920, which may have played a crucial role in his positions on the independence movements against European colonialism. Aydemir recorded his intellectual journeys in *Suyu Arayan Adam*, 204–15.

32   Linda Nochlin, "The Imaginary Orient," *Art in America* (May 1983): 119.

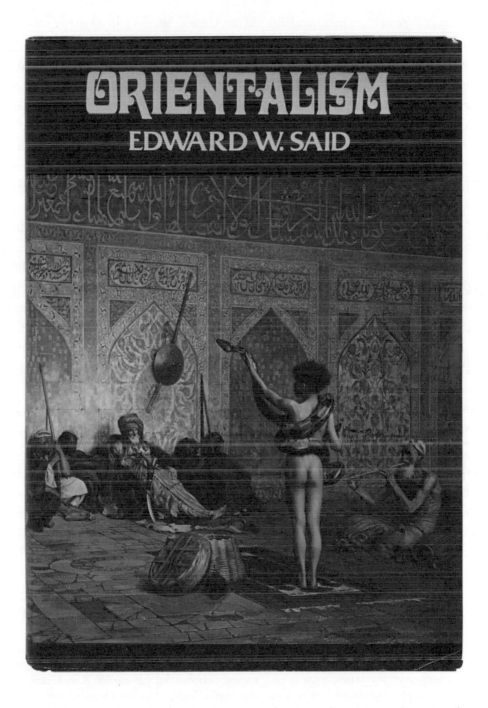

FIGURE 1. Edward Said, *Orientalism*, 1978, cover (courtesy of Penguin Random House)

editions of *Orientalism* published outside the United States or in its many translations—perhaps because its disturbing transparency was considered inappropriate.

Orientalist art had repercussions in the late Ottoman era, centering on the prominent figure of Osman Hamdi (1842–1910) around the turn of the century. Not approached critically for decades, Osman Hamdi's art became subject to long debates in the post-*Orientalism* climate since the early 1990s. Although belatedly, his Orientalist paintings engendered discussion. Conducive to interpretations that allowed for counter-positions, Osman Hamdi's paintings, executed according to Orientalist conventions, turned around favorite topics of Western artists, giving them other meanings even when presented in similar settings. His men in mosques did not display submission to religion, but instead were shown as engaged in discussions in small groups and immersed in theological studies; his women crowded the public spaces and read at home, forming a contrast to the ever-reclining odalisques and hammam scenes of Orientalist artists.[33] Osman Hamdi did not write about his ideas on Western Orientalists or about his own art, leaving his work open to suggestive readings. He received no response in his lifetime. In light of the Ottoman literature critical of Orientalist representations that we clearly encounter in this volume, this silence is troubling, but perhaps may be explained by a lack of art criticism in Istanbul at the time.[34]

While the late Ottoman discourse on art did not address paintings, commentaries and interpretations on architecture and decorative arts abounded. Their common struggle was to define the essence of "Ottoman-ness," and later "Turkish-ness," against the essentializing approach shared by European art historians that saw no distinction between Persian, Arabic, and Ottoman art. In a series of articles published in the newspaper *İkdam* in December 1906 and January 1907, Celal Esad, arguably the first Ottoman art and architectural historian, laid out the distinctions among them. In the first article, titled "Ottoman Fine Arts," he explained that his

---

33   Recent literature on Osman Hamdi's Orientalism is too broad to be discussed fairly here. Among the scholars involved in the debates are Ahmet Ersoy, Edhem Eldem, Mary Roberts, and Wendy Shaw. I had an early contribution to the arguments as well.

34   A similar trend can be traced in Ottoman photography, which capitalized on the modernity of the late-nineteenth-century Empire, extending from infrastructure projects to institutional reforms, such as educational reforms. Set against Western Orientalist photographs and despite the overlaps, the scenes depicted in the Ottoman images can be read easily as counter-narratives. Ottoman photography is also attracting considerable scholarly attention. See, for example, Zeynep Çelik and Edhem Eldem, eds., *Camera Ottomana: Photography and Modernity in the Ottoman Empire, 1840–1914* (Istanbul: Koç University Press, 2015).

rationale was to correct the error of some European writers who, first, considered Ottoman fine arts to be an imitation of Arab, Iranian, and especially Byzantine art, and second, furthermore attributed the origins of the entire art of Islam to that of Eastern Christianity. He then engaged in a discussion of the influences of different artistic traditions on each other. Accepting that Ottoman art was born and developed "in the cradle of" of Arabic, Iranian, and Byzantine arts, Celal Esad nevertheless claimed a careful study would reveal that it did not closely resemble any one of them and instead had developed its own character. In effect, the art of every society had inevitably been affected by those that preceded it. After all, he asked, who could deny the continuities between ancient Egypt and Greece, as well as between Greece and Rome? As the tools of "scientific progress" replaced "subjective opinion," the study of Ottoman art would reveal its original identity, linked to the historic eras of the Ottoman State. The implication was that Europeans did not think scientifically and objectively and that Turks had just started doing so.

In "Arab Decorative Arts" Celal Esad emphasized the distance maintained by the Arabs from ancient Greek and Byzantine fine arts and architecture, arguing that geometry formed the basis of their style. Arabs had created a unique decorative method by using geometric forms in series or in an interlaced manner, which Europeans named "arabesque." Celal Esad identified another feature of Arabic art as calligraphy, which could even take on familiar shapes such as a ship or a mosque. In time, and under Chinese, Mogul, and Iranian influences, Arabs began integrating flower motifs, culminating in the examples found in al-Azhar Mosque in Cairo. Taking on the topic of "Arab Fine Arts," Celal Esad acknowledged that some objective European scholars accepted the existence of an original Arab art, positioning themselves against those who denied any creativity to Arabs and insisted on their reliance on Coptic and Sassanian forms. He maintained that Arab art had registered a remarkable development, and that while having a widespread impact in geographies other than the birthplace of the religion, it also had transformed itself according to local and regional traditions. Among the typical features of Arab architecture were high, conical domes that looked like "eggs," the reasons behind them likely stemming from soil conditions and related structural concerns. Another original element was the "gem-like" three-dimensional geometric treatment of the squinches, the transitional elements between domes and piers.

"Persian fine arts" were so much influenced by Arabs that during the early Islamic era there was no distinction between Iranian and Arab architecture. This was most obvious in mosque plans, with four iwans organized around a courtyard. Nevertheless, once subjected to Indian, Chinese, and Turkish influences, the art of

Iran transformed into a new character, outstanding in its refinement. Its architecture distinguished itself from other "Islamic" traditions by its high, conical domes covered with tiles, the latter testifying to the advanced stage reached by Iranian decorative arts among Eastern populations.

Celal Esad concluded his discussions of the main regions of Islamic art with a longer piece on Ottoman architecture. Attributing its origins to the fourteenth- and fifteenth-century monuments in Bursa and linking the tradition to the Seljuk and Byzantine eras, he charted a chronological development that paralleled the conventions of European art history, with Mimar Sinan marking the peak in the sixteenth century. Sinan's genius was in improving, simplifying, and purifying the principles put into practice by Mimar Hayreddin, the architect of the early-sixteenth-century Mosque of Sultan Bayezid II in Istanbul. Through codification, Sinan had turned Ottoman architecture into a unique art, one that occupied a privileged place in the hierarchy of Islamic architectural history due to its simple and pure forms and spaces. The "rules" of Ottoman architecture, if examined carefully and understood well, would make it possible to critique later shortcomings, such as those resulting from the introduction of *alafranga* styles from the eighteenth century on. In this collection, Celal Esad attempted to clarify the different traditions within Islamic art and architecture, to present them in their historic dynamism, and to periodize them. One of his principal goals was to untangle European misconceptions that conflated the various regional traditions and processes of Islamic art and architecture. Picking up bits and pieces of earlier arguments on a search for Ottoman art and architectural history, he helped shape the conceptualization of the field.

Around the same time he published these articles in *İkdam*, Celal Esad also compiled a dictionary of architecture, *Istılahat-ı Mimariye*. The entries in the volume included European and Ottoman elements, some illustrated (most likely by the author himself). Two sets of figures reiterate, in basic outlines, Celal Esad's message about the character of Ottoman architecture. The first is a generic Turkish house, juxtaposed with a generic European-style house, all components labeled on the drawings in astute technical terms. As appropriate for a dictionary, there is no commentary, and the images are allowed to speak for themselves. The second set of figures compares again two "styles" (*usul-i mimari*): Arab and Ottoman, with a set of drawing for each. Considering the nuances Celal Esad attempted to raise in his *İkdam* essays, the narrow representation of Arab architecture in just four images and of Ottoman architecture in one section of the Mosque of Süleyman I may seem inconsistent, although perhaps not essentially antithetical to his longer discussions.

The page on the Arab style includes five pieces from different buildings, from three different contexts: wooden latticework from the window of a Cairene house, Mamluk mausoleums in Cairo, a minaret of the Mosque of Sidi Ukba in Biskra (Algeria), capitals from the Palace of Alhambra, and the courtyard of a house in Algiers. The collage thus depicted different geographies and variations of the "Arab style." The summation of the Ottoman architectural style by means of the Mosque of Süleyman I accords with Celal Esad's reasoning, since he establishes Sinan's work as the pinnacle of Ottoman architecture. The sectional drawing was most likely selected for explaining best the "spatial rules," practices that had been used famously in *Usul-i Mimari-i Osmani* and by Léon Parvillée in his attempt to unpack the rational design principles of early Ottoman monuments.[35]

Two decades later, Ismayıl Hakkı wrote a thought-provoking and complex article, entitled "Research on Turkish Arts: An Introduction." Ismayıl Hakkı's essay integrated Celal Esad's arguments and, inspired by them, built new ones. His starting point was the concept of "the history of civilization," defined in its broadest terms as the history of social institutions. Art history was one of its branches, specifically the one that exposed a community's most creative characteristics. As Turkish civilization was part of universal civilization, the study of Turkish art would contribute to the history of humanity. Therefore, it needed to be cleared of the myths developed by European writers (including Gustave Le Bon) that no independent Turkish art existed and that Turkish art was composed of Arab, Iranian, and Byzantine fragments. Such superficial verdicts were prejudiced. Given that continuities and influences among, for example, ancient Greek, Assyrian, Egyptian, and Phoenician civilizations were well accepted and respected, why was the same methodological yardstick not applied to Turkish art? Like ancient Greek art, Turkish art had synthesized influences and re-invented them in simplicity and clarity, according to

---

35 Marie de Launay, Pietro Montani, et al., *Usul-i Mimari-i Osmani* (Istanbul: Imprimerie et Lithographic Centrales, 1873); Léon Parvillée, *Architecture et décoration turques* (Paris: A. Morel et cie, 1874), ii–iv, 2. See also, Anatole de Baudot, "Exposition universelle de 1867," *Gazette des architectes et du bâtiment* (special issue), Paris, 1867. De Baudot, a follower of Viollet-le-Duc, discussed in this article the rationalist principles he identified in the Ottoman pavilions erected in Paris for the 1867 Universal Exhibition. Celal Esad was not in complete agreement with *Usul*, but as a critical and theoretical text, it carried enough authority. Celal Esad was not alone to develop ideas on Turkish architecture. Professional architects, among them Kemaleddin Bey, published articles and applied their thoughts to the buildings they designed. Among Kemaleddin Bey's writings, see "Mimari-i İslam," *Hüdavendigar Vilayet-i Salname-i Resmisi* (Hüdavendigar: Vilayet Matbaası, 1322/1906), 142–87 and "Mimari: Türk Mimarisinde Renge Verilen Ehemmiyet-Sırlı Tuğla ile Çini Sanatı," *Yeni Mecmua* 1, no. 7 (August 23, 1917): 129–33.

rational and logical principles. Formulating a thesis that would be echoed later in Oleg Grabar's explorations of early Islamic art in the 1970s, Ismayıl Hakkı postulated that the combination of material elements endowed the newly created object with new meanings and originality that also carried new subjective and spiritual values.[36] Scrutinized critically and analytically from this perspective, Turkish art emerged as an original idiom, generated by an innovative fusion of elements from Arab, Iranian, and Byzantine art. This was not imitation. Ismayıl Hakkı's methodological approach to historic analysis thus called for the need to understand art as a dynamic force, in terms of both its past and its relations to other civilizations. Published in a quiet academic corner in the pages of the journal of Istanbul University's School of Divinity, Ismayıl Hakkı's article was nevertheless a radical invitation to re-think Turkish art against European assumptions.

The newly developing discipline of art history was keen to identify an origin for Turkish art, and that was Bursa. Bursa and the region around it had already been designated officially as "land of the forefathers of the Ottoman dynasty and the seedbed of the empire" in the late 1880s.[37] In 1886, Abdülhamid II commissioned an expedition team consisting of military officers, two photographers, and three painters to document the area. Their work relied heavily on photography. During the half century following the invention of photography, Bursa had already been the subject of the new technology. The importance of this venture was its claim that Bursa was the site where a long process of cultural formation had begun; Ottoman architecture was included as one of its indispensable components.[38]

Preceding Ottoman investigations into art history and theory, Pierre Loti had visited Bursa and written about it. In "La mosquée verte," a long essay published in 1894, he had baptized the city as the "cradle of the Ottomans" and praised its

---

36 Oleg Grabar, *The Formation of Islamic Art* (New Haven and London: Yale University Press, 1973).

37 Ahmet Ersoy, "The Sultan and His Tribe: Documenting Ottoman Roots in the Abdülhamid II Photographic Albums," in *Ottoman Arcadia: The Hamidian Expedition to the Land of Tribal Roots (1886)*, eds. Bahattin Öztuncay and Özge Ertem (Istanbul: Koç University Research Center for Anatolian Civilizations, 2018), 38–41.

38 A recent exhibition on this project organized by Koç University Research Center for Anatolian Civilizations and the accompanying publication, *Ottoman Arcadia*, examined this expedition and its resulting archive from different perspectives. The materials were drawn from three volumes of photography albums presented as gifts to Bismarck, which are now in the collection of Ömer M. Koç. By the time of the expedition, Bursa's monuments had featured as examples of early Ottoman architecture in *Usul*, as well as in Parvillée's *Architecture et décoration turques*.

charming setting, its mosques and Byzantine monuments, its cafés, crafts, and its women looking onto the streets behind grilled windows. He described the Green Mosque (Mosque of Mehmed I) in detail, awed by the "mysterious designs" that decorated the high entrance door, the "lace-like" treatment of marble around the windows that reminded him of the Alhambra, and the tiles of all shades of green in the interior spaces. To his eye, the "real Green Mosque" was the mausoleum of Mehmed I, the founder of the mosque, presumably because of its exterior decoration of green tiles.[39] Loti's account was highly descriptive, without getting into art historical claims that characterized writings on the early mosques discussed above. Nevertheless, penned by a much-admired author in a poetic language, it contributed to the debates about the origins of Ottoman art and architecture. While they did not cite Loti, it would be reasonable to assume that Ottomans writing in the early twentieth century were familiar with "La mosquée verte." Celal Esad's claims that Bursa should be accepted as the place where Ottoman art was born, and more precisely that the Green Mosque marked the beginning of Ottoman architecture, unravel a connection to Loti's idea of "cradle."

The texts included in this volume on art and architectural history may have proposed shaky arguments, based on questionable facts. Furthermore, the self-made scholars who penned them may have lagged in the exhaustive knowledge about the substance and methods of the field that marked their European counterparts. They may also have been caught up in degrees of nationalist ideologies that flavored their positions. Yet, despite their relative lack of scholarly maturity, the authors still mark a key moment in analytical and critical writing about Ottoman art and culture. This is indeed the heralding of a local art history tradition that reveals a passionate search for the identity and originality of Turkish and Ottoman art. Complementing each other, the articles simultaneously provide a critical and deconstructivist overview of European notions of Turkish and Islamic art, and display an uninhibited and perspicacious front to the established authority of the European discourse.

The struggle continues today. Consider, for example, the important work of Gülru Necipoğlu in the 1990s. Her analysis of a late-fifteenth- or sixteenth-century scroll from Iran (in the archives of the Topkapı Palace) reveals rich topics that revise the field from multiple angles, including architectural practice, links between science and art, geometric patterning, conceptualization of architectural design,

---

39   Pierre Loti, "La mosquée verte," *La Galilée* (Paris: Calmann-Lévy, 1896), 211–48. The essay was published first in *Revue de Paris* 1, no. 8 (July 15, 1894). The Orientalist tone of this essay contradicts the analytical proposals in *Usul* and *Architecture et décoration turques*.

and its recording and dissemination. Necipoğlu asserts that the background of the kind of geometric patterning (*girih*) found in the scroll was named "arabesque" in nineteenth-century Orientalist texts—an ahistorical assumption that generated a major literature of its own and that still survives. For her, dismantling this discourse became a mandatory first step before delving into the (actual) historical development of the *girih* mode, in order to identify its associations, and ultimately establish its links to theories of aesthetics and psychology of vision as gleaned from Islamic texts.[40]

"Oriental" Women and Life At Home

"'Oriental' Women and Life at Home," is not restricted to an academic discipline, but instead encompasses popular publications, travel accounts, and novels. This is, of course, one of the particularly loaded themes of Orientalist discourse, imbued with unsubstantiated assumptions, superficial observations, exoticization, eroticization, and flights of fancy. Its strong appeal to large groups of people in the West resulted in a particularly rich repertoire that stretched across literature, painting, and photography. Women became the centerpiece of this other world and, in turn, the discourse on Muslim women became an object of passionate rebuttal from both men and women of the "Orient."

Representations of Ottoman women and their domestic spaces are a prolific area of scholarship, especially among feminist historians. Again, the aftermath of *Orientalism*'s publication has been significant in this regard. This literature, which follows the Saidian path of thinking while taking a critical turn against those of his arguments deemed totalizing, is too broad to survey here with due justice to its multiple and nuanced interpretations. Nevertheless, two main trends can be identified. The first involves close analyses of the depictions found in travel literature, that go well beyond the jaded stereotypes by reading and challenging them through the eyes of European women, especially British women. Scholars who engage in this pursuit include Reina Lewis, Billie Melman, and Mary Roberts.[41] They propose an "alternative" view that emerges from the particularity of the feminine

---

40   Gülru Necipoğlu, *The Topkapı Scroll-Geometry and Ornament in Islamic Architecture* (Santa Monica, CA: The Getty Center, 1995), especially Part 2.

41   See, for example, Reina Lewis, *Gendering Orientalism: Race, Feminity, and Representation* (London and New York: Routledge, 1995); Reina Lewis, *Rethinking Orientalism: Women, Travel, and the Ottoman Harem* (New Brunswick, NJ: Rutgers University Press, 2004); Billie Melman, *Women's Orients: English Women and the Middle East* (Basingstoke: Macmillan, 1992); and Mary Roberts, *Intimate Outsiders: The Harem in the Ottoman and Orientalist Art and Travel* (Burham, NC: Duke University Press, 2007).

experience, itself originating in and intertwined with women's conditions in the West. Writing outside England, they argue, made it possible for women travelers to review and reassess their own conditions at home. As revealed poignantly in Billie Melman's accounts, nineteenth-century English female observers discussed issues of polygamy, concubinage, and cloistered women in an appreciative tone. Using these themes to criticize English norms and practices, they provided an intriguing cross-reference to Fatma Aliye's *Nisvan-ı İslam* (The Women of Islam, 1891–2). Relying only on English-language sources, however, the methodological shortcoming of this school of analysis is its exclusion of the agency of Ottoman women. These contemporary scholars are well aware of the problem and attempt to bring in voices from the East, but they are limited to literature in English (notably, Zeyneb Hanım and Halide Edib in Lewis's texts) and to visual documents (Nazlı Hanım in Roberts). Against their best intentions, their innovative perspectives may hence slip unwittingly into neo-Orientalism.

Without any quarrels with the literature that relies on English-language material, a parallel trend brings forth the voices of Ottoman women. The focus here is not Orientalist representations, but women's history in the late Ottoman era. In her ground-breaking book, *Osmanlı Kadın Hareketi* (Ottoman Women's Movement), Serpil Çakır traced women's activism mainly through women's periodicals of the time and opened a significant press archive that begs to be combed for responses to Orientalism.[42] Abundant with articles on motherhood, education of children, and good housekeeping, these journals align, for example, with Ahmed Midhat's objections to the image of Ottoman women as the ever-reclining odalisque. In an astute analysis of Ebüzziya's almanac for women, *Takvimü'l Nisvan*, Özgür Türesay takes us to English women travelers' observations and Fatma Aliye's lectures to her European guests. Türesay shows that, like them, Ebüzziya saw feminism as irrelevant for Ottoman women, because Islam had already granted to them the very same rights for which Western women were fighting.[43]

It would be appropriate to consider the work of two leading late-nineteenth-century Ottoman intellectuals, Ahmed Midhat and Fatma Aliye, as an intellectual collaboration. Ahmed Midhat was Fatma Aliye's esteemed tutor, convinced by her father Ahmed Cevdet Pasha, himself a prominent post-Tanzimat scholar, to take on the education of his brilliant daughter. The relationship

---

42   Serpil Çakır, *Osmanlı Kadın Hareketi* (Istanbul: Metis, 1996).

43   Özgür Türesay, "An Almanac for Ottoman Women: Notes on Ebuzziya Tevfik's *Takvimü'n Nisa* (1317/1890)," in *A Social History of Late Ottoman Women*, eds. Duygu Köksal and Anastasia Falierou (Leiden and Boston: Brill, 2013), 225–45.

had profound impact on both, the evidence of which echoes in their writings.[44] The accounts from which excerpts are included in this volume were published a few years apart, and while Muslim women occupy only a few pages in Ahmed Midhat's *Avrupa'da Bir Cevelan* (A Journey in Europe), it is the exclusive topic of Fatma Aliye's *Nisvan-ı İslam*. Ahmed Midhat's *Avrupa'da Bir Cevelan* is an exhaustive record of his travels in Europe, including his attendance at the Eighth Congress of Orientalists in Stockholm (1889) and his visit to Paris and the grounds of the international exhibition there. Ahmed Midhat describes in detail cities, geographies, history, culture, and everyday life with a great deal of appreciation and always from a comparative perspective. His controlled tone took an acid pitch, however, on the topic of the "Oriental" woman. Presumably in view of the innumerable paintings and photographs he encountered, he drew her portrait through European eyes as lying lazily on a sofa and smoking a nargile, her thin and transparent garments ornamenting her half-naked body. This imaginary person, he revolted, was nothing but a dream, one that assumed that the woman thus represented was only a servant to the pleasures of her husband, and not the mistress of her house and the mother of her children. He added that such shortsighted statements undermined the role of Eastern women in the education of their illustrious sons, whose historic achievements in the arts, engineering, and warfare were well acknowledged by Europeans. Many pages later, Ahmed Midhat noted the popularity of the rue du Caire on the exhibition grounds, not because of the beauty of the architecture or the displayed artifacts, but because of the bizarre form of belly dance performed by Jewish and Coptic women in "Oriental" garb who falsely embodied Muslim women for exhibition visitors. Revealing his own hierarchical biases, he concluded that the absurd form of the dances was foreign "even" to Egypt or Tunisia.

Fatma Aliye's *Nisvan-ı İslam*, by contrast, is a treatise on European misunderstandings of women in Islamic cultures and society, structured as dialogues between

---

44 Ahmed Midhat Efendi wrote an entire monograph on Fatma Aliye. See Ahmed Midhat Efendi, *Fatma Aliye Hanım yahud Bir Muharrire-i Osmaniye'nin Neş'eti* (Istanbul: Kırk Anbar Matbaası, 1311/1893–94). In her book that covers the era of her father, Fatma Aliye makes many references to Ahmed Midhat Efendi with great reverence. See Fatma Aliye, *Ahmed Cevdet Paşa ve Zamanı* (Istanbul: Kanaat Matbaası, 1332/1916). The close intellectual relationship reflects on the fact that Fatma Aliye's *Nisvan-ı İslam* was translated into French as *Les femmes musulmanes* (Paris: N. Nicolaides, 1893) by a close acquaintance of Ahmed Midhat, Olga Lebedeff, also known as Gülnar Hanım. On this relationship and Ahmed Midhat's travels in Europe, see Carter Vaughn Findley, "An Ottoman Occidentalist in Europe: Ahmed Midhat Meets Madame Gülnar," *American Historical Review* 103, no. 1 (February 1998): 15–49.

women. Defining her starting point as European errors and deficits of knowledge concerning Ottoman society, Fatma Aliye traced the problems to their source, especially to travel literature. She set forth to correct the predominant vision by composing imaginary conversations between Ottoman and foreign women, emphasizing the fact in each that the former maintained their religious traditions and national customs, although they had adapted to modern norms and were fluent in French. The most effective procedure for eliminating misconceptions, she maintained, was to welcome foreign women into the heart of Ottoman houses, into the realm of women. The book purported to record visits by European female travelers to Fatma Aliye's house. The guests came from different walks of life to evoke the widespread nature of opinions held among Europeans. They hence included a European aristocrat, a nun, an English woman, and three French bourgeois women in their twenties accompanied by a spinster. The conversations covered a list of themes central to Orientalist discourse and seemed to address a foreign audience. However, they included at the same time contemporary debates taking place in the Ottoman Empire about late-nineteenth-century cultural and social developments and the search for balance between advancement and preservation of traditional values—the latter being Fatma Aliye's revered agenda for the future of Ottoman culture and society.

The first conversation raised the practice of keeping jariyas in wealthy houses. In contradiction to the European vision of this institution as "slavery," Fatma Aliye presented it as one of benevolence and charity. Polygamy was the subject of the second conversation and the hostess explained that while Islam permitted it, its conditions were so complicated that it was rarely practiced, even in economically prosperous circles. Fatma Aliye criticized men who took more than one spouse, yet argued that the practice could have valid reasons, as in the case of wives not able to bear children. On the topic of "the veil," Fatma Aliye surveyed the long evolutionary progress of the custom and pointed to the fact that Ottoman women dressed exactly like European women, but also covered their heads with a scarf to observe the rule of sharia, the Islamic law. The third conversation devoted a long segment to women's fashion, satirically obliterating the fabricated image of "Oriental" costumes in European visual culture as random collages commonly seen in postcards and photographs. The conversation shifted to marriage customs, once again Fatma Aliye rationalizing the advantages in the East, especially in terms of absence of dowry and women's rights over their property. In her enthusiasm to resituate her culture and society in the eyes of Europeans, Fatma Aliye may have substituted the distorted "truths" of Orientalist discourse with her own distorted "truths." However, truth is hardly the issue here; it is representation that matters and the fact that the book was exhibited in the Women's Pavilion of the 1893 World's Columbian Fair in Chicago affirms its status as an official statement about the Empire's women. Of course, by the end of the nineteenth century, clichés about Muslim women were deeply engrained in the West and fed a market hungry for exoticism and sexual reveries permitted only through bodies that belonged to other worlds. In this climate, *Nisvan-ı İslam* did not have a chance to shake the opinion of the international community. It remained a patronizing, preaching, critical, witty, and amusing historic record.

As witnessed by Fatma Aliye's account and going back to Lady Mary Wortley Montagu's reporting from the early eighteen century, domestic life in Istanbul's upper-class houses was accessible only to a small number of Western women. Entering the Turkish house was a much desired experience, its appeal so well known to the privileged class of Ottoman society that it appeared in one of the earliest critically acclaimed novels in Turkish literature, Halid Ziya's *Aşk-ı Memnu* (Forbidden Love). Mademoiselle de Courton, soon to be the governess for Adnan Bey's beloved daughter Nihal, had long dreamed of "a Turkish life" in a "Turkish home." Her heart beat with excitement as she expected a spacious and domed marble hall, its furniture decorated with mother-of-pearl, its sofas covered with Oriental rugs and populated with bejeweled, bare-footed, kohl-eyed women smoking nargiles or dozing to the sound of *darbuka*s played by black slaves. Never doubting the possibility of an alternative décor and lifestyle, Mademoiselle de Courton's disbelief and feelings of betrayal were complete when she was taken into a European style, small, and chic drawing room, representative of "the entire lifestyle program of the newly-developing bourgeoisie," in the words of Tanpınar.[45] Halid Ziya hence destroyed in a few words the image Mademoiselle de Courton had inherited from Western writers and artists. His insertion of this brief and isolated attack on Orientalism in a long, multi-layered novel accounts for the internalization of criticism among intellectuals.

The persistent circulation of fabricated images of the Oriental woman and the harem continued to poke Turkish intelligentsia in the 1920s. A photographic collage in *Resimli Ay* replicated the expectations of Mademoiselle de Courton and Fatma Aliye's guests, as well as of innumerable others. The caption identified the images as "of Turkish women frequently featured in foreign newspapers and magazines," and referred to the resentment they generated at home. Yet, *Resimli Ay* turned the criticism around and accused the Turks themselves for not putting an end to this

---

45   Tanpınar, *XIX. Asır Türk Edebiyat Tarihi*, 414.

degrading propaganda. After all, the magazine claimed, the center of diffusion was Istanbul and the photographs were of Christian models in Oriental costumes taken forty years earlier in the capital. Yet they still circulated. A few years later, this versatile magazine opened a window to notions of female beauty. A photo-essay, titled "Beauties of the Orient" (Şark Güzelleri) depicted women from Syria, Palestine, Siam, "Arabia," Egypt, and Turkey, taking exception to assumptions that Europeans were better looking than "Orientals." Declaring that "a Chinese woman can be more beautiful than an English woman," *Resimli Ay* launched a contest to choose the best-looking woman in the images. The entertaining tone lightened the message but pushed forward an ideological stand that destabilized readers' values inherited from European clichés.

The Unique Case of Pierre Loti

Louis Marie-Julien Viaud is best known under his *nom de plume*, Pierre Loti. Loti was a French naval officer, adventurer, and traveler who trod the globe across Algeria, Senegal, Morocco, India, China, and the Ottoman Empire, producing a large body of literature on the places he had visited. Loti's two widely acclaimed novels with Ottoman women heroines, *Aziyadé* (1879) and *Les désenchantées* (1906) also found a wide following among Ottoman readers. Especially considering their late translation into Turkish, in 1923 and 1922 respectively, the popularity of the original French versions is striking. The two books were met with conflicting receptions: great admiration and fierce rejection.[46] As Zeynep Kerman noted, the Ottoman and Turkish press has spent much ink on Loti since 1891, celebrating Loti over and over. The foundation of the "Pierre Loti Association" in 1919 was followed by a yearly meeting from 1921 to 1927 at Istanbul University on January 23 to celebrate a lecture Loti had delivered in Istanbul on that day in 1920 while the city was occupied by foreign armies. Indeed, the newly founded Turkish Grand National Assembly (TBMM) even gave Loti honorary citizenship in 1921, accompanied by a letter from Mustafa Kemal that thanked him for supporting and defending the Turkish nation during its war of independence.[47]

---

46   First translations into Turkish: Pierre Loti, *Azade*, trans. Handan Lûtfi (Istanbul: Mahmud Bey Matbaası, 1342/1923); Pierre Loti, *Meyûseler*, trans. Hüseyin Naci (Istanbul: Marifet Matbaası, 1338/1922).

47   Zeynep Kerman, "Türkçede Pierre Loti Tercümeleri ve Hakkında Yazılan Yazılar Bibliyografyası," *Türk Dili*, no. 580 (April 2000): 336–51. Published on the 150th anniversary of Loti's birth, Kerman's list covers the period from 1891 to 1994. Against this background, and fitting into the intellectual climate initiated by *Orientalism*, recent literary criticism has returned to Pierre Loti. See, for example, Zeynep Mennan, "Türkiye'de

ارباب قلمڭ محب ملتمز حقنده کی احتساسلرندن برنبذه

(اسماء حروف هجا ترتیبیله تصنیف اولونمش وهرکسڭ املاسی عیناً محافظه ایدیلمشدر.)

مثلا Les pêcheurs d'Islande ده ...
آتش فشانی حوالی Vers Ispahan ده ایران ...
— Le roman d'un Spahi
Les désen- ...
chantées ...

۱۵ آغستوس ۱۳۲۹

حسین دانش

مبرل نوری

غلطه — ۱۵ آغستوس ۱۳۲۹

جناب شهاب الدین

عیب زاده
حسن حسین

مصطفی نوفیون

قلیج زاده
حقی

۱٦ — ٦ — ۱۳۲۹

مجدول ساهر

برهان نوفیون

جلال الدین عارف

وبو مظلوم ترك اولورسه!
۱۲ آغستوس ۱۳۲۹

مجدول ساهر

FIGURE 2. *Şehbal* 4, no. 81 (September 14, 1913): 168–69.

عثمانلیلرك صنف، منوّری پیه رلوتی حقنده نه دوشونیور؟

(اسملر حروف هجا ترتیبیله تصنیف اولونمش وهر کسك اسلامی عیناً محافظه ایدلمشدر)

مساعده مسئله سایه سنده ، کزوب کورمك و بورازده طویلدیبی قوچاق قوچاق تحف و طرائف شهریه آلهبیلنك کتابنه عائده ملوز نوز بدك؟ که موفقیت عثمانلیك تحصر او اختیار لغدر! ایشته بو موفقیت و موفقیت ، بوسوده ده کامران اولان ذات بوکون مسافر محترم فرانسز ادیب ناسیی موسیو پیه رلوتی در.

فقط ، بو و انسانی ، و بویوك ادبی ایچون فیض قدر دها عاوری دها مقبوط ، دها لایق برقدر شرف لنظر تقدیراغتی ایده نندن لندنك مجاهده حق برستانه سنه ماضی شوقی و محدود ، اقبال استقلالی مساعی ، وكی كاماله سنه وه ورداولان دعا عبطیء له و نوشنمشمه سی وورآله مساله سنا مؤاخ تاریخ ایده مه ملیده مشکر قدر قدرانا ئاتا نیدیم یه ده.

کوز ته — ۱۱ اغوستوس ۱۳۲۹ جالیزاده

اکرم

بندن ، وطننك معزز مسافر و مدافعی پیه رلوتی حقنده کی احساسی مصور بر ایکی سطراو بر فقره ایستیورسنز ، طولوچه ای صدر هیچ رایكسط اله تصور ایه بله بیلریم!

فلاکتردر ، بر ملت اله او قدر خالصانه مواسانت!... بتون ملك مشترك وجدانه اله ایبتداتی حس اجهاداتك پایان در دك حمایه قطره اله تعبیر نهمكن ، هم نی قورققلداه اوله بیلیرك ، کندی فؤاده تحصر ایداردك ، بو عظیم طوفان حس آیجنده شخصیت وجدانته مكتنا ایدك ، فرقت ایمدیم. فقط اورد ذاتاوملته موقوف برخلید (؟) دكی؟

اعراب

پیه رلوتی انسانلقك بوکلمه سنه معطوف اولان حس نیبه باطنا سالی طابعین عرضز بز ، آیمدی ، بزی سیوی ، بزم منافع شخصیتی ، بوشویور دكعطاء سویلی یوكه کیمه ایدربیلر.

ادرنه — ۱۴ اغوستوس ۱۳۲۹

انور

نوك رزرلوك ماني تحقیر لدن جهان قانلرك سلامته ور. مندی عزّ بشان! دئ مظلوم ایدلك ، فقط ینه دنیا دابقادول دیاربارله ، دئمدی بز لـ...دئ كیزآلکمه سی!

یالكیز ... بولودن منتفر وكر-دار:
— تاریخ ، بیل دیووردی و بویوك ناتره لك سبسی ، بیکارده ، تمثله اكتئل تاصنره لغز ظلماتك ، تمصله مدنی ماسر اسیدر.
«نوراب افراشی» اورویانك افراشیدر.

دئیدم بو حق صدای-له! دئیدم آغلادم ، کوز یاشلرله « شاعر » ومئ بر سوكی عزیز آغلادیسیدر. وجداننك یكانه عزیز آشنا سیدر.

۱۲ اغوستوس ۱۳۲۹

انیس بهج

(١) موالانات المذکور حسن الشنكی و طويلاته المذكوره دفی ورواتی ادرو الرینكده ، ایکی وجوده الته عاده اجتماعیه عبارتندده لا صراط علمته ورجداددائر دائر و وجداننه اعتناب انتخاب ایتهدی انا واسی برق براسیوار. اوشتار وستانی وجده یو ترف ایشاه آلهیمه ترقی-له پیه نو دوست. بیرآله یو سقاتر دوستدر. خییرای و خلیل آتماز ایدم ، او بادتك سنده چه خلیل ایدبی لدیری آله ایده-راسته.

اسماعیل حامی

آلچمی بر قاچ ذاته نصیب اولان سیاست حقیقتی شیمدی آرته او تعدیل ایدیور. درك درك مؤمن بنگاكسی اولان افكار عمومیه جهانی تصحیحه اله منظومات دولته ماف یكی بر جیغ اختیاریه برور اوغله شرقی پوزماو قدر حق هیچ برو سیاسی مسعوده نه نصیب اولامشدر ! اسلام اوزنه نامارلوتی الی الابد ذکر ایده جکدر ، بو اروابشمان لدله ولی رمی اولان پیه رلوتی ، بزنك دك آوج بوز بیلیون دره بوزنك مدافع طار — آ کاهندر ... موازنت بین الملل ، دیاوماتك جومله منفعته نور حق ایتارلید-نك سایه سنده بل مبدل اجتهاداتك جومله قطره اله تعبین ایدر ، اونك سایه سنده ایچون ایچمه برچوق وطنی قورلوردر اونك ایچون بن پیه رلوتی بی سوكیلی وطنم قدر سه-یورم.

۲۲ اغوستوس ۱۳۲۹

اسماعیل حقی

بیكرمنجی عصر ممد نیتك بیقدار دانظاری او کننده قرون وسطا وحشتلرینی یاد ایدندری بالقان مظالمی تاریخ ، ارشهادلار لا عوث تصور ایدرك او نام مئلت تجیل ایدمك و او وحشتلرك قارشومهن نظر تایایش مهر تین شیسکوت انجش آیچ اوله ایكن ، برانثای ، پیه رلوتی مدافع حق ... اولمشدر دهبلرك.

افضل الدین

پیه رلوتی نك اولاد درجمی ، آلچی هندستانی انكلیز ماکیندن ، لاافغانیی موسولوف ایده سندردقور. تاراجق قهرمائزه قارشی اولاجق مرحومتك درهمیسله اوقلوله بیلر.

آغا کوندوز

کدرکاه تماشاشنده مضادی مناظر طبیعده نك ، محیط استطلامت اله داخل خاوشات کونه-نك کزودرشراتنده کزلانش اك دقیقی ، اك رودوجور شعریتر ، اك مؤثر ، اك عبرت انكیز حقیقتنی:

کوروب بونی و بونلری بدیع و صریح بر اسلوب رنكینی ، حار ومحركانكار بر طوز حزین اله انتظار اشتیاق و حیرته عرض ایتلك قابلیت فطریه-سیله جهان آرای وجود اولق ده مسعود ومقبول بر مظهردر ... جلاده لده میهادنه کثرویكی مستثنا بازارکندیسنه پاك حق وشروعه اولهده مهم برشهرت و روث تأمین انجش ومالكانه اك بویوك عدل ادبنه جناب عبزل استدعاسی بلا منت احراز موقع اعظام اعلام انجش اسرار غرائیه طبعا معقول اولدیغنه شرقك اقصا مالكنه قدر برجوق بلدیه زی وراده...

عالی حق مذکوره:

سنه معطوف مجاهداته تمیز ایدن موسیو پیه رلوتی ، منتك — مئك تخرب قالدی ، برورده — سوركانه مدافعی مذکوره سكی عالی بولیورم.

دار الفنون عثمانی حقوق شعبه سی معلمنردن

ابراهیم

سوكیلی ملكتك اك فلاكتلی زماننده — نزاحت فكر-لری ور. ماظلرینك ساحنه خیاك ایسندن باشقا برده نجلی ایدمهن — فرانزز آراسنده بولونق بجبورت ایدمه-سكده ، مطلوبتك شاپان تحقیر-ونفرین کور-وك لربی اجماعت اله نابتاولان فرانسده-نك اولان پیه رلوتی بو حكم ظالمانه قارشی بوتون صفوتیله عیصان ایدنلرك برنجیسیدر.

پارس حقوق فاكلتهسی ماندونردن

احمد اسعد

پیه رلوتی ، دنیانك بوتون سهام بغش وعدل ونی اوزرینه هدف ایدنمیسه. چكی پیله هدف تیغ ظلم اولا-دن ني دی-بك بر زمره بیتری-مندافعه-دن چكمه مه یل عالی — طنیتان اراب دهاندندر. غربك

بوتون قوای مادمهسی علیمزه در-له درباره تجاوز اولادیمزه صم-ده ده اله اجلاء اله بزده لهیمزه اجاله قلر ایمدیی جهان معنوی حق — پرستنك حاكم مطلق اولدیغی اثبات ایتمشدر.

استانبول خطباط

احمد جمال

بندماه پیه رلوتیه نام مکرم وغدری بتون توار عنایه واسلامه. دهپتون توار دمرخ انسانیت وده یوقه الاعظم وخلتم برصحیفه تجیل وتقدیس اشغال ایدمدك ، اولام جلیل كافه اهل الملك خاطراندن اصلا سیلنمه یدجك ، حتی عاليمنزانه بالجله عثمانلیلرك واسلاملرك حاصل ایتدیی فرط تعظیمات ومجبت ومنتداری قلیلرنده ایدن ایدن حفظه قالمشدر.

کوزته — ۱۵ اغوستوس ۱۳۲۹
عسکری مؤدمی مدیریه ارکان حربیه فریقی

احمد مختار

استانبولی ، شیراز راستابولی اوهامنه قبال جامعكری سیاه طوغرو بوكسلش برمر نیاز منبری آكدیرن آون ظریف منارلرنك ، فنور وجیددیرك ، کاتری بكسته عالمنك تصور وتزكر بر شان بین الملل اکتساب ایتدی. دنیاده تمقی

ایدمن شهرتكار پیه رلوتی ، سوك عادلانه جلاله-سنده

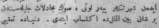

مملکتمزك زبدۂ متفکرینی قارشیسنده پیهر لوتی

(اصطر حروف هجا ترتیبنه تصنیف اولونوب وهرکسك املاسی عیناً حفظه ایدلمشدر.)

عبدالحق حامد

دفتردار عمر نامه

عزت ملیح

علی جانب

علی عبدالله امیر

بیهر لوتی ایله

غالب عطا

فائق علی

فاطمه عالیه

عبدالرحمن شرف

عبدالقادر موفید

Quelle grande consolation pour nous autres, victimes du fanatisme de la croisade balcanique, que, malgré l'iniquité du siècle envers nous, l'élite de la société française tels que Messieurs Pierre Loti, Farrère et Jaurès ait été favorable à notre cause.

Président de la section pénale de la cour de cassation.

OSMAN

عثمان

علی رضا سیفی

FIGURE 3. *Şehbal* 4, no. 81 (September 14, 1913): 170–71.

ملتك پییر لوتی حقنده كی خلاصۀ حسیاتنه ترجمان اولمق ایچون

(اسامی حروف هجا ترتیبیه تصنیف اولونمش وهر كساك املاسی هیئة محافظه ایدلمشدر)

نظارتی حق وعدلك اریكۀ لوانور و احتشامندل برجدای ارشاد عائلهسنه مدینتنك كرش اتباهنه ارسال ایدنلر ایدی معظم حقندهكی مقنوت بردو والضف احمدور رمان وفكر آعمطلب اولو...

دوكتور رضوی علی

عثائلی اقلیمی تضیله ایدل فلاكتلرك توالی ابتدایی و فرانسا علوجانبیه توركك نجاد نفتك عندز دنۀ انطباشتمادیغی و بر بر یته باقلاناشدیغی زمانلرده و عربانك وطئی اولان فرانسانك...

خاطرات ومعنویاتنه وطئی اولان توركایی تقدیم و تعریب یاكنه نیۀ سپاه پیرلوتیدر و بر عمره دكه یكۀ یكا حق ... دی او نلكسندر ...

اونك بورلده شو عصرینك ترق عصرینك احتوا ایدنلكی پالكنی لاقیدی دكل ، حتی مظاهرنه كوردمش وحشت اؤزای آرا كوزری ننالك ، دودلاقلری منقلس كوردیكم زمان ، مبرده اخوت وانسانیت حسلرنك بركون منفعه وسیاستدن دها اؤزرو بویولر موتقاریی اوله بلجكسله نكرار آمد وارواولوبه و بو نجیب وحكیم سیماده سیاده پیكرۀ امیدوار و بر نعمتلی فضیلی سلاملادم.

ادرنه ، ١٢ اغستوس ، ١٣٢٩

حقی الجع

شرفه الاعتصم بر لسان شمرلۀ ترجمان اولان پیرلوتینك صدالی حقنده كی مهجبه بركبلات اعتلا اولمشدر ، ٢٩ كوزاره دیكری دها عائده بو ایك كواش دا بویله ازلی و بر ازئالی

اولان اونك هوین شهشهداری بریۀ مصائف مئندهمبیم بر لهبلك بر دائما آولمۀ قاله حقند

عشقی زاده خالد ضیا

پیرلوتی بزی سومسه بیه بن ۀ اوكی سوكنك كندیی منح ایده مدمم ... دنلو ظلر و حقارته متحق كوردیلمشی وطئی سوددیكی فیتندار قلبی حقنزی مدافنه به آلتعاخذ ابتدایكی دوشنیودم ده بویولك وعظم ایده جكی تعیندن عاجز قالیورم ...

١٢ اغستوس ، ١٣٢٩

خلیل نهاد

فضیلته میل اعلالك ته انسان اولان كافیدر ... فقط فضیلته جنایت عد ایدیلدیكی محائده اونی وكولك ... به بله اجرمدا حاج قاتدنۀ اولق لازم؟ .. نچه پیرلوتی بردنۀ تیی انسانیدر !

فندق اله

بترت ، محاكمك لری حسبات دیله ده اساسلمه نور تارمبله جلك ده یبۀ آمكدیكی وقت ... بالقان مظالمی تارخنهسنده عالم مدینتنه كوشندكی سكوت اولۀ قیدی دلی زش و نظر تلامل

ایدهجك ، وبوجمر ماهسكو اشتراك اجتمعش اولان برزمرۀ قلدیكۀ اركان آراستدنۀ پرلوتینی بوكبل و موفق شرف و مجددر .

١٥ اغستوس ١٣٢٩

سامع

بدبخت ماتماك غرایۀ خون آلودنه یوزبیكارله آسنه ملك ...مشهركه شهق اخریلرینی دیكلركم ، سكریه یاكۀ مظلومك ایدی الری ، ایدی تلمیتلری ، ادیۀ كو زیكنشراله حضور الوهیته جانانسام و ورنتانكه جهانان سیر ایده مك اولدیغم ماثل سنۀ اجنمده بهرتنك حیندان هنوز بر شبیل بكۀ نیبه بیله جكلنه ، جهانده جباب فضیلت شجاعت اولدیكنه اعلان ایده یك یاكۀ بر زمانلرده پیرلوتی نۀ ده درك خاطر ایده یجكم.

١٢ اغستوس ١٣٢٩

سالحه ثروت صیفی

صوك بالقان محا ربی بزه مصیبت اولدیغی قدر اوروپایه وبكرمنی عصرینه ده شاه مظلومۀ اولان شاهرتۀ قلبۀ ده سیۀ وطئۀ معظمنك وباعادیای دوره درك شرف ...

وحنتینی انسان واعمار منتنه ... ۀ قادر آراسنده حساس وبجرمانۀ میانده سایۀ بلندمدر . پیرلوتی او ل طوفرزایۀ وبكرمنی عصرینه پالكر الك بیوك الك نازری دكل ، الك اصیل وبمرد فردی او لدیغنیدر كوستردیكۀ . بوآدمه انسانیت حاضرده عثمانلك كی وعثائللك قدر منتدار اولدی ...

سلیمان نظیف

پیرلوتی استانبولۀ طار واعترل سوقاقلر یریۀ دكۀ جاده اجیادلسنه ۀ ... ۀ اخنال اولار كاركار اولماسنه اسرار انكز قسفرده یریۀ ماهوزر طالباسۀ خلا. بو مدینت غریۀ نامه جهران بله ماجنه پیلان شبیلاركه هیچ شكایت آمیز بر لسانله دبیوركه : دن استانبولك و اوروپا شهری كی كوردنكنن ایستمم .

اونك كندنكه محصوص كوزلیكری واردر . اونۀ بری كی محافظه اتۀلیدر .. مجا اولۀ ؟

سلیم صری

مدینت غریبنده اسلاملره قارشی برمعنای مالك ته موجودبری تصور ایدبلمش دیم بونی آنجی ، مبزز ومحترم اخی بویوكۀ نجیب پیرلوتی جنابلرینی مدافعه حق و حقیقت بواندۀ ...

آنشین مجاهدنك محصول المای اولان قلمنده ، بالبان مظالمی مواجهسنده یكرنجی عصر مدینتنه ، جانیۀ ستا یشفول شناعتدن باشقا ... هر شیكۀ صوصیدیغی زمان یۀ بینه انسایتدن پالكنك برصدای حق یوكسلیۀ لیوردی كه ، بو شائلی موفق مجاهد تاریخ انسانی لایموتۀ لواح مفاخر آله تزین ایدنلشدر . بو بومفتق مشمشه قارشسنده ... ۀ قلبۀ مقتدیرده ، مظالمه قارشی رحیمی بر غیر مقتدر بولونددنده طولولی اودور دمۀ مقتدرم .

مجر١٥ ، ١٥ اغسطوس ، ٣٢٩

پیرلوتی صوك كبری جبۀ طرفندن تشكل ایدن اباربیه نك هیبتنده بر استاندار . لوتی جشاو برباءۀ سكری قبیله الوانی وخطراله نقاب نصاحب ایدن یكۀ بابا در ، بو كوبۀ بابا آشندری نری ناوتقدری اولورسۀ بوجمنده حساسیتنده باشمۀ ، او، نازلكۀ برزازی و برترن حس طائریم سودم ، بونك ایچوندركه بو حقلۀ كدكی عیبم برادای دشدنی زیاده منفعتۀ قاری ، سنتكساردر .

شهاب الدین سلیمانه

وطلتنده یكبرمكمه اولدیغی شو آوان فلا . كنابۀ حقوقروۀ الخری ، مدافعه ایچون ، والقان جنایاتنی جهال بربرنه نشرایدن غالبجنابدن فزنزمسیو فیمۀ لوتیۀ یشبدن ...

وكنور صبحی

بزی هیچ بر غرضۀ مسئلد اولمایوب ، انسائت نامه سمون یولیۀ آرامی لازم ... ۀ ۀ ... پیرلوتی اولدیغنده شون قلبۀ قائم .

ادنۀ والیمی عادل

پیرلوتی ، مهبانه دائر اولان Partou of l'on pleun mon âme a sa patrie(۱) مصراعی ۀ شاعریدۀ والنتاندۀ در . اونۀ پیه لوتی ۀ فرانسه دوغوردی ووبوتودی .

عبدالله بودری

پیرلوتینك قاندلری پالكر فرانسی اماجۀ الجمعار ایدهبیلجك ایۀ جاده كبكش و ۀ بازارك وۀ كك اوروپاینۀ لاقیدی كۀ اوكنده پیرلوتی شیۀ سۀ در مۀ حكۀ تخفیفۀ پرسبب اولایجی . فقط القائدلر طرفدن او روئانۀ حضورنده یۀ كال حضور تطبیق ارنتك وۀ الۀ اعای نام سیستمنۀ ۀ بویولك حكومتنك بحق حرفی سلوی وبردس اولایلر . او روپانۀ مراتب توئینی مدهش وصورتنده جك جك . طبیعتۀ طبیعی لازال بر متعالۀ طاله ۀ ادلشایهۀ اولایجی ، یمدنۀ بزك قۀ فاشۀ بناۀ كۀ عونانندۀ قلیدی . پیرلوتی نۀ شاعر رومی و آملی نۀ توركا قدار نشكر قدم ۀ ایسۀ ۀ ، اوروپا قدر بورلۀ و وطنداشۀ ته حسبۀ خیلندنۀ انسان ۀ ۀ انۀ اعظم ایده ... سودم .

عبدالله بودری

يبرلوﭘ جنابلرينه ، مقدور و مضطرب ايتكڭ مملكتم نامنه
حقيقت و حقوق بهر نامنه اك صميمى تشكرا

استحكام ملازم اوغلردن
طياره چى

يوسف كنعانه

«پيرلوﭘ» دونه
مقدر طبيعى تفرع
و تبهيرده نوعى شخصيته
منحصر بويوك رمصور
عدد اولونوردى ، اونى
اوقوﭘلر ايله تحليل
و تنقد ايدنلرك حاصل
ايتككلرى فكرندن
عبارتيدر .

يالكز شو عال مظهريى ايله جاودانى حيات قازانمش
اولان «پيرلوﭘ» بوكون هركك وجدانانه عائد
حقيقتلرى ينه كندينه خاص بر صفوت و بكارتله ، مدا
فعه ده دخى اٰمالنه بك آز رانسانى اولى وطبيعى دها
زياده بويوديى ، بوكدير .

بونى هركس بايدكه ، شرق اونه نهرى
جار ومنتورو بر حسنله مجلوبيدر . شبمدى شرق ، خصوصيله
تورك ومسلمان عالمى بو بويوك انسانى منتداراً و حرمتكار
برعشق ايله تبجيل ايدييور .

برنس نادى

ﻭ

كتابلرﭘڭ مطالعه
سندن آلهﭬم ذوق
ولذتدن طولايى پير
لوﭘى ذاتا" سودرم ،
طالامز ملتمزك يكيدﭘى
قارنه زنلرده و بتون
مالك زى يخستر ايتدكى
صرده نور كاره كوتردﭬى

الى الايده منتدار ابتدبكى بويوك آدمى شمدى تقدس ايدييورم .
تورك دوستى ، عدل و حقيقتمدافعى بر پيرلوﭘى ، نوركارى
الى الايده منتدار ابتدبكى بوهرك عاليجنابانه سيله كندى
ماﭬى اولان فرانسه ده يكى برشرفه بخش ايتمدﭬى —

يوسف رائى

متفكر و نيكبين
دماغلرك ، ظلم وتعصب
قرانليغنده ايجنده رها
وحقيقتى ايشيقلرى آراء
ينان اقليتى بحرينى :
« حقيقته تورتانيدهر
هيچ بر شى اونى نور —
لكه ده ايدمه يهجكدر »
صده سيله بلككه اك بديعنه هيئت اجتماعيسى اولان عالانليك
آپافر آلتنده ژيكيتنش حقى هر طرفدن يوكسكان آوازهﭬ
غيظ وكين آورسنده متيناً نده مدافعه ايدن محترم بر فرانز اديب —

(١) جلال ساحب بك — پورمنحى عصره —

شرقه منتون اولديمى قدرده عثانليلره مجلوب اولان
جسور و عاليجناب بير لوﭘى به عهماﭘى برتقدمه شكران
اوتى علوهت و عظمت فكرى قارشيسنده مطلقا ً عاجز اولور .
انجون بويله عاليجنان ، مدافع حق اولاد نشهﭘرونه اوفياض
فرانسه ى عثانلى قلبندن بر محبتله سلام واحترام رفيق ايله
متلى أولهبيلورز .

مدير شهبال

جمالى

پيرلوﭘى ﭘڭ حضرته اذلال ايتدﭬى متانت قلبيه ايله
نجابت روحيه طيت بحريه بويوك اولان عثانليلرى بكڭ
ايده جك درجهده اولوندر .

دوشنته ، به وعهدارنى طونى طه ايجون اوزاتدﭬى
دست نجيب وتسلتكارى بتون جهان انسانيتك التعامكه
خلال اولالودر . بويوك پيرلوﭘى نه سويدى نكر ميانده
كوردﭘى استقبال متعالكانه اثبات ايتدى كه وكر بر قصور
يوكسه لسه ، نت بس نست اثناتى اولندكدكدر .

بر پيرلوﭘى طرفندن تقدير ايتلق !
ايشته بن بر حس انه تعليبهﭘم . .

روم ايلى حصارى ، ١٠ اغستوس ، ١٣٢٩

نظام بك عثمانه

بوتون تورك ك ،
تورك ك ملى اعتبام عصرى
اعتداسنده پاشانك غرب
ادبياتك بالكزريى
اونو تيه بيقدرك اوده
پيرلوﭘ يدير .

١٢ اغستوس ، ٣٢٩

يوسف آقچوره اوغلى

مصاحبه

قاديلق دعواسندن

نهﭘ تخطر ايده مهﭘورم ؛ لكن غالا انقلابيزك
طلوعندن همان بوﭺ دورت سنه قدر اول ، انكلتره ده
اوزمان ضعف نسه ، تردى ﭘه چاره بولابلمك نو —
زمره صورت دائمه ده ايشكل ايدن جمعيت مخصوصه ده
فبريقالرك قاديكر سرمفتشه سى طرفندن يازيلان مهم
برراپور قرائت ايديلمش ايدى . بوراپور هنوز بر جهده
ويا داها بويوك چوجقلرى اولان قاديكلرك فبريقا
لرده ، وسائر مؤسسات صناعيه ده استخدام ايدن جهت بحث
ايدييوردى . بو زمان ايسه يله تدقيقات موشكا فانه سنه
عرفانه حيران اولارق قوجا راپورﭘ زوره له اوقو —
ديغم اوجمره انكلتره ده قاديكرى چوجقلو قاديكلرك فبريقا
لرك ، صناعتكاهلر ده جالشديرار دن طولايى كركؤاﭘمه
كرك چوجغه ، كركه حيات عائله به وورولان ضر —
رلرى نموثر و مقنعه تصوير ايتمش ايدى ؛ او درجه ده كه
او زمان هرك وقاديك وظائف متقابلهﭘ . « انقلاب
اجتماعيمز » كبى مباحث كوزلرﭘ ، دوشنجهلرﭘ ،
دماغنى ايشغال ايتمه اوستارلرى در خاطر ايدييورم .

كبكرده قاديك بر جمعيت ملىﭘ انجده هﭘ عائد اولديغى
نقودى بحث ايتمش ايدك ، قاديكلرك طبيعى اقتدارﭘ
حائز اولديغى نفوذ اولديغى ماتي ماده وي معنوى ؤﭘ تأثيرى
در ؛ نهﭘ والدهلرك جمعيته ماده وي معنوى ؤﭘ تأثيرى
فنا والدهلرك ، فنا تأثيرﭘ نشر ايغاﭘﭘ ده طبيعى در .
عموماً تربيت اجتماعيه مزده قاديكلرك تورك ك ،
همه مركز شهرلرك اوضراديﭘ قاتبورلق ، جيلزلق

ايله ادخاله ، بالكز ادخالهده كل ، لاقليه تطبيق و تعليمه
قطعيا ً محتاج ، چونكه بر ذوق شاعرانه خياليمزه
رغما ً قاديكلرنك اك بويوك شعرى ، اك امتياز علوﭘ ،
كندوسنه طبعتا ً طرفندن تخصيص اولينان والده اولمق ، والده قدسى
مشفاﭘنه وظفه والده اولمق ، والدهﭘنه وظائفنى بحق
ايفا ايدبلمكلدر .

ينه رانكلتره ده قاديى بوكا تماس ايدهﭘ بر موضوع
نوزرنده بويورركن دييوركر :

« قيزلرمزك معلومات شعليﭘ وعقل حفظ الصحه وقوقولرﭘ
نقدر بويوك اولسه والده خيازى ، چوجقﭘ بشﭘرورنه
اعتيادﭘرﭘ تحت تأثيرنده طولاﭘ صرف سوق طبيعى تناﭘلف
ايله اعتقادان واعتيادات باطلانه طولﭘ ، اصلى ايشيفى
أرلاﭘﭘﭘﭘ انجون فضله عداوولماز ، بودﭘدكه قوله اعتيادان
اعتقادان باطلهده رك الاٰن هنوز نن مفتاﭘ چوجغورﭘ
هك ، طوز ، شكر وصوت بر خصوصا ً غرى به ايله سيلمك
اصولى شدله مدافعه ايدهر . (١) لكن خصوصيله شيرلرﭘ
نوزاد وجوجغه حيات قارشى ﭘﭘ امان بوقدر دشتنداه محاط
اولان نواحى ، سفله ومسينه ده ؛ يا خود هبرك كوزرك
كوردﭘﭘرﭘ عاليده قيزلرﭘﭘرﭘ معلومات فنيه كشﭘ عدم
رافﭘ نه بويوك غفلت به بويوك جنايت اولور ؟ قاتليفده
امداد اولابليهجكر بعض تشبثات ايلديﭘده ، پيرلوﭘﭘ
ايستهﭘبﭘور ، مكتبلرده . — ايكنجى درجه برابيت وبرلكه
برابر ، اقتصاد واداره ، ال دسترليكنله قوله مقرون اولانﭘ
شيرﭘده تشكل ايدن فتيشاﭘده محبهﭘ داورﭘندﭘ بسﭘ ذواﭘﭘ
مهابانه ً زياد ايتهﭘ ايﭘﭘ مساﭘﭘﭘ وجلدﭘ ده نه اولﭘ ابﭘﭘﭘر .

لكن ايزﭘﭘ ، والده و نو قاديى ايله چوﭘ قاديﭘﭘ قيزلرﭘﭘﭘ
حقله داﭘﭘﭘﭘ وظيفه مقدر قلﭘﭘ ايجون اﭘﭘﭘ پاره واﭘﭘ سﭘ ،
ﭘرﭘﭘﭘنه ايجاب ايﭘﭘﭘ غداﭘﭘﭘ كاﭘﭘﭘﭘﭘﭘ جهت نظر دﭘﭘﭘ
آلﭘﭘﭘﭘ نه امﭘﭘ اولﭘﭘﭘﭘ رﭘﭘﭘﭘﭘﭘﭘ جهان !. . . »

(ماﭘﭘ كﭘﭘﭘﭘﭘﭘ نسخه ده)

كوزﭘﭘﭘﭘم ١٥ اغستوس ١٣٢٩

صالح تروت صفى

(١) انكلﭘﭘ عروﭘﭘﭘ عصبا يرﭘﭘﭘﭘﭘﭘ بر ده يزﭘﭘﭘ داه اطورﭘﭘﭘ كوردﭘ عصبا اﭘﭘﭘﭘ كه دﭘﭘﭘﭘكدﭘﭘ ؟

نهكرى باجﭘﭘﭘﭘق خستهﭘﭘ ده ملﭘك جاﭘﭘ والدهﭘﭘﭘدن
طوﭘﭘﭘده ، ونﭘﭘ بر ﭘﭘ قاﭘﭘ ، نﭘ بر جوﭘﭘ
باﭘﭘ اولاﭘﭘان والﭘﭘﭘ طرﭘﭘﭘدن بوﭘﭘدولﭘﭘﭘكﭘﭘﭘته —
شهمز طوﭘﭘﭘﭘ ﭘاولﭘﭘﭘ — عطف ايدﭘﭘﭘﭘﭘﭘور ؟
نوﭘﭘ ايﭘﭘ صاﭘﭘﭘﭘﭘم ، اﭘﭘﭘﭘدار بر نسل بشﭘﭘﭘﭘرﭘﭘك
ايﭘﭘﭘﭘﭘور ايﭘﭘﭘ اولا ﭘ اوﭘﭘﭘﭘﭘ ماﭘﭘ ومﭘﭘﭘﭘ تربﭘﭘﭘﭘ
ايﭘﭘ يﭘﭘﭘﭘ والﭘﭘﭘ تﭘﭘﭘﭘ كﭘﭘﭘﭘ اﭘﭘﭘﭘﭘﭘﭘكﭘﭘز ؛ يﭘﭘﭘﭘﭘ
اك منﭘﭘ ، اك مﭘﭘﭘﭘ وﭘﭘ اﭘﭘﭘﭘ تﭘﭘﭘﭘ اولﭘﭘ — ﭘﭘﭘﭘﭘ
— اﭘﭘﭘﭘﭘﭘﭘﭘز ، نى بﭘﭘﭘﭘﭘﭘﭘﭘ اتﭘﭘﭘ ايﭘﭘﭘﭘﭘﭘك ، يﭘﭘﭘﭘ
صﭘﭘﭘﭘ ده متﭘﭘﭘﭘ مﭘﭘﭘﭘﭘﭘ ، شﭘﭘﭘﭘ نﭘﭘﭘ تﭘﭘﭘﭘﭘﭘﭘﭘﭘ اﭘﭘﭘﭘﭘﭘ
برزﭘﭘﭘ موﭘﭘ و مﭘﭘﭘﭘ مﭘﭘﭘﭘﭘﭘ منﭘﭘﭘﭘ قﭘﭘﭘﭘﭘﭘﭘﭘم
تﭘﭘﭘﭘﭘ جﭘﭘﭘﭘﭘﭘﭘﭘﭘ اولﭘﭘﭘﭘﭘﭘﭘ قﭘﭘﭘ .

مﭘﭘﭘﭘﭘﭘﭘﭘﭘ ده ورﭘﭘﭘ ﭘﭘﭘﭘ تﭘﭘﭘﭘﭘﭘ ، آﭘﭘﭘﭘﭘﭘ ده نﭘﭘﭘﭘﭘﭘ
عﭘﭘ تﭘﭘﭘﭘﭘﭘﭘﭘﭘ مﭘﭘﭘﭘﭘﭘﭘﭘ علاﭘﭘ اﭘﭘﭘﭘﭘﭘﭘ ﭘﭘ قﭘﭘﭘﭘﭘﭘ
ﭘﭘﭘﭘﭘ داﭘﭘﭘ وارﭘﭘﭘ اوﭘﭘ « نﭘﭘﭘﭘ وﭘﭘﭘﭘﭘ » در ، نﭘﭘﭘﭘ
اﭘﭘ اولﭘﭘﭘﭘﭘ بوﭘﭘﭘﭘ ، درﭘﭘﭘﭘﭘﭘﭘ اﭘﭘﭘﭘﭘﭘ يﭘﭘﭘﭘﭘ ؛ يﭘﭘﭘ
قﭘﭘﭘﭘ و حﭘ نﭘﭘ طﭘﭘﭘﭘﭘ ده اﭘﭘﭘﭘﭘﭘ ؛ نﭘﭘﭘ
درﭘﭘ كﭘﭘﭘﭘ اﭘﭘﭘ ، نﭘﭘﭘ اﭘﭘﭘ بﭘﭘﭘﭘﭘﭘﭘ كﭘﭘﭘﭘﭘ ؛
مﭘﭘﭘ اﭘﭘﭘﭘﭘﭘﭘ ﭘﭘ جﭘﭘﭘﭘﭘﭘﭘ بﭘﭘﭘﭘﭘﭘﭘ غﭘﭘﭘﭘﭘﭘﭘ !
مﭘﭘﭘ نﭘﭘﭘﭘﭘﭘ طﭘﭘﭘﭘﭘﭘﭘ طﭘﭘﭘﭘﭘﭘ ومﭘﭘﭘﭘﭘﭘ حﭘﭘﭘﭘﭘﭘﭘﭘ —
به اﭘﭘﭘﭘﭘﭘ بﭘﭘﭘﭘﭘ ، يﭘﭘﭘﭘﭘﭘﭘﭘﭘ بﭘﭘﭘ متﭘﭘﭘﭘ نﭘﭘﭘﭘ درﭘﭘﭘ
چوﭘﭘﭘﭘﭘ غﭘﭘﭘﭘ ايﭘﭘﭘﭘﭘ هﭘ خﭘﭘﭘﭘ ماﭘﭘﭘﭘ همﭘﭘﭘﭘ
مﭘﭘﭘﭘﭘﭘ به اﭘﭘﭘﭘ اولﭘﭘﭘﭘﭘﭘ قﭘﭘ كﭘﭘﭘ عﭘﭘﭘﭘﭘ اﭘﭘﭘﭘﭘﭘﭘﭘ
كﭘﭘﭘﭘﭘ ؟ بﭘﭘﭘﭘﭘﭘﭘ اﭘﭘﭘﭘ قﭘﭘﭘﭘﭘﭘﭘ ؛ يﭘﭘﭘﭘ ملﭘﭘﭘﭘ مﭘﭘﭘﭘﭘﭘﭘﭘ
والﭘﭘﭘﭘﭘﭘﭘﭘ تﭘﭘﭘﭘ تﭘﭘﭘﭘﭘﭘﭘﭘﭘ وﭘﭘﭘﭘﭘﭘﭘﭘ طﭘﭘﭘﭘﭘﭘ در ، بﭘﭘﭘ
واﭘﭘﭘﭘﭘ مﭘﭘﭘﭘﭘ حﭘﭘﭘﭘﭘﭘﭘ درﭘﭘﭘﭘﭘﭘ بﭘﭘﭘﭘﭘﭘ براﭘﭘﭘﭘﭘ

FIGURE 4. Şehbal 4, no. 81 (September 14, 1913): 172–73.

محافل فكریه من پیه ر لوطی ایچون نه سویله یور؟

(اسماء حروف هجا ترتیبیله تصنیف اولوبنك وهركسك املاسی عیناً محافظه ایدیلمشدر)

یكی تورك تاریخی
پیه رلوطینك نامنی عزیز
تراكیانك ایچنستی
قانلوبی مره سندندایم
حقدر. یكی بر هوسله انسانیت
یكی زولاسی
تاریخی ده اونوتماز.

اساساً پیه رلوطی حقنده دیدیكلریم پك تخیل ایتكلده
ایشته: اوك، نشریاتنده نه قدر اصیل و محتشم و بونكله
برابر نهایت بر انسان اولدیغنی دوشونك: تكرار كندی
سوزنده اصل انسانلرك سوهاری آومسنه ایتكك مجبوریتی
دوغه نجه اصل انسانلرك سقوط تولید ایدر.
بندن سوكیلی دوستك بلنه انسانلقنه ساده نه احترام
وتجیل.

فالح رفقی
۱۱ اغستوس، ۱۳۲۹

فرانسز حیات اد
بیستنده حیوك وممتاز
برموقع سامی اولدیغی
كی هی و ساكیانه
اك شجیع برمدافع
نجیب و اصیل بولنان
پیه ر لوطی قلبًا طا.
شیدبفمز اك دردن
وصمیمی احتساسانك هدف انطاقدر. حقًا وحقیقتله وعلوی
خصلت مدافع غیوره بوتون انسانیت منتدار وتشكردار در.
كامران سری

The collective celebration of Pierre Loti among Ottoman intellectuals is nowhere as explicit as in the September 14, 1913 issue of *Şehbal*. The issue recounted the welcoming of the French author as a "national guest" (*misafir-i milli*) in August and expressed its appreciation for Loti's strong support of the nation during the catastrophic Tripoli and Balkan wars. This was the year in which Loti published *Turquie agonisante*, which looked with sympathy at the Turks' suffering during both of the wars and the earlier 1911 fire in Istanbul.[48] According to a Turkish critic's interpretation two decades later, Loti had assumed that Turkey was on its deathbed and had written this book "as though he was weeping at the death of a friend."[49] The response to the book in France was hostile, though, subjecting Loti to awful insults (*pires insultes*).[50]

The special issue of *Şehbal* was dedicated to Loti as a debt of gratitude for the sacrifices he had made in his "friendship for Turks." The cover featured his full photograph, while other pages depicted his arrival in Istanbul and his visit to Edirne. They were followed by three sets of double-page spreads dedicated to a survey. The magazine had invited a distinguished group of people from elite circles—among them literary figures, government officers, military men, and religious leaders—to offer brief testimonials about the French author. Quotations accompanied photographs of those surveyed, their headshots set in artistically composed round frames. The titles on each page summarized the issue's mission: "What does the enlightened Ottoman class think of Pierre Loti?" "A sample from the opinions of our literary experts on the lover of our nation," "Translating the nation's summary of feelings on Pierre Loti," "Pierre Loti face to face with our most important men of ideas," and "What do our important men of ideas say about Pierre Loti?"

The resulting collection stands out as a graphically powerful statement, with more than four dozen Ottoman intellectuals paying homage to a European literary figure. True to the *raison d'être* of the query, their statements were transparent, repetitive, and fulfilled the mission's goal. They emotionally voiced their gratitude to Loti for

Olumsuz Pierre Loti Eleştirileri," *Hacettepe Üniversitesi Edebiyat Fakültesi Dergisi* 20, no. 2 (2003): 31–40; Yakup Öztürk, "*Aziyade* Romanında Tematik Çerçeve ve Tevfik Fikret'in *Aziyade*'ye Getirdiği Eleştiriler," *Yeni Türk Edebiyatı Araştırmaları* 11, no. 21 (January–June 2019): 131–54.

48   Pierre Loti, *Turquie agonisante* (Paris: Calmann-Lévy), 1913. Loti dedicated a chapter to Macedonian and Armenian massacres committed by Turks. This book was translated the year it was written into Turkish by several translators as *Can Çekişen Türkiye* (Istanbul: Matbaa-i Hayriye, 1329/1913).

49   İsmail Habib Sevük, *Avrupa Edebiyatı ve Biz* (Istanbul: Remzi Kitabevi, 1940), 404.

50   Alain Quella-Villéger, "Pierre Loti et l'Europe balkanique," *Loti en son temps: Colloque de Paimpol, 22, 23, 24 et 25 Juillet 1993* (Rennes: Presses Universitaires de Rennes, 1994), 182.

his devotion to the Turks, for his humanity, for his commitment to civilization, and for standing behind the nation when the entire world was against it. Some referred to his refined writing. Poet and playwright Abdülhak Hamid took an extra step when he qualified Loti as "the unique poet of France." Novelist Halid Ziya, himself skeptical of any kind of exoticism, underlined Loti's importance as "the translator of the Orient in a most glorious poetic language." The East-West dilemma emerged in lawyer and statesman Celaleddin Arif's testimonial. His respect for Loti derived from Loti's struggle to "explain to Westerners and even to Easterners the natural difference between the Orient and the Occident, which they did not understand," his love for Turkey or his desire to make Europeans "love what he loved."[51]

Before this politically driven lovefest, several angry denunciations had polluted Loti's image. Tevfik Fikret had concentrated on him in his broader critique of European clichés about the East in the pages of *Servet-i Fünun*. Reviewing what Loti had written, Tevfik Fikret admitted he had barely touched upon "the lies perpetrated by Monsieur Loti," that is, his pedantic views of Istanbul and Turkish life. He rushed another article to the same journal, which was published in the following issue. Even angrier than the first, the second missive scrutinized *Aziyadé*, a book that Tevfik Fikret faulted for its "oddities [...] regarding our customs and mores," and for its claims that went beyond simple lies and errors, turning into slanders. In a bitterly ironic language, he followed the story line and tore apart assumptions that appeared "on every page" of the novel. He made fun of Loti's learning Turkish in two months, but also expressed fury at his game-playing like a "spoiled child" dressed *à l'Orientale* in a kaftan and a fez, living in a Muslim home in a modest neighborhood under a Muslim name. He fumed at the Frenchman's account of an Eastern woman hosting foreign men and entertaining his lover's guests by playing the *laterna* and serving alcoholic drinks and coffee. Like Halid Ziya's protagonist in *Nesl-i Ahir*, Tevfik Fikret, too, wanted to throw the book away—not only because of its inaccuracies, but also because of its insolence. He concluded that it would be impossible to fit into a few pages a comprehensive criticism of the novel—one that would display European ignorance of the Turkish language, culture, and society and demonstrate that most of its claims were erroneous and defamatory. Tevfik Fikret declared that *Aziyadé* stood as a glaring and arrogant product of this attitude. Nevertheless, the poet in him recognized the charm of the writing and predicted that Loti's books would be admired for a long time to come, since Loti formulated all his lies "not with a pen, but with a feather plucked from the wing

---

51 *Şehbal* 5, no. 81 (1 Eylül 1329/September 14, 1913): 168–73.

of a fairy." His books contained "the enchanting narrative" that gave readers great pleasure, even if they did not believe in them and got angry at them.

Tevfik Fikret's perspective on Loti's language survived for decades. For example, in his 1940 volume, titled *Avrupa Edebiyatı ve Biz* (European Literature and Us), İsmail Habib described Loti as having a melancholic spirit and delicate intelligence. He argued that Loti's original and idiosyncratic language worked like "ash," covering the flaws of the text with the beauty of its sentences. İsmail Habib quoted critic Jules Lemaître, who likened Loti to an "exhilarating machine of emotions" due to the poetry of his expression.[52]

Ömer Lütfi's review of *Les désenchantées* was published in French in *Idjtihad* (*İçtihad*) in 1907. *İçtihad*, a journal of Young Turks in exile, was founded in Geneva in 1904, moved to Cairo in 1906, and finally to Istanbul in 1911, where it was published until 1932. The French language articles targeted a readership that included foreigners. Ömer Lütfi's introductory paragraph praised Loti against the canvas of European writers who associated Turks with only "atrocities and incompetence." Loti's difference was in his appreciation for the people and his love of the beautiful landscapes, especially of Istanbul—all articulated in a poetic language. Nevertheless, *Les désenchantées* had a "thorn": its portrayal of women and the problems they were assumed to face during the process of the country's opening to the Western world. According to Loti, Ottoman women had been sleeping for centuries behind the barred windows of dark harems that were their prisons, but now a wind from Europe was waking them up to pleasures such as spending time in public spaces and enjoying balls, theaters, and ballet. Ömer Lütfi disagreed with Loti's assumption that Ottoman women lacked freedom and asserted that they enjoyed the same rights as European women, as could be observed clearly in their use of public spaces.

Kalem, a weekly satire journal in Turkish and French started after the declaration of the Second Constitution, punished Loti with more ridicule in two subsequent issues, less than two weeks after the regime change.[53] İzzet Melih penned two "let-

---

52 İsmail Habib Sevük, *Avrupa Edebiyatı ve Biz*, 314–15.

53 İzzet Melih was the author of a small collection of romantic novels, among them *Sermed* (Istanbul: Sabah Matbaası, 1918). Pierre Loti wrote an introduction to the French edition of *Sermed*: Izzet-Melyh, *Sermed* (Istanbul: Edition Atar, 1919). Curiously, Loti's introduction oscillated between repeating his former positions and reversing them: "I admire the way in which it [*Sermed*] analyzes delicate sentiments, especially the feelings of women, and the discrimination with which it deals with the shades of emotion. 'Sermed' completely destroys one prejudice against Turkey, namely that Turks consider women as a herd of submissive slaves," quoted in "Izzet Melyh Bey: A Rising Novelist of Turkey," *Current Opinion* 68, no. 3 (March 1920): 384–85.

ters," the first from Loti to a friend in Istanbul, the second from Djénane (Canan), the heroine of *Les désenchantées* to Loti. Loti's alleged letter told a Turkish friend that the Turkish yearning for progress and civilization would lead the country to lose its exotic picturesqueness, originality, and life of total pleasure, without ambition and ideals. Like an "insult on everything Turkish," the letter continued, Turks would end up with senators and representatives. If they were to benefit from paved streets, electricity, automobiles, in brief, "idiocies," they would also ruin Istanbul. The fictional Loti ended his letter, declaring his wish to cry like a child at the loss of his beloved city. Djénane's letter picked up from this point and added that while some admirers of Loti were reading his sentences with teary eyes, "a witty lady" whispered in her ear: "True, our eyes were filled with tears... of laughter." She then told the French author that she and her friends had formed a committee to fight the evils caused by civilization so that his feelings would not be hurt. Tevfik Fikret, Ömer Lütfi, and İzzet Melih's critical essays were published during Loti's lifetime. Giving some credit to Tevfik Fikret's claims about Loti's limited Turkish, it may be reasonable to conclude that if Loti cared to browse through *Servet-i Fünun*, he would not have understood these articles. Most likely, he was also oblivious to the ones written in French.[54]

The best-known attack on Pierre Loti came from the great Marxist Turkish poet Nâzım Hikmet in 1925 (two years after Loti's death). Only twenty-three at the time, Nâzım Hikmet's powerful summary of Loti's understanding of Orientalism begins by sharply synthesizing the Orient he portrayed in a few words, pertly covering the essence of the entire scope of the discourse. The mentality is described in three words: "hashish / obedience / kismet," the corrupt political power is explicated as "Maharaja, padishah, / a thousand-and-one-year-old shah," the obsession with women materializes as they weave with their feet at the loom. Religion is condensed to "Green-turbaned imams singing prayers in the wind." Nâzım Hikmet thus ridicules the Orientalist clichés in a few short lines. The poem then proceeds to convey his anticolonial message. The Orient of the popular books published in Europe is not real, instead, it is the land of violent exploitation. Nâzım Hikmet's finale celebrates the forthcoming end of imperialism, while continuing his attack on the French author for his abandonment of "the olive-eyed Azade" and for his corrupt operations as a textile dealer. Calling him a "bourgeois swine," Nâzım Hikmet longs for the day he would hang Loti's soul on a cross on the Galata Bridge and enjoy a smoke in front of it.[55]

---

54   I could not locate any response from Loti to his critical reception in the Ottoman Empire.

55   Nâzım Hikmet's poetry remained politically charged throughout his life and was always intertwined with struggles in the four corners of the world. Several long poems on resis-

Even though far from bearing the earlier fervor and intensity, fluctuating opinions about Pierre Loti persist to present day in Turkey through diverse venues, extending from conferences on his oeuvre to scholarly and popular journals on literature and history, and covering topics as diverse as memories, vignettes from his life, his love of Turks, and his artwork.[56] He is very much present in contemporary Istanbul in other ways as well: his house in Eyüp has been turned into a museum, the hill where the house sits is called the Pierre Loti Hill, and there are hotels, restaurants, and cafés named after him. The Orientalist hue of his persona is capitalized upon for touristic consumption. The French high school, Lycée Français de Pierre Loti, makes a lonely link to him as a French literary man with strong ties to the city.

Sarcasm as Vengeance

Ömer Seyfeddin's short story of 1919, "Gizli Mabed" (Secret Sanctuary), is a sarcastic exposé of European obsessions with the "real" Orient in Istanbul. The protagonist is not Pierre Loti, but one who resembles him. He is a young Frenchman, clearly an admirer of Loti who was taken by the latter's books about life in Istanbul, especially *Aziyadé*. Disappointed with the modernity that he finds in Istanbul, this character pleads with a Turkish friend to fulfill his desperate wish to find the "real" city. His Turkish friend, the story's narrator, takes him to spend the night at the "authentic" house of his old wet nurse in a remote neighborhood (reminiscent of Eyüp, where Loti lived). Titillated at first sight by the wooden latticework on the windows, the Frenchman goes native, insists on eating his dinner while sitting on the floor, and admires the old books on the shelves without showing any curiosity in their contents. At night, when everybody is asleep, he enters an empty room and discovers "a secret family sanctuary" that contains what he thinks are "undoubtedly" coffins with "the mummies of their loved ones," "relics" of the dead hanging on mys-

---

tance to colonial rule were written during the decade following "Piyer Loti," most notably "Jakond ile Si-Ya-U" (1929), "Benerci Kendini Niçin Öldürdü" (1932), and "Taranta Babu'ya Mektuplar" (1935). For an analysis of Nâzım Hikmet's "solidarity" with liberation movements, see Gül Bilge Han, "Nazım Hikmet's Afro-Asian solidarities," *Safundi (The Journal of South African and American Studies)* 19, no. 3 (2008): 284–305. The three epics mentioned here are from the interwar period. Nâzım Hikmet's interest in colonial struggles goes back to his days at the Communist University of the Workers of the East in Moscow, where there was an international student body. I would like to suggest that even though Nâzım Hikmet was not yet in the Soviet Union then, he may have been influenced as well by the proto-Third world waves that spread from the Congress of the Peoples of the East, held in Baku in 1920.

56 For a comprehensive bibliography, see Kerman, "Türkiye'de Pierre Loti Tercümelerinin Bibliyografyası."

terious ropes, and vessels filled with "holy water, brought from who knows which secret, which sacred corner of Mecca, Medina." Much amused by the misunderstandings, the narrator explains that the "secret sanctuary" is in fact the old lady's storage room. The coffins are clothing trunks, the relics are clothes on clotheslines, and holy water nothing other than rainwater. Alas, undeterred, the Frenchman reacts, "Don't laugh, my dear sir, even your trunk rooms have something mysterious, something incomprehensible, a sacred air about them," adding, "You are blind to it... Obviously you can't see."[57]

Ömer Seyfeddin's humorous dissection of the Frenchman's misconceptions and his refusal to give them up teases the Orientalist trope, but also underscores the Turkish friend's impossible quandary: correcting the errors even in the most concrete and credible manner does not translate into changing mindsets. Even after a few days in Istanbul, the Frenchman can think he knows and understands the local culture better than the Turk himself, a lesson learned from Orientalist depictions by the likes of Pierre Loti. Ömer Seyfeddin's satirical portrait of the Frenchman clearly reflected his attitude toward Orientalism, but it also stemmed from his political affiliation with Turkism, an ideological trend that rejected both Ottomanism and Islamism during the early days of the twentieth century. Ömer Seyfeddin's use of plain Turkish, devoid of Arabic and Farsi words, strengthened his message and conveyed it smoothly.

A decade earlier, an anonymous poem in *Kalem* had drawn a similar portrait of foreign tourists wandering in groups around Istanbul. Foreigners presented strange scenes for locals as they were herded to the usual places, criss-crossing the city, climbing the hills, thirsty and tired. They frequented crowded markets, old walls in ruins, and cafés; they stared at porters wearing colorful vests, at the stray dogs, the constantly weeping beggars, and the "Oriental Belles [...] swaying with childlike grace." The poet suggested that the curious tourist on the hunt should instead be looking for something else: The Oriental who thumbs his nose at him.

---

57 Ömer Seyfeddin, *Gizli Mabed* (Istanbul: Maarif Matbaası, 1926), 11–14. The story was first published in *İfham*, no. 100 (November 10, 1919). Ömer Seyfeddin's criticism of Orientalism has been noted by Turkish scholars. See Hanife Özer, "Bir Oryantalizm Eleştirisi: Gizli Mabet," *TÜBAR* 41 (Spring 2017): 257–75. Bernard Lewis translated this story into English in 1988. See Ömer Seyfettin, "The Secret Temple," trans. Bernard Lewis, *Die Welt des Islams*, New Series, Bd. 28, no. 1/4 (1988): 301–8. It was published without any commentary. In the light of Lewis's persistent attacks on *Orientalism* at the time, following his "The Question of Orientalism" (*New York Review of Books*, June 24, 1982), it is tempting to read his translation as another one of his nagging responses to Said, now in an implicit manner.

Humorist Ercümend Ekrem's account of a fictional trip to Europe, the United States, and Japan, *Meşhedi ile Devriâlem*, mocked the common misreadings and clichés of the East throughout; in one episode, however, it dealt directly with Orientalism. In a bar, the protagonist met an Englishman, who claimed he taught Middle Eastern languages at Oxford and had written a book about six hundred Turkish folk rhymes. In turn, the Turk declared that Orientals had invented a new field of scholarship called Occidentalism. Among the works they studied were the speeches Lloyd George made at the parliament; since they were all the same, they corresponded well to the folk rhymes that the Orientalists valued. His frustration took him one step further, accusing European experts of creating a breed called "Turk," who was not an ordinary human being but an anomaly.

A year after Ercümend Ekrem published his fictional travelogue, Ahmed Haşim constructs another travel account, this time about Bursa. Among the highlights of Ahmed Haşim's visit to the second Ottoman capital is a special trip to meet a certain Monsieur Gregoire Baille who had settled in Bursa about half a century earlier. Contrary to the venerations in the French press about the reclusive art lover, the author figures him out after a few brief words as "a kind of Pierre Loti, though without his 'genius.'"

Monsieur Gregoire's house is unremarkable, except for a wall-piece of imitation tiles fabricated in Kütahya. His pride is his garden that has an intentionally disorderly and ruinous appearance. Turkish art had taught him to love nature, that is, nature without rules. The willows and cypresses are meant to mimic Turkish cemeteries that exuded an air of happiness free from the stress of material anxieties—unlike French cemeteries that spoiled the "sweet and severe" beauty of death. The conical pine trees scattered in his garden resemble the whirling dervishes in a "large *semahane*—heedless, ecstatic—whirling from end to end, to the melodious songs of the nightingale."

The highlight of the garden is "Gurebahane-i Laklakan" (Hospice for Storks), a small structure composed of three rooms. Inspired by a public sanctuary for injured animals in the middle of a shoemakers market, Monsieur Gregoire's hospice also houses a couple of lonely storks under the trees. The first of the rooms, the Sadi Room, is named after the thirteenth-century poet from Shiraz, and features a hitherto unknown poem of his, purportedly discovered in India by an Englishman, and inscribed artistically on one wall. The second room, the Rose and Nightingale Room, is dedicated to women's names derived from the word *gül* (rose), and, like the first room, is crowded with artifacts such as nargiles, water jugs, silver mirrors, and pieces of carpets. The third room celebrates Vefik Pasha, the mayor of Bursa who had restored many monuments in the city, especially the Green Mosque. Just outside the Vefik Pasha Room, a marble plaque amidst the vegetation pays homage to the evening Loti broke fast with the imams of the Green Mosque.

Unimpressed by what he sees, the author, on the contrary, feels hurt by the exoticization of local culture. In response, Monsieur Gregoire turns the conversation to the familiar topic of the machine age and the alienation of human labor. He adds that the opening of the Panama Canal meant nothing to him, but the "primitive" embroideries of a young girl from an Anatolian town did. Ahmed Haşim hence sums up a collection of favorite Orientalist themes: mysticism, fascination with women, lack of order, and nostalgic traditionalism—behind which stood the European men who valorized the Orient, in this case, Monsieur Gregoire.

However, *Gurebahane-i Laklakan* does not merely ridicule Orientalism. It also provides a critique of the period's discourse on art and architecture that was entangled with nationalism. As noted earlier, art historians had gone beyond challenging European clichés on "Oriental" art, simultaneously disseminating a nationalist ideology. Ahmed Haşim's critique focuses on what he calls, "architectural nationalism," which was popular among the young literati in Istanbul at the time. Most likely with Celal Esad's *Istılahat-ı Mimariye* (Dictionary of Architecture) in the back of his mind, Ahmed Haşim blames the contemporary discourse for crowding the language with terms of masonry and carpentry. He mocks the intensity of the debates that promote architecture as the yardstick for Turkish civilization. Inescapably in step with the movement's protagonists, he feels urged to visit Bursa with an "obvious" program: to see the monuments, analyze the decorative elements, think, and take notes. He ironically claims that he would return rich with materials for future discussions, to further the reinvention of the "history" and "aesthetics" of architecture.

Concluding Thoughts

The Ottoman-Turkish critique of European Orientalism that emerges from the diverse texts in the collection does not come across as a theoretically coherent rebuttal. Rather, the multiplicity of the perspectives reinforces the compelling nature of the debates as a whole. Among the common threads that weave them together, perhaps the most prominent is the inextricable relationship between the critique and the internal efforts at self-definition. In an obsessively reactive pattern, Europe always served as the point of reference. Being Ottoman or Turkish was always in response to Europe. This problematic echoed on another dimension of the late Ottoman involvement in Orientalism, namely, "Ottoman Orientalism." Emerging during the last decades of the empire, this trend was infused with notions of social and cultural hierarchies, race-thinking, modernity, and civilization. Ethnic groups were perceived in two-dimensional and often derogatory categories that echoed European colonial practices, stereotypical definitions applied to both genders. Borrowed from European debates, "civilizing mission" entered the Ottoman discourse, aimed at reforming the "uncivilized" subjects of the empire. The upper echelons of the Ottoman elite, seeing themselves in alignment with the civilized world of Europe, produced various kinds of writing and visual documents on the different provinces, ranging from official reports, travelogues, novels, photographs, and paintings to representations of the empire's people in world's fairs.[58] If not the topic of this book, it is useful to acknowledge Ottoman Orientalism, especially because it even intersected with criticism of European Orientalism. Consider, for example, the art historical discourse, which rebutted European interpretations of Ottoman art and architecture, while creating a hierarchy that considered fifteenth- and sixteenth-century Ottoman art and architecture as superior to "Islamic" art and architecture traditions elsewhere—due to its clear, pure, and ornamentally restricted character, corresponding to the standards of European modernity.

Criticism of Orientalism withered gradually after the early 1930s, consistent with historic developments, shifting European colonial forms of domination, and the subsequent major transformations in the world order. If not entirely dead, the discourse on European Orientalism took on other forms and did not manifest itself in its nineteenth-century fervor. Orientalism again became a heated subject of debate following the publication of Said's book, translated into Turkish several times, and published in many editions since the 1980s.[59] A plethora of scholarly articles and theses appeared, in concert with academic productions elsewhere and accompanied by numerous conferences involving different disciplines and the art world. The debates happened across the ideological spectrum, reminiscent of the earlier period. Nevertheless, the post-1980s engagements in Orientalism moved in

---

58 There is a growing inquiry on Ottoman Orientalism, parallel to the growing literature on various aspects of the nineteenth-century Ottoman Empire. Historians do not consider the trend as a straightforward replication of European Orientalism, but attempt to qualify its idiosyncrasies. See, for example, Selim Deringil, "They Live in a State of Nomadism and Savagery: The Late Ottoman Empire and the Post-Colonial Debate," *Comparative Studies in Society and History* 45, no. 2 (April 2003): 311–42; Ussama Makdisi, "Ottoman Orientalism," *American Historical Review* 107, no. 3 (June 2002): 768–96; and Zeynep Çelik, "Epilogue," *Empire, Architecture, and the City: French-Ottoman Encounters, 1830–1924* (Seattle and London: University of Washington Press, 2008), 246–74.

59 On this topic, see Ali Şükrü Çoruk, "Oryantalizm Üzerine Notlar," *Sosyal Bilimler Dergisi* 1, no. 2 (December 2007): 193–204.

different directions. They were framed by popular trends in neo-Ottomanism and neo-Orientalism, as well as strong reactions to them—cutting through different sectors of Turkish society. Although inviting further associational analysis with the materials presented in this book, it is beyond the goals and the scope of my essay to probe the complexity of recent discussions and their political and historical ties. I would caution against drawing quick parallels to today.

I offer *Europe Knows Nothing about the Orient* not as a finished book, rather as an open-ended project. To collect the texts, I combed through the literature to the best of my ability and consulted with many colleagues. Inevitably, there will be sources I missed, and it is my hope that those who identify the lacunae will come forward and add to the reader. Beyond my reach is also the discourse from other "Oriental" contexts, which, I am convinced, is at least as rich as the Ottoman one. The reactions to Renan's "L'islamisme et la science" from India and St. Petersburg are indeed good indications of the presence of many others. On women's status and rights in Islamic societies, as well as the European misrepresentations, Ahmed Midhat draws attention to his colleague, eminent Egyptian scholar Hamza Fathallah, whose work dates from the same time as his own.[60] Hearing more voices would complicate the history of cultural hegemony and help to present a world in which ideas traveled, became transformed, engaged in debates, and even turned into battlegrounds. The open-endedness of this book hence extends beyond the Ottoman-Turkish boundaries. In support of this call, my final reference is to a satirical story, "I Don't Want to Be Arab Any Longer," published in Bône (Annaba) at the height of the colonial rule in 1919, in the French-language Algerian journal *el-Hack*.

> I am an intelligent man, very 'respectable,' but I have the misfortune of belonging to this dirty Arab race. Everywhere I go people speak to me using the familiar, elbow me out of the way, even young French girls make faces at me. Alas, just like the lepers in the city of Aosta, the people of Europe flee from me. And yet I am healthy. I am also very clean, my fez is new and my hair, cut in the English style, is home to no parasite. I shave my beard daily, and my moustache stands proudly above my lips, my teeth glisten like nacre. My eyes are like amethysts. Truly, I am a handsome creature, believe me...

60 Hamza Fathallah, *Bakurat al-kalam 'ala huquq al-nisa'fi Islam* (Earliest Discourse on the Rights of Women in Islam) (Bulaq: al-Matba'a al-kubral al-amırıyya, 1308/1890). Hamza Fathallah and Ahmed Midhat most likely met in 1889 at the Eighth Congress of Orientalists in Stockholm, which they both attended. On Hamza Fathallah, see Ronak Husni, Daniel L. Newman, eds., *Muslim Women in Law and Society* (London and New York: Routledge, 2007), 3–4.

I have even gone to high school...

And yet, in spite of all this, I am still treated like an Arab. What must I do in order to be French, to be able to make eyes at the girls at the counter without feeling guilty...

Let us make haste and go to the most stylish tailor and request of him a suit that is of the latest style: tight trousers, an alpaca or colonial khaki jacket, polished boots, trimmed felt bowler hat, and a cane with a silver knob. I shall be quite decked out in such an outfit, and so as to avoid any possible indiscreet meetings, I would never again have any contact with native peoples...

So it is all one thing: I no longer wish to be an Arab, and I won't be one anymore.

—But your visitor's card very clearly reads "Ali Aghioiu."

Don't worry, I am smart. I am going in today to line up at the civil affairs office so that I may henceforth be called Pierrre Aréoul or even Pierre Martin. I am sure that Mr. President of the Republic, so anxious to see Arabs become civilized and draw nearer to their French city brethren, will do me this small service with great pleasure.[61]

61   Published in *el-Hack*, June 8–15, 1919, quoted in Aldelkader Djeghoul, *Éléments d'histoire culturelle algérienne*, excerpt trans. Sharon King (Algiers: ENAL, 1984), 91–92.

GRAND BATTLES

FIGURE 5. Abdullah Frères,
early twentieth century
(from the collection of Ömer M. Koç)

NAMIK KEMAL

"Europe Knows Nothing about the Orient"[1]

It is indeed strange that so many eminent nations, intent on finding out whether or not there are people in their midst with strong desire to investigate the truth, are advanced enough to keep thousands of scholars busy with various hypotheses and deductions, but they do not see the true character of a land such as ours, which is so close to them that, as the saying goes, it might as well be touching their eyelashes.

But our citizens should not get the wrong impression. It is stranger still when those people strive to uncover the depths of their conscience through the power of the epics of their ancestors lying peacefully in their graves, and yet remain unaware of the character of a nation that lies with them like conjoined twins on the lap of the same earth.

We may excuse Europeans for their ignorance, for they have no source of information about Islam besides the slanders of certain of our friends.

Take the Englishman who visited Istanbul. He heard the fire cannon. He asked his Rum interpreter what it signified. The interpreter pointed at the baskets hanging from the Beyazıd Tower and said, "There, they hung two men, and they are celebrating." And now countless foreigners mistake the tower for the gallows. They are convinced that the Turks always hang people, and that every time they do so, they exclaim their joy.

A fabulist thought up some tales. Thanks to his deceptions, the harem quarters are now believed to be dens of iniquity filled with odalisques and concubines.

Two libertines managed to get themselves published; because of their influence, it is now believed that the lives and rights of non-Muslims here are protected thanks to Russia or England.

A few status-hungry persons, aiming to deprive the general public of the civilized world's sympathy, depicted Muslims as zealots, and now the name "Turk"

1   Namık Kemal, "Avrupa Şark'ı Bilmez," *İbret*, no. 7 (16 Rebiülahir 1289/June 23, 1872): 2.

calls to mind a savage tribe like the bloodthirsty Crusaders who wanted to over-turn the world.

Certain fickle enthusiasts, having learned a handful of French words, attempt-ed to ignorantly and crudely mock Islam, which is the epitome of justice and wis-dom. Inspired by them, now there are those who wish to make a plaything of the precepts of our religion.

We have yet to see any books on the Orient written in European languages that are worthy of study. Those who truly wish to learn the character of the Orient, by what means might they achieve their goal and abandon these misconceptions? For instance, in French, the most scholarly study on our political organization, events and national morals is a book by one D'Ohsson, and the most factual of the studies treating our past and our customs is, as you know, Hammer's *History*. Whichever of these one happens to read, one is astonished by the abundance as well as the strangeness of the ignorant fables within.

For example, in D'Ohsson's view, Muslims have no rights whatsoever before the state. Sunnis believe in the moral purity of the imam; Shiites follow the con-sensus of the people. Imam Ali is the guide of the Shiites, and Omar is the lead-er of the Sunnis. This same writer has Fatih Sultan Mehmed make a certain law against fratricide and has the ulema of the period approve such a law. "The word and order of the sultan is immutable so long as he lives," he says. He believes that "the Padishah is free to dispose of the property and lives of those in his command." In sum, as one reads this book, one is unsure if the author is discussing the laws brought down by Muhammad or the laws of China.

With this sort of scholarship, how can one gain knowledge about the wise laws and just decrees of the *fiqh*?

At the very beginning of his *History*, Hammer has Sultan Osman execute his uncle, while batteries and cannons are sent from here to Kosovo. He turns pro-gressives such as Selim I and Köprülü into vexing souls, remembering them with denunciations befitting monks. He transforms decadents such as Bayezid II and arrogant men such as İbrahim Pasha into angels of good works, describing them with the kind of exaggeration the Persians are known for. In his description, Fatih is crueler than Ghengis Khan. To savages like Alexander and Hunyadi Janos, he ascribes a mildness and mercy approaching that of the Apostles. According to his telling, wherever we go, we go in multitudes of hundreds of thousands, while our enemies merely number in ten to fifteen thousand. In fact, he counts a mere five thousand soldiers standing against Fatih's entire army. In the Battle of Mohács, he brings only twenty-five thousand Hungarian soldiers to face Sultan Süleyman's army of three hundred thousand.

He preposterously attempts to explain away Charles V's flight from Venice to Spain upon hearing of the Ottoman offense, and worse yet, his failure to join the battle against Süleyman the Magnificent, by claiming that the king didn't deign to the encounter. He presents Fazıl Ahmed Pasha's retreat with ten thousand advance troops—who, upon his orders, cross the waters of the Raba—as a great slaughter that might have ushered in a new era in the art of warfare. Whenever we are victorious, he suddenly finds an accident to explain it. Whenever we are defeated, he extols our enemy's extraordinary heroism. Any decision concerning Christians, whether based on the sharia or issued by the council of state, he attributes to zealotry. Every conflict is a sectarian uprise. He characterizes the Vienna campaign as a "breach of treaty" even though it was rightly proclaimed by Kara Mustafa Pasha at the time through the office of foreign affairs, while he characterizes the Polish king's despicable breach of treaty in that same campaign as "just warfare." While attempting to explain ritual prayer and the injunction against beginning prayer exactly at sunrise, noon, and sunset, he offers the nonsense that, according to Islamic belief, at those times "the devil is holding the sun." When he tries to translate passages from Arabic and Turkish, he misreads the word *ferec*, which means "lightness of heart," with a quiescent letter *ra*.[2] He renders the word *gidi*, a term of insult, as the familiar *kedi*.[3]

Given information such as this, how could you learn of the Ottomans' heroic eminence and the beauty of their morals?

While Oriental languages are essentially of no use to the Europeans, some do learn these and make modern grammars for Arabs and modern dictionaries for Turks. These are not perfect, but they at least serve their compatriots who wish to produce their perfect works.

Although Western languages have for us become indispensable, none among us is able to learn a language as well as Seyyid Mustafa did in the time of Selim III, so that anyone might read what we get to write.

So long as the mirror of our reality consists only of the books written by the Etnik-i Eterya,[4] we cannot be less obscure to the Europeans.

---

2   As *ferc*, which means cleft or vulva. —Trans.

3   *Gidi* means pimp while *kedi* means cat.—Trans.

4   A Panhellenist organization founded in 1814 and dissolved in 1899.—Ed.

When we are finally able—like the Russians, the Poles, the Greek—to counter the aspersions cast upon us in other languages by expressing ourselves in those same languages, then the general public in Europe will quickly get to know the Orient, and just as quickly render to us our due.

At the same time, the fact that the Orient is not completely known in Europe does not, in my opinion, pose any great threat to us. For Europe properly understands the significance of our future, and it is perfectly known that we are true to our word.

But we should repeat: our citizens should not blame us for things that are not our doing and hesitate to work for our commonweal because their own lives and posterity, more than ours, depend on such work.

Let everyone take note: Is there another state in the world where every community speaks its own language? Where so many creeds are safe and free from assault? Where so many peoples have continued to live together? If one considers the condition of the Poles or that nothing at all remains of the Armenians in Hungary, one will understand that every nation here relies on the independence of the Exalted Ottoman State.

We have always held the adherents of other religions under our protection. We have honored every promise we have made. We sacrificed our security for their sake, sacrificed wealth and lives by the millions, to guard their wealth and their lives. In return, we expect that they, too, honor their word. We desire that our common homeland be held sacred, and safe from self-interested motives and malice.

We are pleased to see that this tendency has set in among certain groups. It is our hope that it will soon spread among all of them. Sound ideas are like the daylight: when it dawns in one part of a land, it is natural that, before too long, it spreads across the rest.

Translated by Gregory Key

EBÜZZİYA

"Europe Knows Nothing about the Orient"[1]

In an important article of his, Kemal Bey illustrates how the Europeans are guilty of either exaggeration or deficient knowledge: "In Europe, one encounters scholars who can assess the depth of the rivers on the moon and prove their claims scientifically, yet who are oblivious to the dimensions of the Maritza River, which is in Europe."

In truth, there are learned Europeans who willingly face a thousand perils in ardent pursuit of the truth but whose knowledge and inquiry concerning the Orient are, on the whole, not free of defect and exaggeration.

As fresh evidence in this case, I submit the following excerpt from a column published in the August 21 issue of the newspaper *Tabaat* in Paris, which I purchased:

Excerpt

Monsieur Ernest Mayer,[2] whilst enumerating the periodical organs of the religion of Islam, says:

"In Istanbul there is a press that prints a small newspaper. This paper has a daily circulation exceeding one hundred thousand, and it wields extraordinary influence.

"Said newspaper is run by a Syrian, and parcels that contain its issues are sent all around the Muslim world. These papers are found everywhere from Samarkand to Mogadura.[3] They have correspondents in numerous countries: India, Morocco and throughout the Arabian Peninsula. Even in Timbuktu they have a correspondent by the name of Şeyhül-Beham."

The question of whether there is any such paper in Istanbul does not, in my view, merit even mention. However, any European reading this may be excused for be-

1   Ebüzziya, "Avrupa Şark'ı Bilmez," *Mecmua-i Ebüziyya* 5, no. 49 (November 30, 1886): 1551–553.
2   Ernst Heinrich Meier ?—Ed.
3   Mogadura is a city and port on the Moroccan coast.—Ebüzziya.

lieving it, because Ernest Mayer is counted among those scholars whose words are trusted by all of Europe. In view of this, is it not an act worthy of censure to expound on a thing which does not exist?

This, then, is what truly merits mention as well as discussion. Thoughts expressed on a subject, as we know, stem either from sincerity or from an ulterior motive. Remarks made in earnest, even if they suffer from inaccuracy or exaggeration, are excusable so long as there is no malice in them. In other words, they are to be forgiven on account of good intentions.

Now, what needs to be determined here is the intent with which Ernest Mayer wrote this article. No malice is evident in the tone of the above excerpt, and indeed the esteemed gentleman is one who serves the good of humanity and not the malicious ends of some nation. This being the case, one must conclude that the aforesaid has been the victim of deception, an affliction to which persons of excellent morals are frequently susceptible.

Specifically, because the greater part of European scholars who travel to the Orient do not know the Oriental languages, all that they learn about us comes from guides, to whom they give the name cicerone. One may well imagine what manner of knowledge and morals are possessed by those who seek their livelihood in acting as guides to anybody and nobody, and how accurate is the information that they offer. The fault in this again lies with us, for we have produced no work that might serve as a reference for earnest Europeans who have cultivated an interest in researching our country. Whatever the Europeans would learn of us, they have recourse only to the deceptive publications of our enemies, or to the fabrications of the guides whom they happen upon.

Translated by Gregory Key

"Foreigners and Our Turkish"[1]

The letter from London published in last week's issue of *Servet-i Fünun* discusses how rare the use of our language is in England. It aims to show the extent to which the English locals are ignorant of our language, of our customs and ideas, and of our circumstances and dignity:

> [...] It would be no exaggeration to say that, from their parliamentarians all the way down to their common village priests, among those who opine and declaim on affairs of the Orient, there is not one who knows Turkish, nay, who has even heard of the literature, education, or customs of the Turks. In fact, there are few who would know us from our outward appearance. If one of them should see you in frock coat and trousers, he would never imagine you to be a Turk, what with no quilted turban on your head, no woolen cloak on your back, and no scimitar at your hip. And should you happen to be fair-skinned, you could never convince them of your Turkishness were you to produce ten witnesses; as far as they are concerned, anyone without dark hair or skin cannot possibly be a Turk. When at a gathering it is found out that I am Turkish, some ask me such questions that I cannot help but laugh at their vacuous opinions; at times, however, I feel like crying out of rage. In sum, the English know neither us nor our language. And one cannot convince them of this...

It would not be unwarranted or too rash to apply, verbatim, this description of facts to the French, Germans, Italians, and Spanish of Europe, or to accuse the Americans of suffering, in their way, from an even greater ignorance of the Orient. If you ask an Ottoman who has returned from living among any of those people, you will receive this answer: "Europe does not understand the Orient!"

Since a lengthy inquiry into the social factors underlying this lack of knowledge is beyond the scope of a literary exchange column such as this, I leave the matter aside. Still, it must be confessed that knowledge of the Orient has not been

---

1   Tevfik Fikret, "Ecnebiler ve Türkçemiz," *Servet-i Fünun*, no. 401 (5 Teşrinisani 1314/ November 17, 1898): 165–67.

so harmful to Europe as knowledge of Europe has been to the Orient. To say that Europe does not understand the Orient is to say that it knows nothing of its languages and customs; else it would be naive in the extreme to presume that it does not understand the commercial interests it has in the Orient. In any case, my object is to discuss the civilized nations' disregard for our language and their ignorance of our literature; let us now return to this object.

The Frenchman Pierre Loti is well-known. Five or six years ago, on the day this man of letters was elected to the Académie française instead of the late Octave Feuillet, he gave his customary speech, which was met with a response by the secretary of the Académie, Monsieur [Alfred-Jean-François] Mézières. During the welcoming ceremony for his new associate, Monsieur Mézières spoke approximately the following words:

> Thanks to you, the Orient and the Far East [Aksa-i Şark] are known to the French. You roam about there as though it were your private excursion spot, and you take us along. Lifting layer by layer the veil of mystery that covers the customs and circumstances of the Orientals, you reveal before our eyes myriad secret marvels. [...]

These words suffice to demonstrate that Monsieur Loti is renowned amongst his countrymen for his considerable knowledge of the Oriental world; as corroborating evidence, we may refer to *Capitals of the World*, the series printed by the renowned French publisher Hachette, in which the description of Istanbul was entrusted to Monsieur Loti. For each capital, the writer most knowledgeable about that place was commissioned to write the description. The pages pertaining to Bucharest were penned by none other than the Queen of Romania herself. It would appear, then, that in France the most knowledgeable, or one of the most knowledgeable, about Istanbul and about us is Loti. He says as much himself: "I have been to Istanbul many times. I have learned Turkish well. I have assimilated to the Turks, and resemble them so much that, when I entered their midst in disguise, they were none the wiser..."

In fact, Monsieur Julien Viaud—Loti's true name—was here for a time in military service aboard the attendant vessel of the French embassy, and later visited our country once or twice more. In view of his natural Western aspect, he may well have donned Turkish clothing on one or two occasions, but it is doubtful that he fooled himself, much less any of the Turks to whom he presented himself in such garb. It is certain, however, that he managed to completely fool his compatriots. They believe him, thinking that Monsieur Loti—as he relates in his novel

Aziyade—truly met with a girl in Salonika and later in Istanbul, and that he lived with her for several days in the vicinity of Eyüp without giving away his French identity... For one who has believed this much of the fairytale, is it not even easier to believe that he speaks Turkish as though it were his mother tongue, and that he has thorough and complete knowledge of the Turks and Turkishness? And yet look at what Monsieur Loti says, he who claims to know Turkish and the Turks so well and who sells himself and his books on that reputation:

> [...] And now, amidst this human tumult, I gleefully shouted "*Bestur! Bestur!*"[2] as I had done before, driving my animal on at full gallop [...]

These lines are taken from his description of Istanbul. The author is going through Galata on horseback one Ramadan evening. The street is crowded, yet he does not hesitate galloping through. Lovely. But what about those *besturs*? Would anyone who speaks Turkish like a Turk pronounce *destur* in that way?

Loti's knowledge of our customs and circumstances is no better. For example, while narrating his cohabitation with Aziyade, he writes that, on rising from bed every morning, she would expend some effort in painting the ends of her nails with a red dye, that she perfumed her room with varieties of incense, and that (as far as I can gather) she used opium. Poor besotted Loti has apparently heard that henna is used in our lands, that it is applied to the fingers, and although he has learned its name, alas, he has failed to learn its manner of use. While writing his novel, he must have given this much thought, and ultimately decided to declare that women paint their nails with henna every morning. This is what he wrote and of this he convinced his compatriots, indeed, to such a degree that the high Académie was obliged to applaud his considerable expertise in the customs and circumstances of the Orient.

Virtually every line that Loti wrote about us, with the purported Turkish words interspersed amongst them, loudly attests that he does not have the least knowledge of the Turkish language and that he understands nothing of Turkishness. These works are comprised of the above-mentioned description of Istanbul, *Aziyade*, and its sequel *Fantôme d'orient*.

Aziyade is a pitiable young woman who, forming an amorous bond with Loti in Salonika, comes to Istanbul in pursuit of her lover; here they meet and cohabitate for some time, intoxicated and absorbed in an amorous life. During the same period Loti has moved to Eyüp, where he speaks and interacts with the neighbor-

A READER

---

2   "Make way! Make way!"—Trans.

hood folk in coffeehouses and bazaars, and no one realizes that he is foreign. In the end he leaves his Aziyade behind and returns to his country.

Now, when a Turk reads this story, is there any doubt that he will begin his criticism with the very name? "Aziyade"... Has any name, any word such as this ever been heard in our country? Upon *Aziyade*'s publication, a person of wit remarked, "There is no such name in our language, but we have a word: only the 'A' is *ziyade*!"[3] Someone must have pointed this out to Loti, for he attempts to correct the problem in *Fantôme d'orient*; supposedly, he wished to keep his beloved's identity secret, and so invented the name, made it up. In point of fact, there is little of the story that is not made up. When one reads the book carefully, it appears that poor Monsieur Loti was a plaything in the hands of his Jewish interpreter. This cunning Jew practiced deceit upon deceit; he took him to Balat and told him it was Eyüp, he dressed him up in a knee-length jacket and told him it was Turkish attire. No matter what Loti inquired about or tried to learn or see, this Jew misdirected his attention with some trick, some sleight of hand, keeping the poor man in a perpetual state of disorientation.

I read *Aziyade* when it was first published; naturally, the details are not entirely fresh in my mind; however, I have always remembered the foregoing fundamental details, and hence am aware that one must exercise prudence in treating as accurate the stories, novels, and even travelogues written by Europeans about Far Eastern lands, for instance, India, China, and Japan. And to be sure, it goes without saying that novels written in our country with the claim of full knowledge of European countries are chock-full of amusing errors, and that if one of these should be translated into French, English, German or, in sum, any European tongue, it would be laughable to the Europeans!

One happens upon many such errors in all the works that Europeans write about us, even in books on geography and even in encyclopedias. Some of the fault lies with us. We write nothing to make ourselves known to Europe. Even though many individuals among us are conversant in foreign tongues, none of them takes the trouble to write corrections of European authors' erroneous ideas and claims about us in those tongues. In fact, no serious, comprehensive work has so far been written about our literature. Several years ago, our men of letters were the subject of an article bearing the signature of Charles d'Agostino, published in *Revue encyclopédique*, and a similar piece appeared in the April 1 and 15, 1894 issues of a peri-

---

3   The Turkish word *ziyade* (of Arabic origin) means "excessive, superfluous," and thus the Turkish sentence *A ziyade* means "the A is superfluous."—Trans.

odical entitled *Revue des revues*. The signature beneath the latter was of one Garabet Bey. It is apparent from these articles that both signatories had quite good French. Yet one laments the fact that neither was versed in our tongue, let alone our literature; this, too, is proved by their writings. We get the impression that one of our literary luminaries must have sat them down before him and given an account as he understands, as he knows, as he wishes, and as he pleases: and they, believing the information thus gathered to be sound, wrote it all up in articles in French, which they sent to those periodicals... In truth, nothing will come of this; there may or may not be any among the French who have read those articles carefully; yet were such writings to multiply in close succession, they would be likely to attract attention; if so, is it not better that they be truthfully written rather than falsely?[4]

But what fault have the authors of the articles? They wished to provide a service to the country where they found themselves and, by the strength of their pens, they labored and wrote these pieces. If the authorities whom they consulted have deceived them, then the true fault lies with those who provided this unsound information.

In sum, it is certain that Europe does not understand us, and the responsibility for this ignorance in part falls on us. Would it not be for the better if the much-famed sagely writers, who presume to relate events and stories taking place in European countries, abandoned this laughable undertaking and instead took pains to remedy this grave deficiency of understanding? But they will say: So what if Europe does not understand us? And indeed, what can one say to such true words?

Translated by Gregory Key

A READER

---

4   I shall take these matters up again in another column.—Tevfik Fikret.

HALİD ZİYA

The Last Generation[1]

After covering his mouth with the back of his left hand to conceal a yawn he had
been struggling to suppress, he let fall to his lap the book that had been growing
heavier in his right hand, as he shifted slightly in his tall wicker chair and looked
around him.

Whenever he picked up a book on the Orient, particularly one on his own country, a disquiet such as the one he was feeling right now would compel him to put
it aside. As he witnessed the false and laughable ideas of the Western writers who,
audaciously fearless that their falsehoods might ever be exposed, depicted a life that
they strove to observe through the haze of a language they did not comprehend,
who were dazzled by the effulgent colors in the Oriental sky to which their eyes
were not accustomed, he would, with a deep heartache, lose patience and close the
book with a yawn meant to suppress his anger, until such a time as he would find
the strength to pick it up again, whenever that might be.

[...] After this prologue, Nüzhet described his dismay in short sentences: His
objection to the book was different. Besides, the author's fame alone would suffice
to lead the reader to seek objections elsewhere. He was a poet who created marvels, in this book and wherever he should apply his talent. The same pen that had
indelibly etched into the minds of all readers the northern seas, the African deserts, the skies of the Far East [Aksa-i Şark] and the horizons of Istanbul, here, too,
had painted superb tableaux of such splendor and glory that the eye was dazzled
and the mind deluged with the colors and magnificence outpouring from them.
Nüzhet of course recognized the superb quality of the art and would perform with
utmost deference the duty of veneration owed to the poet's pen. He did not quib-
ble about the small errors, the laughable minutiae concerning the customs of the
country, nor did he wish to dwell on the author's peculiar weakness towards youth

---

1   Halid Ziya, "Nesl-i Ahir," *Sabah*, no. 6808, part 1 (August 25, 1324/1908): 2; no.
6813, part 6 (August 30, 1324/1908): 2. This novel first appeared in serial form in *Sabah*.—Ed.

and his amorous aspirations, and even were you to insist, he would not speak a word about the overly lengthy passages, the repetitiveness that would weary even the most indulgent reader, or the formal excesses that could not elude even the most charitable critique. He simply objected to the overall philosophical conclusion that the reader was to draw from the book as a whole, from the manner in which events were narrated. In such an important field, on such a significant topic of social relevance, something other than poetry was to be expected of that pen. What did the book contain other than women who remained hidden under their veils, houses hidden behind lattice screens, and nebulous feelings left unspoken or unexplained? Out of millions of people, ten or fifteen exceptional faces are chosen, and around them are drawn deceptive scenes of Oriental skies and moonlit nights, and after all traces of reality have been drowned in equivocation, we are made an appeal, to our sensitivity and compassion, in order to bolster a theory that cannot persuade our reason, and so we are brought to the bedside of people afflicted with consumption. In truth, Nüzhet agreed fully with some of the book's theories, but he wished that their soundness were not established through misleading methods.

And the men... You would find not a single male heart alongside those phantasms of women held inside the folds of black garbs and living the mysterious life of indistinct shadows. Does this country consist solely of women dying a slow death behind lattice screens, their lips twisted in sorrow and distress under their veils? Where, oh where were the men?

Translated by Gregory Key

NAMIK KEMAL

Refutation of Renan[1]

In response to a lecture given by Ernest Renan in which he
argues that Islam has supposedly eliminated progress and
opposed the sciences and the arts, this work is a refutation
that contains incontestable evidence based on clear logic
and religious law, to extol Islam's exalted glory.

For quite some time, a lecture titled "Islam and Science" that was delivered and
published by the esteemed French writer, Monsieur Ernest Renan, has been a topic
of discussion in the newspapers.

I recently received an original copy. Although the lecture is short, its contents
are fit to be criticized in a few hundred volumes of books; I am therefore certain
that by writing out my opinions, I will not have indulged in the useless task of repeating what has already been said.

Regrettably, I do not have with me all the books needed to prove that Islam is
not an impediment to learning but, rather, fosters it. Nevertheless, the author of
the lecture provides so much evidence in his own words for the baselessness of his
claims that it obviates the need to consult other books in writing this response.

[...] Now if we add to his religious perspective his utter ignorance about the
topic of his lecture, it might give us an idea of how nonsensical his essay must be.

Given Monsieur Renan's extensive knowledge of Oriental languages for which
he has earned his distinguished position in the Académie française, do not think
it strange that I contend he is ignorant in matters pertaining to Islam.

I can easily prove that, not just Ernest Renan, but all Europeans known for
their interest in the Orient are astonishingly ignorant about the religion of Islam.

---

1   Namık Kemal, *Rönan Müdafaanamesi* (Istanbul: Mahmud Bey Matbaası, 1326/1910), 2,
4–24, 26, 27, 30–46, 54–56.

Even Joseph von Hammer-Purgstall, the author of *The History of the Ottomans* [*Tarih-i Osmani*], is as ignorant when writing about Islam as are foreigners who have never read a book about the Orient. Hammer's ignorance is even stranger since he lived for many years in Istanbul and, in addition to his Arabic and Farsi, acquired enough proficiency to write beautifully in Turkish, which is likely more difficult to learn than other Islamic languages because it requires Arabic and Farsi, and its grammar is not adequately codified.

Note this passage on pages 400–401, in the tenth volume of Hammer's *History*:

> According to Islamic precepts, the noon prayer is not performed when the sun is at its peak, but a few minutes after. This is because, if one is to trust the hadith of the Prophet, every day precisely at noon Satan takes the sun between his horns, wearing it boastfully as the crown of the "Sultan of the Realms," but when he hears the sound of "Allahu Akbar," he relents. It is on account of this that the Ottoman court historians have said: "During the reigns of Sultan Murad IV and Sultan İbrahim, and especially during Sultan Mehmed IV's childhood, the devils of arrogance, debauchery, rebellion, and strife had worn the sun between their horns."

Is there a single word to this effect in the hadiths of the Prophet that have reached the community of Muhammad? It is impermissible to perform any of the five daily prayers before their appointed time; therefore, no one can perform the noon prayer before the sun has passed its peak. That Hammer only had to ask an ordinary novitiate to learn the truth instead of assuming that this travesty (who knows where he heard from) was an Islamic precept, what is this if not the proof positive of his total ignorance of the norms of Islam? While a horned devil is seen in some churches, where in Islamic books do you find Satan portrayed in the form of an animal?

No! Nor is there a single Ottoman court historian who says that "During the reigns of the three sultans, the devils of arrogance, debauchery, rebellion, and strife had worn the sun between their horns." Moreover, this expression does not even make sense that it can be legitimately attributed to an Ottoman court historian. However, even if one had said something so ridiculous, it does not necessarily follow that there is an Islamic belief associated with Satan holding the sun between his horns and wearing it like a crown.

One who has succeeded more than anyone else in informing Europe about the nature of Islam and whose book, *Bibliothèque Orientale*, still ranks among the most respected resources in Europe on Islamic sciences and Oriental languages, is the famed D'Herbelot [Barthélemy d'Herbelot de Molainville], who writes in his chapter on the Quran:

> Muslims who worship their Prophets greatly venerate this Book, (that is, the Holy Quran). They say that the Quran, at the beginning of Creation, was transcribed from the tablets containing God's original revelations, and it was safeguarded on one of the seven heavens found right below the fixed stars, and brought down sura by sura to the Prophet Muhammad (PBUH) by the hand of Gabriel, who belonged to the first order of angels.

Needless to say, neither such a thing has ever been uttered nor any Muslim would fall prey to such a belief. In Europe, many industrious people spend their entire lives determining, for instance, the genus and the species of the tiniest insects, and making unimaginable discoveries with the power of their mind. Thousands among those intelligent and skilled Europeans keep working with Oriental languages, and yet, how come the true character of Islam remains a mystery to Europeans when the people of Islam have, for the past 1300 years, dominated a large part of the world, when hundreds of thousands of manuscripts are widely available, within easy reach? Is this situation not truly perplexing?

[...] Apart from these examples, Europeans have strange beliefs, some of which Monsieur Renan nicely demonstrates in the following passage of his lecture, which I have been busy responding to and translating:

> When a Muslim child begins his education in religious matters around the age of twelve until which time he had been inquisitive, he suddenly becomes fanatical, filled with foolish arrogance, believing that he has attained everything he takes to be spiritual truth, and he considers himself fortunate, as if privileged, when in reality he is inferior to others. This insane vanity is Islam's most basic perversion.

Such people think that Muslims see themselves as better than other nations, but favoring the opposite, they treat the Muslims as inferior. Taking seriously the beliefs of such an insignificant tribe would, for them, mean wasting time on trivialities; therefore, most of the scholars on Oriental matters approach Islam as an enjoyable hobby as they do the belief systems of certain savage tribes.

Another matter worth considering is that, for a foreigner, obtaining proficiency in Oriental languages can be one of the most challenging tasks, whether due to the breadth and difficulty of the grammar or because of the nature of the script.

So much so that Hammer, recognized as one of the most skilled scholars of the Ottoman language in Europe, fails to understand the meaning of the common-place insult, *gidi*.[2] In his *History of the Ottomans*, when translating the following refrain by the tower guards in a folk-poem,

> *Yoktur sizinle viremiz*
> *Eğrili, gidi Eğrili*

Hammer assumes the word is the Arabic *hirre*, and translates it as "cat."

Monsieur Renan, famous for his "comprehensive knowledge" of the Arabic lan-guage, asserts that the Arabs pronounce the word *feylesof* (philosophe) by putting the short vowel "i" sound after the letter "f," followed by a long "y" with a pause on the letter "l"—resulting in the following vocalization: "fiyīlsof" rather than *feylesof*. Some Europeans who are interested in Islamic languages but haven't been able to learn them from the standard grammar manuals are putting together their own grammar rulebooks to more easily instruct others in these languages. Some people actually believe they have learned these languages by reading such manuals. The things being learned and taught are so strange that, when I was in Paris and found myself attending a Turkish lesson open to public, I could not understand a single word of the teacher's recitation. Had I not heard a few Turkish prepositions here and there, I would have thought the language being taught was one about which I knew nothing.

Additionally, concerning European scholarship on Islam, one must reserve a sizable space for half-scholars. When those with superficial knowledge read books on topics they cannot understand, even when the topics are presented truthfully, is it not natural for them to perceive what they read as gibberish?

Now, a European views the exalted religion of the Prophet Muhammad—the essence and value of which requires years of deep study and reflection—as an obsta-cle to freedom of thought and to civilizational progress, and he therefore dedicates his investigation to forcibly uncover irrational beliefs. If he thinks he can justify his opinion simply by casting a superficial glance at every issue he comes across as though—lest we suggest a comparison!—he was dealing with the Zulu sect, and if he is shown that he cannot even properly pronounce the words of languages he has purportedly been studying, is it rationally possible that what he writes would be anything other than delusional?

---

2   *Gidi* here is a derogatory term meaning "bastard, pimp, son of a bitch."—Trans.

Let me acknowledge a fact: we cannot say that no one in Europe is proficient in one or more Islamic languages; yet, those privileged few endowed with such knowledge—like the majority of those giving lectures and writing treatises out of a desire to know the Orient and to educate others—do not show the willingness to examine and critique the effects of Islam's cultural and scientific development in a mere forty-page essay.

The above explanation shows plainly all the reasons for European Orientalists' complete ignorance of Islam as a religion and possibly most of its other attributes. Nor should it be overlooked that Monsieur Renan is one more reason for the spread of false information and inadequate scholarship on matters pertaining to Islam.

I do not think I need to elaborate further to demonstrate the disposition of both the speaker and his contemporaries. Therefore, I now turn to the content of his lecture.

Before reading Monsieur Renan's lecture, I never imagined that so many errors could be packed into so few pages! Let me enumerate them one by one.

The speaker begins his talk by observing that societies do not retain a fixed identity—a truth everyone knows—as if it were a newly discovered, secret wisdom, and mentions his desire to clear up the confusion concerning terms such as: Arab learning, Arab civilization, Arab philosophy, Arab arts, Islamic sciences, and Islamic civilization. By his reasoning, this confusion has resulted in some inaccurate opinions which, in turn, have caused grave errors in thinking and even actions!

Clearly, however, there is no confusion concerning the terms he mentions. Nevertheless, the author is content to simply assert this a priori, so as to lay the ground for the assertions he will later make to summarily reject Islamic sciences, civilization, philosophy, and arts. As for the inaccurate opinions or grave errors resulting from said confusion, he asserts that they exist but does not provide any evidence.

And that he does not provide evidence should not come as a surprise because every word spoken about us by European scholars of the same ilk as Ernest Renan is for them patently self-evident and needs no further proof. When we ask for proof concerning their views on topics pertaining to the Orient, the most frequent response we receive is, "I said so."

Following this groundless claim, Monsieur Renan presents another:

> Everyone who knows something about our contemporary world can clearly observe the underdeveloped state of Islamic countries, and judge as lacking

in intellectual acumen those who derive their education and learning only from Islam. Those in the Orient or Africa are trapped inside an iron circle, as it were, that narrows the believers' outlook, closes off their minds to the sciences, and deprives them of the ability to learn or welcome new ideas.

Concerning intelligence and learning, Monsieur Renan, who sees no need to provide evidence for his views, can then perceive Muslims as the least among the human species, worse than those who worship fire in China or animals in India, those cannibals in uncharted territories or ocean archipelagos. However, if he hopes to earn his readers' trust with these absurd claims, he shows a naive confidence in his scholarly reputation.

How strange! Because we are Muslim, it seems, we have an iron ring clamped around our heads, and that ring keeps our intellect closed off to all forms of knowledge, all forms of learning, all forms of new ideas—and we still do not even know it!

How can Monsieur Renan deny that wherever Muslims can find schools to attend, despite myriad limitations in educational resources, they always outperform their classmates from other nations? Or given his reputation for not using evidence himself, would he simply ignore the evidence shown by his critics as a matter of his own method of argumentation?

As understood from his lecture and apparent in his views addressed further below, Monsieur Renan thinks that a Muslim who is familiar with the natural and mathematical sciences is also one who must turn away from the values and sensibilities of his religion. However, had he spoken with learned Muslims, he would have found them to possess a sounder understanding of religion than most other believers. Muhammad's followers who study mathematical and natural sciences see the exalted verses of the Quran as clear proof: "The Sun, too, runs its determined course laid down for it by the Almighty, the All Knowing."[3] "Did We not send water pouring down from the clouds..."[4] and "Did We not create you in pairs?"[5] In their eyes, these verses add further strength to their faith.

In the paragraph discussed earlier, Monsieur Renan had begun with the phrase "A Muslim child..." and concluded his statement with "Islam's most basic perversion."

Let us not leave him unanswered:

---

3   *Qur'an: A New Translation*, trans. M.A.S. Abdel Haleem (New York: Oxford University Press, 2004), Sura Ya Sin, verse 38. All references to the Quran are from this translation. —Ed.

4   *Qur'an,* Sura Al-Naba, verse 14.—Ed.

5   *Qur'an,* Sura Al-Naba, verse 8.—Ed.

Does the speaker believe Muslims alone think that their religion is more noble than other religions or that their community is more honorable than others? Is it at all possible to argue that those who believe in Christianity or Judaism, or worship fire or idols think that their own religion or their own community is less than or equal to others? Of course not. Why should Muslims but not Christians or Jews be considered as inferior among the nations for believing that they have the true religion and are more holy than others? A topic as important as Islam's scientific advancement, is it to be summed up through this type of conjecture?

Again, the author says: "The simplicity of their religious observances gives Muslims an unwarranted sense of superiority over other religions."

Even if Monsieur Renan does not know it, it is abundantly obvious to learned people that Muslims have never thought whether their religious observances are easier or more difficult, and they never would. No Muslim looks at other religions scornfully either. From the perspective of Islam, those religions that are based on the divinely revealed scriptures are not inferior but rather superseded. Of course, there are the idol-makers who worship those idols as their creator; these adherents of false beliefs, in the eyes of Muslims, Christians, Jews, and even those without religion, are not only inferior but also deserving of scorn.

Monsieur Renan, who himself does not belong to any religion, excuses Christianity and Judaism for rejecting Islam as a true religion, but then how come Islam's view that it supersedes Christianity and Judaism is a reason for attacking it? Regarding idol and fire worshippers, I think Monsieur Renan cannot admonish only Muslims for an idea shared by all People of the Book, even by those without religion. Also according to the author's own illusions, Muslims believe that God grants success and power to whomever God desires, regardless of personal merit, and it is because of this, he argues, that Muslims look disdainfully at science and learning, and at all the virtues that have shaped Europe as an ideal. Is it wrong to believe in God's benevolence or that God is free from all kinds of conditions and constraints? If our esteemed speaker can profess that all who have success and power in this world are people of skill and virtue, and that all people with skill and virtue attain positions of success and power, then he will have to remove from every library the entire human history and every theory heretofore developed so as to convince scholars that this is the case, and, furthermore, he would have to find a way to conceal the contemporary human condition from his listeners.

Besides, why should this particular precept suggest that Islam looks disdainfully at science? Is knowledge only to be used in order to achieve power and success?

A READER

In the past when it was nearly impossible to acquire a position of power or success unless one was a member of the French aristocracy like Monsieur Renan, what kind of power and success did scholars like Descartes and Pascal strive to achieve when endowing their souls with so much learning? Did Copernicus aspire to become the king of Poland or Galileo the pope in Rome when either man dedicated himself to science?

Knowledge is such a subtle passion that those caught in it expend their entire lives to attain it. As for those who try to use science for personal gain, we can never know whether they achieve a position of true privilege or wisdom.

There is no need for these rational arguments. Deeds alone suffice as real proof. If Muslims had looked disdainfully upon learning, then no scholar would have emerged from their midst. Now, if Monsieur Renan thinks there are no scholars in Islam, let him say so and we will discuss accordingly. But be forewarned, Monsieur Ernest Renan's thinking grows increasingly strange.

This is what follows the above-mentioned claim that Muslims scorn science and learning and all the virtues that have shaped Europe as an ideal:

> Inoculated with Islamic dogma, this affliction grows so powerful that it eliminates all of the differences between nations and peoples once they accept Islam. Berber, Sudanese, Circassian, Afghani, Malaysian, Egyptian, or Nubian, as soon he becomes Muslim, then he is no longer Berber, Egyptian, or Sudanese but only Muslim.

Whoever uncovers the logical connection between the introduction and this conclusion certainly deserves a handsome prize!

Let's see: Muslims apparently believe that all success and power comes from God, therefore they look disdainfully upon science and learning, and therefore, due to this affliction, whoever becomes a Muslim loses his ethnic identity and remains only a Muslim!

Now, is there any relation between looking down at science and Muslims losing their ethnic identity? For a man who makes a living as an author, it is shameful to say such ridiculous things, never mind when giving a lecture, even if he were delirious.

It is a historical fact that almost all the communities incorporated into Islam as a result of conflicts between states have been able to preserve their identity. Yet if you ask, say, a Circassian or an Afghan, he will first identify himself by his religion, as will the members of other religions.

Nevertheless, let us ask the speaker: if Islam had destroyed ethnic identities and therefore eliminated to the extent possible one of the barriers to human unity and understanding, would that not be a philosophically laudable outcome?

Once again, the author:

> Only Iran is an exception to this situation as they have been able to preserve a manner of thinking specific to them alone. This is because Iran has assumed a special place in Islam. Iranians are more Shi'i than Muslim.

What does it mean to be more Shi'i than Muslim? Is there a Shi'i who is not Muslim? These kinds of word games may be permissible in literary banter, but it is inappropriate to trade in meaningless words in a serious study.

Monsieur Renan sees Shi'ism as a sect specific to Iran, a characteristic that gives Iranians a special place among Muslims!

If he had a good understanding of Islamic history, he would have learned that there are no Islamic lands or ethnic communities where Shi'ism is not present.

We know that the establishment of Shi'ism in Iran is an event no older than three centuries, and it is also historically true that until it was established, much blood was spilled and hundreds of thousands of Iranian lives were lost. There are also many areas in the Islamic world where people adopted Shi'ism centuries before Iran and still preserve those Shi'i practices today.

What else can be said if, contrary to evidence, Iranians are still considered to have their own special position within Islam and that they are still seen as more Shi'i than Muslim?

After putting forward such strange ideas, Monsieur Renan then turns to those who invoke the past so as to trust the future, those who say: "This now (in their opinion) much-diminished Islamic civilization once shone brightly, as it produced many scholars and philosophers and for centuries was the teacher of the Western Christian world. This was once the state of things. Why can it not be so again?" Their perspective is not to Renan's liking: "This is the point I was originally trying to make," he says, positing, "Were there truly any Islamic sciences or at the very least a science permitted or accepted by Islam?"

As he begins formulating his answer, Monsieur Renan does admit at first that, for about three centuries, outstanding scholars and physicians lived in the lands of Islam, and that during that time, the Islamic world was scientifically more advanced than the Christian world, but he argues that, to avoid drawing erroneous conclusions, one must analyze the civilizational history of the Orient century by century, so as to identify and differentiate the various conditions and character-istics that allowed Islam to achieve its temporary superiority. His analysis begins:

> If there was a time unfamiliar with science and philosophy, then it was the first century of Islam, following the several centuries of sectarian conflicts that left the Arab conscience vacillating among various monotheistic paths.

What do you know! Even before Islam, supposedly there were among the Arabs struggles emerging due to "various monotheistic paths"!

This view, that monotheism existed in the Arab world and that, consequent-ly, struggles—even wars—broke out between tribes several centuries before the emergence of Islam, this "truth" uncovered and put forward by Monsieur Renan, is heretofore unrecorded in any book, it has no proof, and no one in the world, be-sides Monsieur Renan himself, would accept it.

In the first century of Islam, was science not widespread among Muslims? If science refers only to mathematics and the natural sciences, then it certainly was not. But is it logical to conclude that Islam is an obstacle to science? Did the reli-gion of Muhammad find learned people across the lands it spread and led them to ignorance?

As for philosophy, had Monsieur Renan consulted the books that record the words of the Prophet's companions, had he read at least *Nehcü'l-Belaga*,[6] I do not suppose he would have made his claims so easily.

The author then mentions—without cause or context—that the Bedouins were poets, but not scholars. Then, although he concedes that Caliph Omar (may God be pleased with him) did not actually set fire to the Library of Alexandria, he nev-ertheless tosses in the nonsensical assertion that Muslims, while working for the triumph of the exalted principles of their faith in the world, have also allegedly destroyed works of scientific investigation and scholarship. Renan then strings to-gether the following:

> Everything changed around the year 750 when Persia emerged as the domi-nant force following the Abbasids victory over the Umayyads. As a result, the center of Islam moved to the lands between the Tigris and Euphrates, a region that was at the time covered with remains and artifacts that attested to one of the brightest civilizations seen in the Orient. It was the Sassanian

---

6   *Nehcü'l-Belaga* is a collection of sayings from Imam Ali, the fourth Caliph, cousin, and son-in-law of the Prophet Muhammad, compiled by al-Sharif al-Radi in the eleventh century.—Trans.

state of Persia, which had reached the apex of its civilization during the rule of Anushirwan. Advancements in technical arts and crafts had taken place over centuries and Khosrow added intellectual advancement to the mix. Philosophy, banished from Istanbul, took refuge in Persia. Khosrow had books from India translated; Christians, the largest percentage of the population, knew the Greek sciences and philosophy; medicine was also entirely in their hands; the clergy knew both logic and geometry. It is related in the *Shahnameh* (*The Book of Kings*, which attained its most consummate character during the Sassanian period), that when Rüstem wanted to build a bridge, he summoned the *caselik* as engineers; in Nestorian Christianity, *caselik* means "Catholicos" i.e. members of the clergy or the Patriarch. If Islam's violent assaults had put a stop to Persia's advancement for at least a century, then it was the reign of the Abbasids that once again revived the splendor of Khosrow's time. Those responsible for the revolution that brought the Abbasids to power were Persian soldiers operating under the command of Persian rulers. Abu al-Abbas, the founder of the Abbasid dynasty, and Mansur especially, always surrounded themselves with Persians. It was as if the Sassanians themselves had been revived. The privy councils, imperial tutors, head ministers and generals were all Barmakids, descendants of an ancient Persian lineage, learned men who had half-heartedly accepted Islam very late while they still remained faithful to the traditions of their people. The Nestorians, too, surrounded these half-pious Caliphs and assumed the privilege of serving them as head physicians.

We are listening to so much chatter offered as proof that Islam is an obstacle to science. The author's assertions are bereft of any evidence, and his one true statement serves to refute the slander perpetrated by the clergy that Caliph Omar (may God be pleased with him) had the Library of Alexandria burned down. It is also correct that some Christians did serve as physicians to Abbasid Caliphs.

As for his other points: To begin, what effect would moving the Caliphate's capital to Baghdad have on the development of Islamic civilization? The Sassanian Civilization that Monsieur Renan imagines had lasted a mere thirty to forty years in Iran, reaching its nadir with the emergence of Islam. Why should the noble Arab people need the Sassanian civilization to obtain the benefits of knowledge? Why would the Arabs, when the seat of their power was still Damascus, not have learned from the Greek civilization which, for more than a thousand years, had produced great and beautiful works, and earned the status as the origin of philosophy and civilization for all of humankind, in fact, the very civilization to which, in the words of Monsieur Renan, even the Sassanians owed their intellectual development?

I wonder if the remains of Persian civilization between the Tigris and Euphrates were more numerous than those of Greek civilization found around Damascus?

In looking for evidence that Persia had achieved a position of advanced learning in the time of Anushirwan and Khosrow, we see nothing other than Monsieur Renan's empty words. Benefiting from Greek philosophy for a few years, having a few books from India translated, would these suffice to bring a nation to an advanced level of intellectual development?

When asserting that the Sassanians had accumulated enough knowledge to transmit to the Arabs, what scientific and literary works does Monsieur Renan have in mind? If the Persians were highly developed in the sciences, then where are their books now? Or is this going to be another deceitful fabrication: that the Muslims burned these books, too, as they did the Library of Alexandria?

How come an advanced nation wants to build a bridge but cannot find an architect among their own people and must turn to other nations' clergy for help?

Monsieur Renan asserts that Persians of that time had science and technical knowledge. However, Imam İbrahim, the first of the Abbasids to lay claim to the Caliphate, did not share this belief at all. He would send orders to his deputies in Khorasan, saying: "Do not leave any Arabs there alive. Their intelligence and knowledge prevent them from being easily controlled; however, the locals are ignorant like the animals; hold them by the rope and lead them wherever you want."

I wonder whether Monsieur Renan thinks he knows about the intellectual abilities of the Persians during the rise of the Abbasids more than those who directly experienced it.

[...] Monsieur Renan contends that neither Abu al-Abbas as-Saffah nor Abu Ja'far al-Mansur were total believers; in fact, as almost every paragraph of his article makes eminently clear, he cannot imagine that a Muslim believer can also love learning. Yet, in the Holy Quran there are many verses to the contrary. "Whoever is given wisdom has truly been given much good."[7] "We endowed Luqman with wisdom..."[8] "God will raise up, by many degrees, those of you who believe and those who have been given knowledge."[9] "Say, 'How can those who know be equal

---

7   *Qur'an*, Sura Al-Baraka, verse 269.—Ed.

8   *Qur'an*, Sura Luqman, verse 12.—Ed.

9   *Qur'an*, Sura Al-Mujadala, verse 11.—Ed.

to those who do not know.'"[10] "Say, 'Lord, increase my knowledge.'"[11] The venerable records of the Prophet's hadith say: "The scholars [ulema] are the successors of the prophets..." and "The death of a scholar [*âlim*] is like the death of the world [*âlem*]," and "Seek knowledge even unto China," and "Seek knowledge from the cradle to the grave," all of which definitively prove that Islam bestows honor upon scholars and calls every believer to seek out knowledge and philosophy.

When the people of a nation are commanded by their religion to seek out knowledge and philosophy and yet someone still insists that they cannot be so inclined unless they distance themselves from their religious principles, is this not a preposterous position, as obviously illogical as arguing that darkness ends at dusk?

Let us assume for a moment that the author's presumptions are correct, that there were no true believers working in the service of science and philosophy among Muslims, and that, moreover, Muslims even scorned knowledge itself; however, if so many divine and prophetic commands honor knowledge and philosophy and stress the importance of learning but the people do not heed these commands, can we really conclude that the religion itself is deficient?

The author maintains that when Baghdad became the capital of a revitalized Persia, it was impossible to stave off the language of the conquerors or to deny their religion, but that the emergent civilization was a mixture of existing cultures, with the Christians and the Persians together controlling the administration, and the Christians almost entirely overseeing security operations.

God have mercy! If the Abbasids had gotten rid of Arabic, what language would they have spoken? Having achieved the world's greatest seat of power, the Caliphate, should they have then busied themselves looking for ways to reject the language of their religion and the religion itself, in effect, destroy the very foundations of their state?

The names and titles of all the Abbasid viziers, government officials, and heads of security are listed in historical records. Can Monsieur Renan find and show us one Christian name amongst all of these? Is it acceptable to prove one's claims by falsifying historical facts?

[...] Monsieur Renan devotes many pages of his treatise to presenting deficient information about the level of scientific knowledge the Arabs attained by translating sources. He squeezes some remarkable details into his discussion. For example,

---

10   *Qur'an*, Sura Al-Zumar, verse 9.—Ed.

11   *Qur'an*, Sura Ta Ha, verse 114.—Ed.

he states that the Arabs referred to learned men as "philosophers"—which he misspells as "filizof" (philisophe)—and that this title was apparently as dangerous as "zindiq," or unbeliever, frequently punished by death or persecution!

The Greeks, the founders of ancient civilization, executed Socrates, who was the true inventor of philosophy because he believed in the unity of God.

Although the Italians, responsible for the revival of civilization during the Middle Ages, did not execute Galileo who was working to prove a new kind of astronomy, they did torture him to the verge of execution. Closer to our times, in the cradle of intellectual freedom, the French not only had Jean-Jacques Rousseau's *Émile* burned—a book he was not supposed to have printed—but also wanted to arrest him.

We continue to witness these events in history. Can Monsieur Renan find for us an individual either executed or tortured for studying "philosophy" during the heyday of Arab learning? Can one compare the life stories of al-Kindi, Farabi, and Ibn Sina—whom he also mentions—to what befell Socrates, Galileo, and Rousseau?

Again in this long paragraph, the author says that the Andalusians began studying science after Baghdad, but he does not indicate that the rulers of Andalusia, like their influential counterparts in Baghdad, were "free of religious sensibilities." Is he silent because he knows that a thousand counterproofs can be offered? Or does he think that his view—i.e. "if a person is a Muslim, he cannot be inclined to scientific knowledge"—is commonly held among his listeners?

In yet another strange statement, Monsieur Renan declares that Arab philosophy should in fact be called "Sassanian and Greek philosophy," but that it would be even more correct to call it "Greek philosophy." Will Monsieur Renan make up his mind? Is Arab science in fact Sassanian science, as he asserted in the beginning of his article? Or is it a mix of Sassanian and Greek? Or will he only look through the lens of Greek philosophy? He should say whatever he means because no one should struggle this much to figure it out.

We need to ask a question here: Let's assume that Arab philosophy and sciences were received from both the Sassanians and the Greeks, should we then ignore the intellectual strides made by Arabs because they did not entirely invent them? If we do, then how do we also prove that the sciences and philosophy that other nations received from Greece were wholly created by the Greeks? How can we deny that the Greeks also transmitted many things they received from other people who came before them—which is a demonstrable fact—or do we acknowledge that this body of knowledge is also "Greek sciences and philosophy"?

Or are we to assume that the Arabs were content with what they received from the Greeks alone and that they have contributed nothing to it?

Monsieur Ernest Renan declares that when the torch of human thought, its spiritual flame, is extinguished in the hands of a nation, it is taken up by another nation that can reignite it, and this is why, he argues, at the moment when Ibn Rushd [Averroes], the final Arab philosopher, passed away dejected and abandoned in Marrakesh, Abelard had just begun publishing his own investigations.

On the one hand, Monsieur Renan contends that the history of philosophy and sciences in Islam was limited to only three centuries, yet, on the other, he accepts that Ibn Rushd was the final philosopher amongst the Muslims.

The Abbasid era began in the year 132 Hijri [749/750]—which according to Monsieur Renan also marks the beginning of Arab philosophy; Ibn Rushd died in the year 595 Hijri [1198/1199] according to one account, or 603 Hijri [1206/1207], according to another.

We wonder how, by his calculation, the time between these dates only amounts to three centuries.

[...] Ernest Renan has no compunction about asserting that philosophy was always disesteemed among Muslims, that since 1200 it has been entirely squelched in the lands of Islam, and that historians and scholars who acknowledge the existence of philosophical practice among Muslims speak about it as an evil that has been rooted out!

Of the two greatest Arab philosophers, Ibn Sina [Avicenna] and Ibn Rushd, the former served as grand vizier for two Islamic states, and the latter as chief justice for two states as well. These facts actually prove whether philosophy in Islam has held a place of scorn or a place of honor.

The schools of medicine built by Sultan Mehmed the Conqueror[12] are still standing in Istanbul, near the Fatih Mosque. Never mind those, today, in every one of our blessed mosques we can witness for ourselves that philosophical texts are still being taught. When a field of knowledge is permitted even inside our houses of worship, how does it follow that it was completely rooted out?

That the philosophy presently studied in the lands of Islam is not the same philosophy currently circulating in Europe should not be a reason to denigrate it. The

---

12   In the original text, *cennet-mekân* [may he dwell in heaven] *Sultan Mehmed Han-ı Gazi.*—Ed.

philosophy that Monsieur Renan believes was rooted out is the very same philosophy inherited from the Arabs and fostered to this day.

We are certain that, if asked, Monsieur Renan would not be able to name a single known and renowned scholar or historian who speaks about philosophy as an evil that has been rooted out from the Islamic world.

He says: "Hand-written philosophical manuscripts have become rare because they had been destroyed; as for astronomy, its teaching is allowed only as an aid to locating the qibla for prayer."

I wonder whether Monsieur Renan wants to blame Islam for the loss of thousands of books that were burned by Tatar infidels in the Orient and the fanatic Crusaders in the West?

Had Monsieur Renan recognized that Islam permits astronomical calculations to determine not merely the direction of the qibla, but also the times for the five daily prayers, then he would have shown us some generosity!

I might be wrong but, in the Samarkand observatory that Uluğ Bey began building in 823 Hijri [1420/1421], didn't Muslim scientists work for thirty years and create the Uluğ Bey Star Charts [*Uluğ Bey Zîci*]?

During Süleyman's era, was the Ottoman fleet only guided by astronomical knowledge of how to find the qibla when it managed to reach the shores of Spain and India?

[...] If Monsieur Renan were a little fair, he would admit that it was not the followers of Islam but the Crusaders and the Tatars who set fire to hundreds of thousands of irreplaceable books and trampled under their horses' hooves many thousands of scholars across the Muslim world in places like Cordoba, Granada, Baghdad, and Samarkand!

After being invaded by barbarian tribes, Europeans, too, remained blindly ignorant for centuries. Was it Christianity rather than the Goths, Huns, and Avars that ruined science and philosophy in Western countries?

If it was not Christianity, then why is it the Muslims rather than the Crusaders or the Tatars that allegedly brought about the destruction of science and philosophy?

I do not know what Monsieur Renan expects to gain from a lecture that treats so superficially one of the most important historical questions of our time. However, I am certain that in the eyes of his peers, he ought to have lost perhaps 90 percent of his reputation as a scholar of Oriental affairs.

Voltaire, known as one of the greatest enemies of Christianity, had written a play called *Mahomet* for self-interest as well as to criticize the pope, and he had completely distorted both the history and the moral norms of Islam, while also adding the letter "p" into the Arabic alphabet, thereby demonstrating the extent of his ignorance and making himself into a laughingstock the world over.

I do not know whether Monsieur Renan is looking to find an object of criticism or to score a win that he goes to great lengths to fit thousands of lies into a forty-page article!

But obviously this much chatter should not go unchallenged.

Later in his exposition, Monsieur Renan appears as if fair-minded when he says, "I do not want to diminish the effects of Arab science"; yet, promptly resuming his original perspective, he declares that what the Arabs and the so called Arab science have in common is only language, and that people like Ibn Sina and Ibn Rushd are Arab in the way Bacon and Spinoza are Latin.

During the golden age of a nation, individuals who may be ethnically different but who nevertheless share that nation's religion and culture are not the same as those who, despite their nationality and native language, write books in a dead language; the impertinence of drawing comparisons among them does not befit an individual purportedly engaged in philosophical discussion.

Just as Napoleon is French when he is part of an Italian family or Bismarck German when his ancestors are alleged to have been Slavs, can anyone doubt that Ibn Sina, Ibn Rushd, and Farabi are considered Arabs?

Monsieur Renan makes an exception for al-Kindi yet asserts that none of the other Arab philosophers are actually Arabs, adding: "Even intellectually they have no relation to being Arab." Since we do not understand what he means by "being intellectually Arab," how are we to verify what he says!

Is it even conceivable for people to possess an intellect exclusively their own, besides the one they share with everyone else? Monsieur Renan then makes another very strange assertion:

> These philosophers employed the Arabic language but with much difficulty. Stylistically Arabic is well-suited for poetry and certain forms of elocution, but as a tool for metaphysics and theology, it is very difficult to use. Arab philosophers and scholars were especially poor writers.

Coming from a person who is incapable of pronouncing Arabic words correctly, this kind of opinion should not surprise us. What is truly surprising is that he attempts to evaluate the Arabic language, Arab science, and Arab philosophy with his level of knowledge, that he succeeds in passing off all of his errors and fabrications as some kind of truth that he shares with the civilized world. Certain experts accept that Arabic is suitable for literary expression as much as any other language, and they also admit that, given the linguistic clarity of Arabic and its relative facility of Arabicizing foreign words, no language, other than ancient Greek, comes close to Arabic in writing scientific works. Anyone—Monsieur Renan included—willing to ask a person truly knowledgeable about Arabic would easily learn that Arabic books on metaphysics and theology are the most beautiful, and Arabic books on science are the clearest.

Once he convinces himself with his scholarly posturing that he has proved there is no such thing as Arab science or Arab philosophy, the author goes on to say:

> If this science is not Arab, then is it at least Islamic? Has Islam demonstrated any stewardship for philosophical research? No, it has demonstrated no such thing. The beautiful striving for learning was entirely the work of Iranians, Christians, Jews, Harranians, Ismailis, and those Muslims who privately resisted their religion. These philosophical studies have been perceived by Sunni Muslims as anathema. Ma'mun, the Caliph who showed the most interest in adopting Greek philosophy, was fully condemned by the theologians, and the misfortunes that plagued his sultanate were seen by them as punishment for giving free rein to other beliefs.

The degree to which Islam both guards and conserves science and philosophy is proven by a litany of Quranic verses and hadith which I cited above. Is Monsieur Renan brave enough to deny the existence of these verses and hadith? If he is not, how can he prove the claims he makes in his article?

In the era of Arab enlightenment, a few Christian, Jewish, and Harrani names appear among the philosophers and scholars, but historical records show that in comparison to great Muslim scholars, they were one in a thousand, perhaps even one in ten thousand.

In this case, is it right to attribute philosophical works of the time to the Christians, Jews (most of whom were Sabeans), and Harranians rather than to Muslims?

[...] Following these empty words, the author once more repeats his assertion that Islam always worked toward and eventually succeeded in destroying science and philosophy. He adds the following:

Islamic history ought to be divided into two periods. The first period begins with Islam's origins and lasts until the twelfth century, while the second period extends from the thirteenth century to the present. During the first period, Islam was weakened due to the Mu'tazili school, a relatively moderate school of thought with a position similar to Protestantism; as a result, this period did not achieve the level of order and zeal known in the second period, when the nation fell into the hands of the Tatar and Berber tribes, who were known for their vulgarity, brutality and ignorance.

It is a fact unique to Monsieur Renan that Mu'tazilites were a moderate school of thought in Islam, given that they did not consider Muslim those who had committed major sins!

We can in no way fathom the basis for the author's observation that during the first period, "Islam could not achieve order"!

It was the learned men of this first period who had collected and organized all of the religious rulings and publicized the denominations and schools of thought active within Islam. At this time, what is called zealotry in the Ottoman language was not just lacking, it was entirely absent.

The Islamic faith did not condone fanaticism, so how would such an evil exist during the nation's age of learning and advancement?

These, too, are the author's words: "It is among the characteristics of Islam that later generations of Muslims were much stronger believers than their predecessors."

Not a single being created throughout Islam has ever declared to be superior to the first generation of Muslims. However, even if Renan's statement was correct, does it then follow that Islam is somehow lacking?

[...] Monsieur Ernest Renan says: "Proponents of freedom who defend Islam do not know what Islam is; Islam means no separation between religious and worldly powers, and therefore, the sovereignty of religious faith; it is the heaviest chain that humanity has had to bear until now."

If proponents of freedom do not know Islam, then how well must Monsieur Renan know it! Political principles of Islam are already in perfect accord with reason and philosophy. The legal principles developed and compiled through intensive study and great effort over three thousand years by Greek, Roman, and European philosophers are also public knowledge... Granted, marital matters are determined according to denominational rules, but those notwithstanding, is it possible to demonstrate a fundamental conflict between Islamic *Fiqh* and these other traditions of law in the areas of transactional law and penal codes? If so, do we consider

European legal practices as superior because they do not depend on religious precepts? Is it rational to argue that the laws found in Islamic *Fiqh* are like chains of captivity just because they are based on religious precepts when in reality they do not differ substantially from European legal practices?

Separating religion from politics is considered as one of the greatest achievements of Europe's most recent revolutions because, even though Christian polity was originally based on the principle, "Render unto Ceasar the things that belong to Ceasar," the clergy gradually imposed themselves on worldly affairs, causing the common people untold suffering, which, in turn, made it necessary to separate religion from politics, or, stated more truthfully, to force the clergy back into the confines of religion proper.

If this were viewed as a general rule and various political judgments, no matter how valid they may be, were then disallowed because they were dependent on religion, does the practice not amount to choosing oppression over justice?

[...] The readers of this imperfect lecture naturally expect Monsieur Renan to offer a conclusion, but I am afraid they will be disappointed because the conclusion has absolutely no connection to the original topic!

After Monsieur Ernest Renan has argued that the scientific and philosophical advancements in Baghdad, Samarkand, Cordoba, and Granada, advancements that spurred the development of modern civilizations, do not belong to the Arab society, that they were neither influenced nor patronized by Islamic peoples, that Islam is against learning and for this reason remains inferior among the nations, he closes his lecture with a paragraph that offers a few words about the benefits of science, and ends with this little thought:

> What was not said about firearms when they appeared! And yet, they have proven useful in the victory of civilization. Personally, I believe in the beneficence of science and that science alone can offer the defensive weapons against those who use it for evil ends. Finally, science never serves anything other than progress. The goal is true progress inseparable from respect for freedom and the individual.

I think the connection between his lecture and his conclusion is as clear as that between the lines of this familiar couplet:

> *Bahçeye vurdum kazmayı*
> *Güzeller bağlar yazmayı*
>
> *I dig the garden with the pickaxe*
> *The comely maiden wears the scarf.*

If Monsieur Renan's advice on the merits of science is intended for the Muslims, is it not a repudiation of his own views? What benefit can this advice have for a people already condemned to inferiority among the nations?

Or, if, by insisting that Islam is an obstacle to learning, he is only looking to motivate Europeans to be passionate about science, choosing such a strangely circuitous route does not at all befit a person famed for his knowledge and his many distinctions.

In our opinion, the only result Monsieur Ernest Renan can achieve from this lecture, which is full of delusions born of total ignorance, is to reveal his own hostility towards religion. In his outright attacks against Islam, too, he does little else besides inventing new forms of proof, as worthless as they are repugnant. The only response his work can elicit in the Muslim world is nothing other than contempt and condescension for the cluelessness of this misguided professor of the Academy whose ignorance and malice I have exposed in this essay.

Translated by Aron Aji and Micah A. Hughes

AHMED HAŞİM

"A Conversation with a Foreigner about Istanbul"[1]

[...] You are right in seeing Istanbul as you see it. This city has no peace of mind to offer a civilized person. Your compatriots who have loved this city were not civilized at all. "Civilized" is what we call those without a soul, or those who have relinquished theirs. Gérard de Nerval, Chateaubriand, Gautier, Loti, Farrère, Régnier and others, these were men who resembled our half-mad dervishes, who, after wandering the earth along lonely trails of exile, found themselves one night in the great domed-city with cypress trees jutting out ostentatiously on the golden horizon, and who thought that they had, at last, found their homeland. These were men who had also seen Beijing, Tokyo, Benares, and Samarkand, and who, upon leaving those places, could forget all the temples, towers, the fragrant aromas of Asia, the pearls, and divine dances—and the only country for which they felt a deep homesickness until their dying breath was this country of minarets and sunsets. For this reason, we know them as one of us.

[ ] We live thus under the effects of such strange poison. This is why our music knows how to find the soul's pathways. Why the veil that our women wear is [...][2] enchanting. And why our complexion is pale and warm. And what is more, our houses, which seem so confining to you, are familiar and spacious to us. Our torn-down streets do not wear out our shoes. You ask why we do not leave our houses at night, why our streets are deserted and dark. We would not venture out even during the day unless we have to. For, outside, we have not an ounce of happiness to beg for between us.

I am doubtful that you have understood the explanation I have given you, my dear traveling companion. I have said these on behalf of those of us who were poisoned. Had you discussed the topic with someone else, most probably he would

---

1   Ahmed Haşim, "İstanbul Hakkında Bir Ecnebi ile Muhavere," *Tarik*, no. 105 (7 Teşrinisani 1335/November 7, 1919): 1.

2   Word illegible in the original.—Ed.

have told you—and you would have understood—something entirely different. To understand me, you had to have a soul, and that soul, unlike the soul of Yakup Kadri,[3] had to have been poisoned beyond cure. Yet your golden eyes staring at me belong to a body that does not accept the poison. Have you met Yakup Kadri? No? What a pity!

Translated by Micah A. Hughes

---

3   Yakup Kadri (1889–1974) was a well-known novelist, who also wrote poems and non-fiction. The reference is most likely to the polemic between Ahmed Haşim and Yakup Kadri on poetry. Ahmed Haşim criticized Yakup Kadri for ignoring the role of the "soul" in interpreting poetry. Yet, he argued, it was the "soul" which allowed different individuals to read different meanings in the same poem. See Özden Apaydın, "Ahmed Haşim'in Politikasına Göre 'Vuzuh'un Mahiyeti ve Değeri," *Turkish Studies* 8, no. 1 (Winter 2013): 747–54.—Ed.

AHMED HAŞİM

"The Library"[1]

[...] I do not know whether it is because the period of capitulations has had an effect on our mindset and made us perceive any flush-faced blond person with a hat we encounter on the streets of Beyoğlu and Galata in recent years as though he was a sacred Egyptian ox, but every foreigner makes us feel as though he was an entire civilization on to himself, and we think every foreign language is an ocean of knowledge. So much so that, for many of us, just being able to read and speak English and French is sufficient remedy for lack of intellectual discipline. What else but blind fate can account for the translators' penchant for all these worthless books they have been translating into Turkish lately, books whose sole merit is that they were written in one of the European languages.

In a country where Kant's *Critique de la raison pure*[2] remains untranslated, what could be more depressing than seeing the efforts of brilliant minds bent over stacks of meaningless pages, sweating over them to give life, in the form of a Turkish sentence, to ephemera found in such works as Baron Stack's [?] *Book of Manners* [*Muaşeret Adabı*] or Gustave Le Bon's stillborn fantasies, the aesthetics of this or the history of that, books that do not even form a single ring in the chain of intellectual civilization.

Translated by Micah A. Hughes

---

1   Ahmed Haşim, "Kütüphane," *İkdam*, no. 11135 (April 22, 1928): 1.

2   The original refers to the French title.—Ed.

"Are Our Movie Theaters Tools of French Imperialism?"[1]

FIGURE 6. The French officer in Arab garb stabbing an Arab youth, in the film *The Brave Cavalryman.*[2]

We should pay a bit more attention to the foreign films being imported into our homeland!

Most of the films become tools of foreign propaganda.

French has no place on Turkish movie screens!

Not one, not five, not fifteen... Every month, among the new films playing in the theaters, we find several "dramas" that ridicule Asian and African nations' in-

1   "Sinemalarımız Fransız Emperyalizminin Aleti mi?", *Resimli Ay*, no. 1 (March 1929): 25–26.

2   The captions are taken from the original text. The references in this article are to the 1928 American silent film, titled *Beau Sabreur* and directed by John Waters. It takes place in North Africa and features Gary Cooper as a French Foreign Legion officer.—Ed.

dependence struggles while defending their homelands against the invaders. These films are very harmful because of the ideas they promote.

Some of the worst examples are set in the French colonies in Africa, like Algeria, and they are an insult to the eyes of a nation like ours which shed its own blood to defend its homeland against foreign invaders.

While French imperialism breathes like a rabid monster right on our Syrian border, we cannot tolerate watching the same monster ridiculing African patriots who are shedding blood to save their homeland at any cost. If France is outraged that its colonial army, drafted from the bandits of seventy-seven nations, its planes, cannons and tanks cannot beat a handful of heroes who are fighting with flint-locks in their hands and unshakable faith in their hearts, and if it takes its revenge by ridiculing them on the screen, Turkish movie theaters cannot be an accessory to this imperialist entertainment.

Not one, not five, not fifteen…

Let's look at an example.

The Brave Cavalryman!

The "Brave" Cavalryman is a French officer. This rascal busies himself with plotting against Moroccan patriots fighting French oppression and shedding blood to gain their independence. Some Arabs who have sold their souls to the French

FIGURE 7. From the film *The Brave Cavalryman*: Arab patriots kidnapping an American girl and the brave cavalryman, that is the French officer, saving her from the "savage" Arabs.

are helping the young officer with the plot. On the opposite side, we see a young Arab patriot who wants to save his homeland. This Arab youth, who is in reality the brave hero but portrayed as a rude and violent monster, is killed by the sword of the plotting cavalryman of the invading French army. This slaughter is portrayed in such a manner that one feels like applauding the French officer!

The entire film, from start to finish, praises French imperialism and ridicules Arab patriots who are struggling against this invading monster.

Another matter we do not understand:

Why do we have French subtitles in films shown in Istanbul? Is Turkey a French colony that we need to read French subtitles while watching the films in our mother tongue?

In America, films are shown only in English. In Germany, only in German. In France, only in French. Why are films shown in Turkey both in Turkish and in French? We need to stop this travesty.

If the French subtitles are supposed to encourage foreigners who live in Beyoğlu to go to the movie theaters, this is not a good reason. A lot of foreigners live in Paris and in New York; yet the films are shown only in French and in English there.

A READER

FIGURE 8. From the film *The Brave Cavalryman*: Two young Arab collaborators hugging the French officer who killed their companion fighting to save his homeland...

We need to save our movie theaters from the French language, and from being used for foreign imperialist propaganda. This has now become a national duty. Because we should never forget that cinema is one of the most influential propaganda tools.

Translated by İlker Hepkaner

HALİDE EDİB

Turkey Faces West[1]

[...] Turk is being widely discussed all over the world—especially in the Asiatic and Moslem world. I do not know whether the religious nature of any people is subject to satisfactory definition. But in the case of the Turk the attempt has led to a series of contradictory conjectures. Western writers on Ottoman history differ widely. None among the historians attempts to define the religious nature of the Turk below the surface. One set of writers speaks of the Turk's religion as mere fanaticism—defining him as a being who kills everybody that refuses to accept his own religion. A charming American woman said to me after a lecture with a humorous twinkle in her eye: "My idea of the Turk was that of a man with a dagger who seizes you wherever he meets you, asks you to accept his religion, and if you refuse his request cuts your head off." This proved that the type of historian I have mentioned had done his work most thoroughly. As this fanaticism is not confirmed by historical evidence, another type of western historian speaks of the tolerance of the Turk in his religion. The second type usually tells us that this tolerance is due to indifference rather than to virtue. But very few have given any serious study to the religious nature of the Turk apart from its political bearing

[...] In his family life and in his attitude toward women the common Turk was less influenced than the Ottoman by Byzantine or even Islamic ways. Polygamy was included as a custom, but in a very restricted sense. The seclusion of women, although a fact in the palace and among the higher classes, was practically unknown up to the eighteenth century. We find royal decrees of the first half of the eighteenth century ordering women (the common ones) to veil. The harem, which to the European means a place where the women are herded together for the pleasure of one man, to the Turk simply means home and an apartment for women. From it the Turkish women ruled the domestic side of life when they ceased to take part in the nation's life.

---

1   Halide Edib, *Turkey Faces West* (New Haven: Yale University Press, 1930), 7, 46, 60.

[...] The western press uses two terms for the inhuman act of slaughter in the Near East, in individual or collective cases. If the sufferers are Christians it is martyrdom inflicted on Christians by the barbarous Turks; if the sufferers are Turks, or even Moslems, they are merely slain by the civilized Christians in some just and holy cause. The Greek Patriarch, who was involved in the Greek insurgent movement, was condemned to death and executed. The Turks in Chios massacred a few Greeks; European public opinion which had watched the great massacre by the Greeks in silence broke out into fury at these Turkish reprisals.

ŞEVKET SÜREYYA

The Ideology of the Revolution
"Bankruptcy of Europacentrisme"[1]

The concept of "Geocentrism"[2] was a human error, and ever since Ptolemy, who shaped it into a field of science, and until Copernicus, who deemed it as unscientific, this error ruled human intelligence for a full twelve centuries. Throughout these centuries, although the earth was a small and only part of the wider system of the universe, it was considered the center and axis of this very system. Every inquiry, every decision, and every fact was centered around the earth and was meaningful only in relation to the earth.

Europacentrism[3] is a similar error. Even though modern Europe has subjected the social sciences to laboratory-based inquiry, this error still dominates human intelligence. According to this concept, which originated among the Greek pedants and has endured until our times, European history, although a small and only part of the wider world history, is considered to be the center and axis of this very history. Every inquiry, every decision and every fact is centered around Europe and is meaningful only in relation to Europe.

Just as Ptolemy considered everything outside the earth to be linked to it and condemned human intelligence to narrow-mindedness and falsehoods for a long period of time, Europacentrism, too, has played a regressive and negative role in human intellectual history by treating the non-European parts of the world only in relation to Europe.

The periodization of human history into several eras such as the Antiquity, the Middle Ages, the Early Modern Age, and contemporaneity, is actually quite recent. Be that as it may, this periodization has become well-established and sacrosanct in

---

1   Şevket Süreyya, "Europacentrisme'in Tasfiyesi," *Kadro*, no. 7 (July 1932): 5–10.

2   "Geocentrism" is the theory of conceiving the earth as the center of the universe.—Şevket Süreyya.

3   "Europacentrism" is the theory of conceiving Europe as the center of the World History.—Şevket Süreyya.

the European illuminati's understanding of history, so much so that now one assumes that the historical eras are not the products of human history but rather that human history is the product of these narrowly construed historical eras.

The first characteristic of this periodization is that it is exclusively European, in other words, Europacentric. In this classification, the entire progress and all breakthroughs of world history and human civilization have been placed on the relatively smaller axis of European history—which in fact started later—and anything outside Europe, such as the civilizations of Asia Minor and Egypt, has been either considered "incipient stages of civilization which had failed to mature," or they were banished to oblivion in the dark pre-European period, and were denied legitimacy.

*   *   *

Just a few sentences to reveal the attributes of this periodization [...] as instructed to us by the mistake called Europacentrism, would give us an idea of how this classification is conceived from an exclusively European perspective.

Europacentrism sees the Antiquity as the period when human civilization was born and founded, and this civilization unfolds, from its dawn to its dusk, on the European horizon. Along this trajectory, every event happening outside Europe is coarse and immaterial, weak and short-lived, and pales in comparison to the European civilization's miraculous self-birth.

According to Europacentrism, the civilizations of Antiquity derive their ingenuity from the Greek miracle, "*Miracle Grec*," while their prowess comes from the Germanics, the epitome of everlasting blood and brute strength of the "Indo-European" race.

Again from the same perspective, the sacking of Rome by the Goths, Vandals, and once more by the Goths between 410 and 476 spelled not the collapse of European superiority, but in fact, the glorious marriage between the human intelligence maturing in the Greek miracle and the human strength maturing in the Germanic blood, and naturally this marriage bears the embryo of the "renaissance."

In Europacentrism, the Antiquity connects to the Middle Ages through a frozen Aristotelean philosophy, which provided the foundation of a rigid church scholasticism. The history of the Middle Ages, this philosophy which became the spirit of religious and worldwide feudalism, is the history of millions of agrarian slaves animated around this philosophy who were then sacrificed in mass to the interest of the church, or the castle, or the predacious wealthy class living in trading port cities. The quill of the European historian gives this history the form of a saga which is presented to the whole world as an exemplar of pure faith and idealism.

In this saga, any human face outside Europe or opposing Europe is perceived as barbarian and destructive.

The relationship between the Renaissance and the Greek miracle is clearer. The humanists of the later age found the source of humanism somehow again among the Greeks, and they wished to present this source to all of humanity as the "dawning of history." However, it was also during this new age that Europacentrism assumed aggressive and violent characteristics. The discovery of new continents, the opening of new trade routes and new markets, and the conclusion of colonial wars fought along these new routes, new continents and new markets really seemed for a while as though the fate of the whole world was tied to Europe. Colonization, unfettered pillage of non-European countries, and the flow of national trade capital from everywhere to Europe, almost prepared the foundation for this continent's universal hegemony. As routes and commerce centers shifted, the lifelines of the world began to center around the little continent, giving the appearance of a centralized system around Europe.

The Industrial Revolution which, according to the Europacentric periodization of history, inaugurated the period often called the Modern Age, broke up national and local economies everywhere by flooding them with cheap and abundant industrial goods, thereby firmly establishing the metropole's hegemony, a condition that would characterize the entire nineteenth century. The French Revolution was the felicitous cause and ideological expression of this system that reached its apex in the nineteenth century, so much so that the revolutionary ideals that were exported in every direction as if they were universally true as well as universal truths resulted in consecrating the reputation of Europecentism everywhere, and Aryanism became a sui generis expression of this political and economic hegemony.

This periodization by Jules Michelet may, to some extent, describe the stages of Europe's progress. However, it is completely inadequate as well as inconvenient in explaining either the global civilizational progress or the stages that characterize the history of the Turks.

First of all, the principal currents and developmental stages of our history cannot be explained according to the Europacentric periodization. The European historian approaches the Migration Period only from the Roman perspective and describes the role of the Turkic race only as negative and destructive. Seen from our perspective, however, the Migration Period began while Europe was still living in the amorphous darkness of pre-history, and it made possible the spread of the earliest techniques of animal domestication, crop cultivation, and mining throughout the world and especially in Europe, thus evolving as a progressive current that brought about the earliest world civilizations with common roots and characteristics. This explanation, contrary as it is to the narrow and abstract explanation of Europacentrism, is entirely consistent with the actual emergence of world civilizations. The Migration Period, which started in AD 375 and is considered to have ended with the fall of Western Rome, is an episode and a portion of a long progressive current, and in fact, the role of the Turkic societies in this event has never been what Europacentric history tells us.

The history of the Turks undoubtedly had a pre-history. However, this period ends centuries before the beginning of history as understood by Europacentrism, and the history of the Turks observed its own continuum that does not correspond in the least to the Europacentric periodization.

When the antiquity starts for the Turks and when their middle ages end, these are not known. This much is clear, however: these stages in our history have completely different characteristics from Europe's Antiquity and Middle Ages. How can we explain our antiquity by the classical standards of a brief period that starts with the Greek miracle—an origin attributed to gods and therefore unknown— and ends with the fall of Rome?

By such standards, the intellectual, technical, and artistic aspects of our first age would be utterly lost.

How can we locate the Europacentric Middle Ages within the history of the Turks? During the Middle Ages, Turkish history had already completed its own Renaissance. Later, you have a sixteenth century in the Turkish history that neither matches any Europacentric standard nor coincides with any of the so-called European centuries. In European history, the sixteenth century was the most characteristic period of religious and global feudalism, scholasticism—which had not yet endured the assault by the seventeenth-century critics—and of technological backwardness and national disunity. Yet, in Turkish history, the sixteenth century marks the height of a civilization that coincided with a boundless world sovereignty, a civilization of unparalleled scientific progress and artistic achievement.

What kind of commonality can be found between the institutions and intellectual outlook of the sixteenth century in Turkish history, and those stagnant institutions and outlook in Europe in the same century?

And concerning the French Revolution and modern times, the standards and method of periodization employed to justify European interests and their struggles for those interests across the globe are completely inconvenient and insufficient in explaining the historical development and nature of Turkic nations, nearly all of which were condemned into becoming colonies or half colonies or forced into economic regression. In fact, this is why, in this era of national independence movements, the European intellectuals have neither the conceptual standard nor the vocabulary to explain the real nature of the struggle being witnessed in Turkic societies and in most other countries which have been under Europe's political, economic, and cultural hegemony.

The history which starts with Europe and ends with Europe is both a narrow perspective and an incorrect framework, and it has thus far either exiled us outside history or left us outside civilization. Europeans, while writing history, first and foremost catalogue events concerning the development of their national identities on their own soil because their aim is to present themselves as the first autochthonous peoples and founders of the culture that is the noble continuation of the Greco-Roman civilization which had presumably developed exclusively in Europe.

However, the material and intellectual basis for this representation is being shaken further and further every day. The Greek miracle or *Miracle Grec*, once considered as an original thing, the Greco-Roman civilization, and the pure German blood, the more they are examined, the more we are discovering the non-European ingredients of these amalgamated notions. The sacred Aryanism of the nineteenth century, which had excited that century's intellectuals in the same manner as religion once did, is eroding with each passing day. The apostates of this belief system have now joined the ranks of real scientists who are discovering the origins of technology, culture and the arts outside European soil, thereby retracing human origin back to its true homeland, and making it possible to understand the world civilization as whole and universal. It is an event of historic magnitude that this major intellectual movement, which recounts our own history and concerns us, finds its best synthesis at the center of the Turkish revolution today, its finest manifestation in the hands of the Turkish revolutionary. As we chronicle our own history, we rightfully find the most momentous events of world history in our own history, and we are proud of it.

Turkish history as the beginning of world history and the Turkish revolution as a historic reaction to European history in the twentieth century: that ancient past bound to our contemporary reality. In this continuum, we find all the elements of a widespread national excitement. Bringing to light this movement in its entirety, all of its significance, and bolstering with each passing day our "national history thesis," all of its methods and means, are the duty and debt of being a revolutionary intellectual.

Translated by İlker Hepkaner

ART AS MEASURE OF CIVILIZATION

Dictionary of Architecture[1]

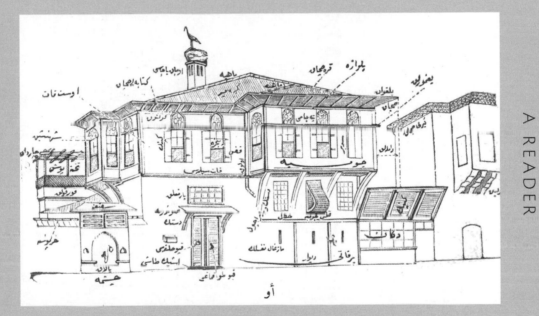

FIGURE 9. House[2]

---

1 Celal Esad, *Istılahat-ı Mimariye* (Istanbul: Matbaa-i Ahmed İhsan, 1324/1906–7), 11.
2 The labels are taken from the original text. —Ed.

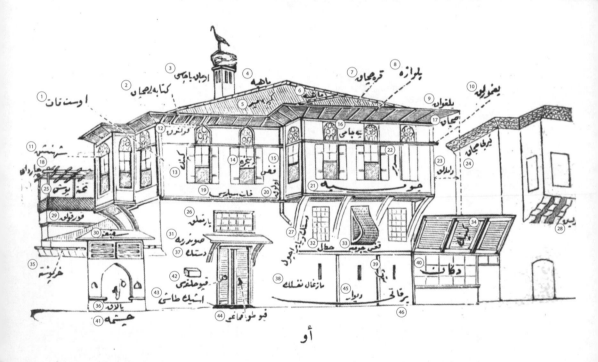

1. top floor (üst kat), 2. eave with inscription (kitabeli saçak), 3. chimney (ocak bacası), 4. ridge (mahya), 5. roof shingles (kiremit), 6. ridge (mahya), 7. exposed eave (kara saçak), 8. braces supporting the eaves (pelvaze), 9. fascia (yelkovan), 10. rain drain (yağmurluk), 11. oriel (şahnişin), 12. eave support (koltuk), 13. shutter (kepenk), 14. window (pencere), 15. latticework (kafes), 16. bull's eye (tepe camı), 17. eave (saçak), 18. pergola (çardak), 19. horizontal molding (kat silmesi), 20. gutter (oluk), 21. bay window (cumba), 22. blank wall (sedir), 23. space between the eaves of neighboring buildings (damlalık), 24. eave with bricks in a zig-zag pattern (kirpi saçak), 25. wooden terrace (tahta puş), 26. grating (parmaklık), 27. wood bracket or iron bracket (destek veya paraçol), 28. curled brace support (kırik), 29. railing (korkuluk), 30. canopy roof (sakifa), 31. lean-to awning (sundurma), 32. beam (hatıl), 33. bay window with latticework (kafesli cumba), 34. shutter (kepenk), 35. coping (harpuşta), 36. basin (yalak), 37. support (destek), 38. vent (mazgal nefeslik), 39. vertical support (dikme), 40. shop (dükkân), 41. public fountain (çeşme), 42. ring pull (kapı halkası), 43. threshold stone (eşik taşı), 44. door knocker (kapı tokmağı), 45. wall (duvar), 46. ground floor (yer katı).

Celal Esad's entry in *Istılahat-ı Mimariye*, humbly titled as *ev* (house), marks the beginning of a discussion in Turkish architectural history. His seemingly simple and generic annotated sketch is loaded with layers of meaning. Reading the image closely and thinking through it reveals some important arguments put forward by the author. It is published in Celal Esad's pioneering "dictionary" of architecture, which attempted to systematize the vocabulary of construction as part of a broader proposal to scrutinize architecture in a scholarly (or "scientific," *fenni*) manner. The modest structure thus makes a case for an inclusive history of architecture that expands beyond monuments. The identification of each one of its details with a proper technical term conveys the message that the building type is worthy of scholarly attention and respect. Indeed, it is some of these very same elements that were revived in discussions of the "Turkish house," famously theorized and put into practice by architect Sedad Eldem from the 1930s to the 1950s. Furthermore, the sketch opens a subtle window on to domestic life. For example, the blank facade of the lower level refers to the utilitarian spaces behind, whereas the fenestrated second and third floors indicate them as the main living spaces of the house, with the third floor as the piano nobile. The wooden latticework of a window on the second floor points to the privacy of the family life, protected from the street view. The shutters are environmental control devices regulating light and noise. The terrace links the interior spaces with nature and the high garden wall gives a hint of what is hidden behind. In addition to the private realm, a few details about public life are glimpsed: the street fountain attached to the garden wall is a charitable offering to passersby and the small shop caters to everyday needs of the neighborhood. Finally, the stork on the chimney alludes to domestic bliss by celebrating the folk belief in this cherished bird as good omen. In brief, Celal Esad's drawing inserts *ev* into art historical discourse and, along the way, quietly destabilizes Orientalist clichés about life at home.

ZÇ

A READER

CELAL ESAD

Fine Arts in the Orient
"Ottoman Fine Arts"[1]

European scholars lacking in careful analysis tend to view Ottoman art as nothing more than imitation of Arabic, Persian and especially Byzantine arts, and argue that, even Arabs adopted the arts from Christian Copts who inhabited the lands of Egypt long before the arrival of Islam, and since Coptic art developed under the influence of Byzantine art, European scholars wish to trace the origin of all Islamic art back to the art of Eastern Christianity.

How different artistic traditions have influenced one another is, of course, a perennial topic that has kept the scholars of the arts particularly busy, and depending on which artistic tradition the scholar has dedicated his career to researching, he has seldom been able to resist being partial to demonstrating the influence of that artistic tradition over the others. Especially concerning the influence of Byzantine art on Western art, obvious among the surviving works, many scholars have nevertheless attempted to refute it, causing longstanding disputes among art historians.

Again because of their partiality, some scholars do not even acknowledge the body of Ottoman art in plain view today, summarily treating it instead as an amalgam of Arabic, Persian and Byzantine arts.

In truth, Ottoman fine arts were born in the cradle of Arabic, Persian and Byzantine arts and have continued to evolve under their influence. Upon close inspection, however, Ottoman art does not bear exact resemblance to any one of these artistic traditions and develops its own distinct character.

Is there any artistic tradition in history that is truly unique and has not been influenced by preceding traditions or even those that have outlasted it? Can any art historian disavow the influence of Egyptian art on ancient Greece, of Greek art on Roman art, of Chaldean art on ancient Persian art and of Persian art on

---

1   Celal Esad, "Osmanlı Sanayi-i Nefisesi," *İkdam*, no. 4502 (December 13, 1906): 3.

Byzantine art, or overlook the similarities between each pair? The museums are filled with surviving examples of all these artistic traditions, dated and displayed.

As scientific progress steadily overcomes subjective opinion and we investigate the arts of certain cultures that had been heretofore neglected, many truths begin to emerge, making objective contributions to our knowledge.

For a long time, Byzantine art and artworks had not been studied as closely as they are today, and persistent differences of opinion had only overshadowed the efforts with a kind of partisanship. Likewise, Jews have long been perceived as lacking in artistic skills; that even Jewish art has found its place in art history today serves as proof that previously held assumptions about its value are disappearing.

Undoubtedly, the further Ottoman art is studied, the more its uniquely Ottoman style and character will be recognized. Among the primary reasons why it has been thus far neglected are: the wholesale representation of the Ottoman artistic tradition based on partial studies that have considered many Ottoman artworks as derivative of Arabic and Persian arts; the absence of a comprehensive collection of Ottoman art that can serve as resource for scholars of art history; and the fact that many of the works that would complete such a collection have not yet been examined because they are currently scattered among European museums and elsewhere.

Although some European scholars claim that our artists were neither trained nor supported because Islam forbids representations of the human form, theirs is a false reasoning. Just as Christians have encouraged and trained the artists who adorned their churches, Islamic artists, too, have been trained to adorn their sacred mosques with calligraphy, engravings, tiles, woodworking and other forms of ornamentation.

Among them are masters of aesthetics who have astonished even the most accomplished painters in the West with the compositions and elegance they have successfully created in such visual fine arts as architecture, engraving, sculpture, carving, and ornamentation. Among the surviving works, it is possible to find examples that undeniably prove the artist's ability to truly feel and express such harmony and beauty, formal grace, pure and elegant detailing as the likes of which have not been seen even in the works of painters who have mastered the beauty and proportions of the human form, the most excellent of all created beings.

Yes, we can truly speak of Ottoman art, and one with distinctly Ottoman identity, that has evolved throughout the ages of the Great Ottoman Empire. Yet, contrary to some scholars' assertions, Ottoman art was not born solely of Arabic or Persian art. It may have evolved in the geography of these cultures. But as a fine arts tradition, it demonstrates that the Ottoman architecture, literature, engraving, calligraphy, even music possess a distinctive and distinguished character.

The history of Ottoman art began when Bursa was made the capital, the construction of mosques and other buildings commenced, and the Ottomans began to gain power and renown. It is not as easy as it may seem to chronicle the discrete stages and achievements of Ottoman art due to the abject scarcity of historical sources. It would take an expert dedicating his time and effort exclusively to such an undertaking.

The primary sources necessary to complete such a history are extremely difficult to find in libraries. A significant project like this requires extensive research and analysis that would be possible only when scholars of art history successfully date and classify all Ottoman art by its periods. Serving in the benevolent shadow of The Rightly Blessed and Great Sultan, the honorable director Hamdi Bey of Müze-i Hümayun [Imperial Museum] has, with expert effort and selfless diligence, opened a section on Ottoman art and exhibited a considerable number of valuable artworks; however, the current collection is not yet comprehensive enough to support such research.

We will not therefore attempt here to chronicle the Ottoman art history—a subject of considerable challenge that would fill an immense volume; rather, we will limit our scope to alerting researchers that, were they to investigate the body and aesthetics of this artistic tradition, they would find themselves beholding such a tradition that, much to their astonishment, had not heretofore received their attention, a tradition that is different from the Arab and Persian arts, its so-called precursors, an art that is endowed with its own forms and idiom. However, to appreciate such distinctions, we must first discuss Byzantine, Arabic and Persian arts briefly and respectively.

Translated by Nergis Perçinel

A READER

CELAL ESAD

"Arab Fine Arts"[1]

Certain scholars with prejudice who refuse to credit Arabs for their achievements concerning the fine arts assert that Arab art originated from the Christian Coptic art of Egypt and from Sassanian art; however, the objective scholars who give pre-Islamic Persian art and Egyptian Coptic art their full due refute this assertion, and observing that the arts of these cultures had little relation to Arab art, they acknowledge that the Arabs had their own preexisting artistic traditions. The historical evidence leaves no doubt that the Arabs had their original arts even before they converted to Islam. These arts, having evolved broadly and proliferated with the advent of Islam, might be viewed as the work of Islam alone.

From this vantage point, Arab art can be considered foundational to the arts of the tribes who later converted to Islam. However, it cannot be said that it was the sole source of those later arts or that these all arose from Arab art. Although Arab art, throughout the regions it spread, did exert an influence on the arts of the societies that revered and respected Islam, and to a certain degree altered their distinctive forms to make those forms resemble Arab art, it never directly gave rise to any local or regional art forms.

With the advent of Islam, Arab art attempted not to mimic the art of the Christian East, which Islamic art regarded as idolatrous, but rather developed its own unique artistic form. Nonetheless, Egyptian Coptic art, deviating from Byzantine art, resembled ancient Egyptian and Assyrian art more than Byzantine and ancient Greek art, and had a considerable impact on Arab art.

Although some European scholars have asserted that surviving buildings and remains dating back to the sixth, seventh and eighth centuries in Egypt provide evidence of this influence, nothing is conclusive so long as the dates and historical periods of such ancient works are definitively ascertained. It is worth investigating why the Egyptian tribes, which belonged to Eastern Christianity, distanced themselves from Byzantine art.

1   Celal Esad, "Arap Sanayi-i Nefisesi," *Ikdam*, no. 4507 (December 18, 1906): 3.

[...] This much is clear: no art of any culture can evolve and develop on its own, entirely exempt from the influences of the arts of its neighbors. The impact of neighbors is therefore manifested in the Arab fine arts just as it is in architecture. With the spread of Islam, as scientists and artists made their greatest discoveries in algebra, geometry, history and letters, commensurate progress was made in the fine arts as well.

Of all the Arab arts, as in the artistic traditions of nearly all societies, architecture holds the most prominent place.

[...] The Arabs built domes in the shape of cones, unlike the low domes of the Byzantines. The exact motives behind their preference are not fully known.

One reason was to keep the mosques from resembling the spaces of worship of other religions. Another and the most compelling reason was the nature of the materials used and the method of construction. Arab architects did not build their domes as the Hagia Sophia's dome. A broad and low dome required walls with supporting columns, and since the terrain was generally not very solid, the Arabs may have aimed to distribute the domes' horizontal thrust vertically, and perhaps to avoid the use of wooden frames in constructing these domes. Apart from these, it bears noting that high domes had the effect of reducing temperatures indoors. Although some experts have claimed that the Arabs must have based this oval shape on the watermelon, this cannot be the case. If they had based this shape on any natural form, it would have to have been the egg instead. However, in all likelihood, neither of these assumptions is correct. The Assyrians had adopted such domes much earlier than the Arabs.

The most striking aspect of Arab architecture is the use of the *arc brisé* or pointed arch, which in fact had never been employed in any other style of architecture.

During the half century following the Hegira, Arab architecture began to be influenced by the Sassanians. Furthermore, during the construction of the Ummayyad Mosque in Damascus, Byzantine architects and laborers were employed, resulting in the intermixing of Byzantine art and Arab art.

Thus, under the influence of both Byzantine and Sassanian art, Arabic art began to flourish and transform itself, eventually achieving its unique character. Unlike the Byzantine mosaics, the Arabs embellished the curved surfaces in the corners of the vault, called pendentives, with geometric designs. To preserve the harmony between the dome and the square walls and to lend a sense of depth to flat surfaces, they decorated such parts with gem-like forms. This style of decoration is the best means of transitioning from polygons of eight or more sides to the circular dome. The origin of these gem or crystal forms, seen first in Arab architecture, must have been the Assyrian zigzag eaves and mouldings made with bricks. The Byzantines employed another form of this in their eaves. At some point in history, Arab architecture used octagonal shapes in order to transition from the square form to the circular dome. In later times, the dome was positioned higher, atop eight, then sixteen-sided prisms, again to gradually transition from square to circle. In the first period of Arab architecture, the external facade of the building was decorated, but, later, the interior decoration obtained greater emphasis, following the adoption of glazed tiles. In Egypt, the Mosque of Sultan Hassan with its magnificent dome above the mausoleum is a good example of such decoration. The structure extends for 150 meters and includes a 33 square meter central courtyard; its largest hall [iwan] includes a minbar and a mihrab. Thereafter, Arab architecture began to change in form and style, incorporating elements of Ottoman architecture.

Translated by Nergis Perçinel

CELAL ESAD

"Arab Decorative Arts"[1]

The Arabs strictly avoided the ancient Greek and Byzantine artistic traditions and chose to employ instead geometric figures as decoration both in their art and architecture. In the first period of Islam, the patterns included squares, triangles, pentagons, and other geometric shapes, arranged in rows or interwoven for aesthetic effect. By incorporating nearly all elements and principles of geometry into decorative designs, the Arabs invented an unprecedented style of geometric art that is known around the world as "Arabesque." Yet, the use of geometric designs itself is not unique to Arabs. Certain shapes found in Babylonian art reveal that the Babylonians must have used similar forms much earlier than the Arabs. Nevertheless, no other culture excelled as much as Arabs have in developing this decorative style to create designs as delicate and ornate as theirs. In architecture, this form of decoration was made as stone inlays or, in places where building stones were in short supply, they were most often created from plaster.

Attentive observers may notice the geometric patterns that embellish the balustrades of the mausoleums and the carved doors of mosques and detect intricately interlaced combinations. While following a certain pattern, the surveying gaze notices another pattern made of the same lines while losing sight of the other, and depending on its observation skills as well as the power of its imagination, the gaze discovers myriad patterns invisible to the common eye, as if wandering endlessly in a fantastic realm. The European experts view this decorative style as reflective of the Arab imagination.

Some experts consider this decorative style as science rather than fine art, given its reliance on geometry. Yet this is an inaccurate view because the patterns do not merely follow geometric principles. The artist who arranged and created these patterns considered first and foremost the aesthetic beauty that they will evoke for the observer; as such, the decorative style should be considered as fine art rather than mere geometry.

---

1   Celal Esad, "Araplarda Sanayi-i Tezyin," *Ikdam*, no. 4513 (December 24, 1906): 3.

Arab artists, highly skilled at replicating, extrapolating, or interlacing vertical patterns, were masters of the art of creating intrinsically harmonious designs to bring about a desired effect on the human soul.

The Byzantines employed mosaic to depict human figures on the walls of their buildings. The Arabs, however, after they embraced Islam, never depicted any living form, human or animal, in decorating buildings, objects or books.

Rather than expressing ideas or exemplary conduct through figurative forms, the Arabs preferred calligraphy as the most appropriate medium to translate religious and spiritual sentiments that, by nature, resist materiality. After geometric forms, calligraphy was the most fundamental element of Arab decorative arts. From walls and textiles to household objects and armors, calligraphy became the most popular form of ornamentation, even including calligrams that, from a distance, resembled, say, a ship, or a mosque with its minarets.

The Arabs also began to employ vegetal patterns to diversify their style that otherwise relied only on calligraphic or geometric form. This form of decoration developed under the Chinese, Persian, and Mongol influence, and the al-Azhar Mosque in Egypt is one of its best examples.

Buildings, objects or armors were not the only things decorated. The Arabs adorned their Holy Quran in the same style, by illuminating the sura headings and page margins with verses and *şemse*[2] motifs, developing thus a singular style of manuscript illumination that differed significantly from the European *enluminure* style. Rare samples of surviving Quran illuminations in Arab ornamental style are on display in various museum collections.

Unlike the European *enluminure*, the Arab illumination style does not include figurative representations, and uses instead geometric patterns and only stylized vegetal motifs painted in diverse colors and gold leafing. In Christian manuscripts, the initial letters are ornamented, whereas they are never in Arab manuscripts. Such ornamentation is employed only in the sura headings and between the sacred verses indicated by stop marks in illuminated Qurans, and in *şemse* motifs and *vakfiye*.[3]

On the question of whether painting is used as decorative art by the Arabs, the noted Arab historian al-Maqrizi offers detailed accounts about Arab painters. Although the author asserts that many painters were trained in the cities where the

---

2   Sun-like illuminated motifs.—Trans.

3   A court approved deed in writing that dictates the operational rules of an endowment (*vakıf, waqf*).—Ed.

arts flourished, painting has always remained outside the bounds of Arab decorative arts, evolving as a separate art form.

Persian and Turkish Arts

Persian art before the advent of Islam echoed the art of ancient Assyrians. Under the rule of Anushirwan, Persian art had been influenced by ancient Greek art and the various Asian artistic traditions, experiencing a period of renewal during the Persian Empire. After falling under the sway of Islam, however, Persian art underwent a complete transformation. In the fifteenth year of Hegira [636/637], when Persia was incorporated into the Islamic realm, Arab arts influenced local practices, gradually leaving no trace of the ancient Persian arts. In the first period of Islam, Persian architecture was no different from Arab architecture. Persian buildings shared similar features with Arab buildings in Baghdad and Kudüs-i Şerif [Jerusalem]; the Mosque of Isfahan featured for the first time columns similar to those in the Mosque of Amr ibn al-As in Egypt. During the period of Arab domination, Persian mosques, like those in Egypt, followed the traditional four-part design, featuring axial iwans[4] surrounding a vast hall or courtyard delineated by columns. The impact of Arab arts on other art forms was not as significant as it was on architecture. Later, when the Mongols and the Turks extended their dominion across the lands of Persia, India and China they adapted some of the local artistic practices into their own, and by synthesizing among these and the Persian practices, they brought about a new artistic idiom.

During the Ghaznavids, the Persian lands expanded into India and with Indian influences, their art obtained more refined expression; and later, because of the elegance the Turkish artists lent to Persian arts, an entirely new artistic expression emerged, bearing no resemblance to either the ancient Persian or the Arab arts. This new expression has no relationship to the ancient Persian arts and evolved in manners that all but eliminated any Arab influences as well. Around AH 622 [1225/1226], progress lost its momentum for a while, although later gaining a new splendor. During that period, Chinese influence is quite evident. Persian tile and porcelain decorations produced at the time were undistinguishable from the Chinese wares. The Islamic art produced in Persia developed to such a degree as to compete with Baghdad, Damascus, and Egypt. At the start of the sixteenth century, however, the arts experienced a dramatic decline, almost ceasing to exist. Later, in AH 883 [1478/1479], attempts to revive them led to numerous construction projects

---

4   A vaulted space with an arched opening on one side.—Ed.

A READER

that filled Isfahan with buildings, and the artists invited from elsewhere succeeded in bringing fresh perspectives to the arts, effecting, in turn, significant progress in rug, textile, metalworks and tile designs. During that time, the works of an Indian painter named Mani gained much renown.[5] During later times, however, with the death of the great artists who had mastered some of those aesthetic principles and elegant techniques, these arts began to disappear, as they did in most of the Orient, and the art that followed, imitations and random pastiches of old originals, lacked in aesthetic beauty and began to decline.

The elegance and subtlety in the surviving works of Persian art is nothing more than the legacy of the Chinese, the Indians, and the Turks. Accordingly, Persian art can be classified into three periods. The first period is influenced by Arab arts, the second by the Turkish and Mongol arts, while the third is the period dating from 750 to 1000.

[...] The arts, and especially architecture, differed across the periods of Persian history. The distinctive features of Persian architecture after the period of Arab influence included mosques with pointed domes, expansive portals extending up to the base of the dome, cylindrical minarets, and long rectangular facades decorated with tiles. The domes built by the Persians were different in shape from the Arab domes. To enhance the outer appearance, they constructed double-tiered domes, that is, domes with an outer and an inner shell. In short, in the context of the Orient, Persian art flourished and excelled especially in decorative arts.

[...] The similarities and connections between Persian and Ottoman arts are considerable. The Persian artistic tradition never freed itself from the influence of the arts of the Seljuki Turks—also viewed as the origin of the Ottoman arts—and the Persian arts can be seen as a conduit in the transmission of the Turkic and Chinese arts to the Ottoman Turks.

We will address later those features of Persian arts that have been transmitted to Ottoman arts. Beforehand, however, it is appropriate to discuss Seljuki arts as the origin of the Ottoman arts. Absorbing Arab, Persian, Indian, Chinese and Byzantine influences, Seljuki arts are Turkic arts.

The architecture of the Seljuks of Rum reached its zenith especially in the eleventh and twelfth centuries. Examples of this architecture survive to our day. In Konya, for instance, the Seljuks created numerous buildings. The Seljuki art can

---

5   Some claim that this painter in fact is Chinese.—Celal Esad.

be perceived as an intermediary between the Arab, Persian, Byzantine arts and the Ottoman arts.

The Seljuks of Konya modeled their architecture after that of the Arab and Persian Seljuks, and absorbing Byzantine influences as well, their architecture succeeded in forging its own distinctive idiom.

Much valuable information on Seljuki architecture can be found in the "Islamic Architecture" section written by the chief military officer and chief architect Kemaleddin Bey, for the *Hüdavendigar Salnamesi* and later published in *İkdam*.

To transition from square spaces to spherical domes, the Seljuks could have employed, like the Arabs did, squinches with muqarnas or triangular forms, and they could have mounted their vaults and domes on square rather than round columns. In fact, even the Ottomans employed square columns in their early buildings. Round columns in Seljuki architecture were used along the window and door frames as decorative features, and their capitals were ornamented with leaf motifs. Like Arabs, the Seljuks adopted geometric and interlaced vegetal motifs for decoration. Building interiors and exteriors were decorated with faience mosaics like those found in Persian buildings during the Seljuk period. They applied porphyry marble to the surfaces and arrises like the Byzantines. In short, Seljuk arts, as a wellspring of inspiration for Ottoman arts, is among the most cherished of Turkic arts.

Translated by Nergis Perçinel and Aron Aji

A READER

CELAL ESAD

"Ottoman Architecture"[1]

When the Ottomans designated Eskişehir as the capital during the reign of His
Eminence Sultan Osman, the brave son of Ertuğrul Gazi, they began to construct
numerous mosques, madrasas, schools, hammams and residencies. The structures
that belong to this period recalled the Byzantine and Seljuk architecture.

It was during the sultanate of Hüdavendigâr [Murad I] that many specialists
from foreign lands were invited to train artists and artisans in an endeavour to im-
prove the architecture of the empire, and the rewards of this effort were harvested
under Çelebi Sultan Mehmed Han I.

However, because Sultan Hüdavendigâr employed mostly Byzantine architects
and craftsmen, the buildings shared similar features with Byzantine architecture.
After the construction of the mosque [Mosque of Hüdavendigâr (Murad I)] in
Bursa's Çekirge district, Ottoman architecture began to assume its own character,
and developing in tandem with the fame and grandeur of the Ottoman State, it
eventually assumed its position of distinction as a form of fine arts. Previous practice had overlooked the decoration of building facades. Later, more artistic forms
were used, and decorative tiles were applied including on wall surfaces. Among
the works that reflect the architectural achievement of this period is an extensive
bath, mosque and imaret complex in Iznik, built in honor of Her Highness Nilüfer
Sultan, the queen mother of Sultan Hüdavendigâr. The early Ottomans had considered the Seljuk architecture as precursor and emulated its techniques. With diligence and advocacy on the part of Sultan Çelebi Mehmed, Ottoman architecture
was elevated further, and developed into a distinctive art form.

Sultan Mehmed I embarked upon reconstructing the cities of Bursa and Edirne,
following the work by his predecessors, Sultan Hüdavendigâr and Sultan Bayezid
I, and, along with restoring various buildings in Bursa and other cities, as well as
completing others started by distinguished ancestors in Edirne, Sultan Mehmed I
commissioned the Green Mosque in Bursa, which is considered as the beginning

1   Celal Esad, "Osmanlı Mimarisi," *İkdam*, no. 4523 (January 3, 1907): 3–4.

of a distinctly Ottoman architecture. This noble and glorious Sultan was especially interested in the arts and a most generous patron to artists.

One of the most renowned architects of that period was Mimar İlyas Ali. Recognized as a pioneer for lending a distinct form to Ottoman architecture by building the Green Mosque, he had mastered his art during Sultan Mehmed I's glorious epoch.

Works from this first period of Ottoman architecture differ considerably from those in Istanbul and Edirne. The domes in Bursa mosques, similar to those found in Byzantine and especially Seljuk buildings, feature an oculus twenty to twenty-five *kadem*[2] in diameter, enclosed with wire mesh to keep the birds out; positioned right below the oculus was a water fountain. The Green Mosque also has the same type of water fountain. The lantern in the oculus zone above the fountain is similar to lanterns in some Istanbul hammams. The use of lanterns whether for illumination or for ventilation was a common practice among the Byzantines and the Seljuks. Dome exteriors are covered with lead panels. This technique, also common among the Byzantines who used both lead and brass panels, was first developed by the Persians.

When compared to the surviving examples of Seljuk and Byzantine architecture, the Green Mosque recalls the Seljuk style rather than the Byzantine. The ornate tiles decorating the said mosque and especially its mihrab are Ottoman in origin and constitute the first examples of Ottoman tile art. The mosque's main gate facing the mihrab leads to *son cemaat mahali*, the section reserved for the congregants who arrive late. Although Mimar İlyas had used one or two columns salvaged from an abandoned Byzantine structure, the columns are placed in the recesses of the main hall, and remaining in the dark, they do not disturb the authenticity of the mosque. Also found in the mosque's interior is the masterfully built water fountain bathed in light coming from the tall dome above it. The water flowing from the stone fountain at times catch the light rays from above, and the rainbow colors reflecting on the already ornate tilework create a transcendent view that is irresistible to watch.

The interior walls are wainscoted up to two meters with tiles that depict multicolored vegetal designs against a cobalt background, and above these is the row of dark blue tiles with a Quranic verse inscribed in white jeli script. The ornamental motifs where the walls meet the dome are of such dazzling beauty that they were later used, with slight modifications, on column heads by Mimar Sinan.

---

2   Equivalent of 30 cm.—Trans.

Used in the various sections of the mosque and mausoleum complex are wooden divan and door engravings, iron balustrades detailed with curvilinear patterns, glazed tiles, multi-colored glass and porcelain panels adorning the windows, calligraphy and stone inlays, all of which are prototypes of Ottoman architecture.

The Hüdavendigâr province hosts many such examples of Ottoman architecture. When closely observed, the buildings from this first epoch in Bursa show that the Ottomans had already diverged from the principles of Seljuk architecture by using square columns rather than the round ones used by the Seljuks. In short, the architectural style of these early buildings in Bursa is notably different from that of the buildings later constructed in Istanbul. Among the major architectural works of this era are the Tiled Mosque [the Green Mosque] in Iznik, built by Çandarlı İbrahim Pasha in honor of his father Çandarlı Hayreddin Pasha; the Seljuk style mausoleum in Bursa commissioned by Bayezid Pasha; the mausoleum of the mother of Sultan Selçuk; Nilüfer Bridge and the Kayağan [Kayıhan] hammam in Bursa. The architectural works in the period from Çelebi Sultan until Fatih Sultan Mehmed (may he rest in heaven) show little change, emulating the style of the Green Mosque. The Fatih Cami-i Şerif [the Mosque of Mehmed II] commissioned by Fatih Sultan Mehmed following the conquest of Istanbul, marks a departure from the prevailing artistic idiom since the local masters and craftsmen recruited during its construction aimed to emulate the Mosque of Hagia Sophia rather than the mosques in Bursa. Mimar Hayreddin, the chief architect of the Mosque of Sultan Bayezid II, reharmonized the rules and geometric designs characteristic of Ottoman architecture and introduced columns and column heads in a style of his own invention.

His masterpiece, the Mosque of Sultan Bayezid II, is among the most beautiful mosques in Istanbul. Close attention to its architectural style, whether in terms of composition or ornamentation, reveals that it recalls the style of the Green Mosque in Bursa—rather than the other Istanbul mosques. An attentive and learned observer will easily recognize that the Mosque of Sultan Bayezid II epitomizes the onset of a new era in Ottoman architecture.

Mimar Hayreddin is known for applying stalactites, used by Arabs in domes and corners, to column capitals and hence substituting the Seljuk style leaf motifs, for determining column heights and widths according to overall aesthetic design, and for creating elegant and harmonious exteriors; credited for inaugurating the new era, he gained unparalleled recognition for regulating its new architectural idiom. As the one who gave Ottoman architecture its singular Ottoman identity, he rightly deserves the honorable title of the inventor. After Mimar Hayreddin, many architects succeeded in becoming masters in their own right, and among them, Mimar Sinan, has come to occupy a place of extraordinary distinction.

[...] While devoting his life to the military rather than to architecture which would later earn him great renown, Sinan served the royal army by constructing military structures such as bridges and fortresses, for which he earned the rank of *subaşı*, the commander of the infantry regiment, as well as the position of the chief architect. Sinan's first architectural commission in Istanbul, the Mosque of Selim I, inaugurated a career that would last through the eras of Sultan Selim, Süleyman the Magnificent, Selim II and Murad III, and produce eighty-one grand mosques, fifty-one prayer houses [*mescit*], twenty-six libraries, seventeen public refectories, two asylums, seven aqueducts, eight major bridges, eighteen caravanserais, six major cisterns, thirty-three royal mansions, thirty-five hammams, seventeen shrines, numerous fountains and other structures.

[...] The Great Sinan, architect of cities, further refined Mimar Hayreddin's rules and principles, and by simplifying them, codified Ottoman architecture to levels heretofore unseen in any nation other than the Ottomans. He can therefore be considered as the epitome of Ottoman architecture. This great architect whose hundreds of creations can be seen across the cities outside the imperial capital also trained many pupils who, in turn, travelled to foreign lands to construct numerous palaces and other buildings. Among the most famous of his pupils, Mimar Yusuf earned world renown for his buildings, including palace-forts in Delhi, Lahore and Agra. In short, Great Sinan's school of architecture has produced magnificent works throughout the Islamic world.

Rightfully, this is the most radiant age of Ottoman architecture. What followed was the Mosque of Ahmed I, a notable departure. As in most other countries, the local masters assumed that progress in art meant transgression, the invention of entirely new forms, and renounced the principles that Mimar Hayreddin, Great Sinan and others had established; failing to understand their own incompetence in recognizing or appreciating aesthetic harmony, they nevertheless turned toward a new style. A glance across the interior of the Mosque of Ahmed I would easily reveal that its architectural style does not resemble that of Bayezid II, Süleyman I, Selim I or other imperial mosques. The columns supporting the central dome of the Mosque of Süleyman I are square whereas they are round in the Mosque of Ahmed I.

The interior walls of the Mosque of Ahmed I are decorated with Iznik tiles and showcase the most consummate artistry of Iznik tileworks, an industry that has been active since the beginning of Ottoman architecture. During the reign of Sultan Murad IV, two new mosques were built: the Yeni Valide Mosque in Istanbul and the Atik Valide Mosque in Üsküdar.

Sultan Ahmed III commissioned, among other structures, several fountains, including the ones in the districts of Ayasofya, Azap Kapısı, Tophane and Üsküdar, which are exquisite expressions of Ottoman architecture. An accomplished calligrapher himself, the Sultan is rumoured to have drawn the sketch for the fountain in Ayasofya, and that the inscription on its chronogram features one of his own compositions.

The artistic revival begun during the reign of Ahmed III did not last long. After Mahmud I, and due to the influence of French engineers brought in for the construction of certain dams, the Ottoman artists gravitated toward *alafranga*, the new, foreign, and highly fashionable style at the time.

As our discussion above suggests, the Ottoman architecture can be divided into four major epochs:

The first epoch extends from the construction of the Green Mosque under Çelebi Sultan Mehmed to the time of Sultan Bayezid II, that is, the construction of the Mosque of Sultan Bayezid II in Istanbul.

The second from the construction of the Mosque of Sultan Bayezid II to that of the Mosque of Ahmed I.

The third from the construction of the Mosque of Ahmed I to the reign of Sultan Ahmed III.

And the fourth from the reign of Sultan Ahmed III to the present.

Some authors claim that art cannot be confined to scientific or geometric rules, and that if it does, each artwork would completely duplicate the other and artists could not be distinguished by their artwork; however, their perspective can be refuted through observation and reflection.

[...] [Eugène Emmanuel] Viollet-le-Duc, renowned French architect and connoisseur of fine arts, studied many of the architectural principles historically used by different nations, and showed scientifically that they corresponded to actual buildings still in existence.[3] Accordingly, Viollet-le-Duc asserted that the compo-

---

3   (M) Viollet-le-Duc, *Entretiens sur l'architecture*. Page 402, 404.—Celal Esad.

sitional aesthetic and color harmony particular to the character of Turkish art and architecture followed a set of basic principles that were known to artists who created them, and that, to date, these basic principles have not been explored. Another French architect, Léon Parvillée, who undertook the task of sketching and analyzing the architectural section drawings of Bursa mosques, revealed that in the Green Mosque and the Green Mausoleum, and even in the Ottoman ornamentations therein, the Ottoman artists had used certain isosceles triangles with eight-to-five base-to-height ratio that conformed to the triangles found in ancient Egyptian buildings, and that even the height-to-width ratio of the domes, the alignment of windows and other design elements followed certain geometric and fixed principles.

If we were to study the Ottoman buildings in Istanbul by taking careful measurements and by producing precise drawings to conduct geometrical architectural analysis, it is most certain that many of these underlying principles heretofore unknown would be uncovered. Without bringing these principles to light, it is impossible to revive Ottoman architecture. Merely taking pictures of some buildings and haphazardly rearranging fragments of disparate structural details can never suffice to bring any Ottoman form back to life.

Today's architects, when they fancy building something in the name of Ottoman architecture, create their works by combining disparate elements selected piecemeal from copies or photographic reproductions of original sketches. While the various parts may each recall discrete traditional forms, the overall aesthetic of the building, the relationship of the parts to the whole, bears no resemblance to Ottoman art, and clearly asserts that the building is merely an imitation.

The resemblance would not be unlike that between a piece of calligraphic art created by a Turkish *hattat* and its imitation by a foreigner as if reproducing a painting. While someone unfamiliar with the art of Turkish calligraphy may observe a resemblance, those familiar with the art would naturally observe that the difference is significant.

Translated by Aron Aji and Nergis Perçinel

Dictionary of Architecture[1]

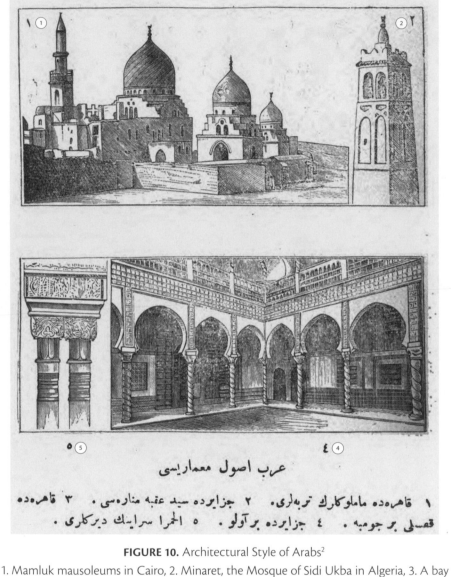

عرب اصول معماريسى

١ قاهره ده ماملوكلرك تربه لرى. ٢ جزايرده سيد عقبه منارهسى . ٣ قاهره ده قصرلى بر جوميه . ٤ جزايرده برآولو . ٥ الحرا سرايك ديركارى .

FIGURE 10. Architectural Style of Arabs[2]

1. Mamluk mausoleums in Cairo, 2. Minaret, the Mosque of Sidi Ukba in Algeria, 3. A bay window with latticework in Cairo

4. A courtyard in Algiers, 5. Columns of the Palace of Alhambra

---

1   Celal Esad, *Istılahat-ı Mimariye* (Istanbul: Matbaa-i Ahmed İhsan, 1324/1906–7), 82–84.

2   The captions are taken from the original text.

(٣) ③

FIGURE 11. Ottoman Style Architecture, the Mosque of Süleyman I

Translated by Nergis Perçinel

ISMAYIL HAKKI

"Research on Turkish Arts: An Introduction"[1]

This essay focuses on the methodology of research concerning Turkish arts. The main points I would like to discuss are as follows: Why is it important to research Turkish arts? What are the principal forms of Turkish arts? Misperceptions about Turkish arts. How should they be researched? What are the underlying principles of such research? How Turkish arts can be defined? What should a research institute dedicated to Turkish arts look like? What are the benefits of such research from the perspective of scientific inquiry and culture?

Historians often assert that "the history of nations is not the history of their rulers, but rather the history of their civilization." But what is meant by "history of civilization"? Or even prior to that, what is meant by "civilization"? In the broadest sense, civilization is the sum-total of the social institutions that a society has developed. What are these social institutions? Language, ethics, law, economy, technology, the sciences, and the fine arts. Together, these institutions that originate in a society comprise the civilization of that society. Civilization can be understood more narrowly, for instance, one that is based on the sciences and other universally recognized fields but not on the rest of the social institutions. While the narrower definition would change our understanding of civilization, it would not change the necessity to research the "history of civilization." For history can be fully understood only as the history of all social institutions. Military history or political history is partial and incomplete... For a complete sense of history, all social institutions ought to be studied. In this respect, art history is a subfield of the history of civilization because the full scope of history also includes art history. But when the history of Turkish arts is viewed in the context of this full history, the matter obtains even greater significance. Since this art history is a subfield of Turkish civilization and Turkish civilization is, in turn, part of human civilization, then research into Turkish arts concerns itself with a segment of humanity. And yet the

---

1   Ismayıl Hakkı, "Türk Sanatlarının Tedkikine Medhal," *Darülfünun İlahiyat Fakültesi Mecmuası*, no. 2 (March 1926): 135–57.

history of Turkish arts is arguably among the most obscure and darkest chapters of Turkish civilization. Therefore, researching Turkish arts is, in a broader sense, researching an obscure and dark chapter of human history. The findings of such a study will belong not only to the Turkish nation but to humanity at large.

What essential truths can Turkish art history reveal about the past of Turkish life? The answer to this question ought to be sought in the nature of art. Art is not an institution like the sciences that entail objective reality and proven theories. Neither is art a random outcome of a reflex activity like the imagination. Perhaps art is not faithful to life and reality like, or as much as, the sciences are, but it is a subjective activity that mostly derives its material from the external world and conforms in part to the real circumstances of that world. In which case, the substance of art is made of both the real and the unreal.[2] If, to understand the nature of art, we must compare it to something else, then, to some extent, it is reasonable to compare it to play. Like art, play, too, is part real and part unreal.

While binding its players with certain strings of reality, the play ushers the soul to an imaginary and fictitious realm. And like play, art, too, has its feet on the ground while its head strives to free itself from reality! Although it does not completely divorce itself from reality, art strays from it. What then is the social function of art, made as it is of the real and the unreal at the same time? Such a weighty question is not possible to answer precisely and definitively. However, given some of the familiar attributes of art, one may note, in sum, that art is the spirit's reaction against the deprivations and inadequacies of life, and its reclamation of its freedom, albeit under fictitious circumstances, in the domain of the imagination. This is why research in the arts carries great social significance. Such research may not reveal to us how we come to know nature, but it will reveal the shape of our collective imagination and how it functions in time and space. To begin with, which of the fundamental precepts and values of society has this imagination felt the need to remain faithful to, and without disrupting their order? In other words, to what extent is art the work of a truthful intellect?

Conversely, at what points and angles has this imagination diverged from society and succeeded in creating a separate, fictitious world? In other words, to what extent

---

2   Additionally, concerning aesthetic works, there are no definite norms or criteria to link truth and imagination in a reasonable and logical manner. In art history, these two may resist each other, and, occasionally, one overpowers the other. To illustrate, when we draw a comparison between the entrance of Kara Dai [Karatay] Madrasa and the entrance of the Great Mosque in Divriği, we see that the architecture of the first foregrounds reason and logic, whereas that of the second foregrounds sensation and imagination.—Ismayıl Hakkı.

٢ — ديوريكده جامع كبيرك مدخلى .

(رسنه فوطوغرافخانه‌سنك قولكسيونندن)

FIGURE 12. Entrance to the Great Mosque in Divriği (from the collection of Resne Photography Studio)[3] (Ismayıl Hakkı, "Türk Sanatlarının Tedkikine Medhal," figure no. 2)

---

3   The captions are taken from the original text.—Ed.

is art idealistic? When does this collective force called art yield to natural forces? At the same time, in what manner does it resist these forces? Most assuredly, it is the study of art that will answer these questions. The function of art is not simply to offer solace or compensation for life's deprivations. Art is an organizing institution that, through its works, spurs the inscrutable and chaotic forces of real life to excess and even brings order and control to this excess. For instance, the inspiration for mosques is, in essence, pious life. Not the moribund, withered part of pious life, but its excessive, exuberant part. Consider the splendor of the sarcophagi: is it not emblematic of the extent to which the dead are revered by a society? What is this bounty and joy that we see in architecture and ornamentation if not the exuberant outpouring of a bounteous and joyous life? In this sense, art serves the freedom and natural flow of life not only through dissent and compensation, but also by helping us to live this present life as abundantly and idealistically as possible, and by turning it into the richest and most freely flowing adventure.

Works of art, by their nature, reveal to us the secrets of the innermost (hence the richest) life, which are neither visible on the surface of society nor discernible in daily happenings, and they entrust us with the inexhaustible wellsprings of life. In this way, they guide us to discover the most creative regions of the collective soul and the most peculiar inhabitants living therein. Architectural works are the vessels of the life they make possible inside them. Mosques are enclosures, made incarnate according to the necessities of pious life they protect inside them: The various facets comprising a mosque have been appraised separately, each adorned with a different degree of due reverence and rank. The main entrance of a mosque is unlike its other entrances, rather, it is constructed with the utmost care. The mihrab and the minbar are the most precious parts of a mosque, materially and spiritually. The house of an ascetic is not the same as that of a layman. The body of a house can be understood only through the nature of the community we call the family. Accordingly, the techniques employed in architectural works ought to be studied also from this perspective.

To illustrate the importance of scientific study in the field of Turkish arts, I would like to bring up a persistent myth concerning this field. Some foreign authors such as Gustave Le Bon and indeed certain Turkish authors as well have supposed that Turkish art does not have an independent tradition, rather, it is an amalgam of Arabic, Persian and Byzantine elements. This is so because, they claim, the Turks adopted elements from the nations they were in contact with, and they mixed elements from the artistic traditions they knew.

٤ ــ بورسه مراد خداوندگاره عطف ايمبلن أوك ايجى .

(استانبول تورك اوجاغنك قولكـيونندن)

FIGURE 13. Interior of a house believed to belong to Murad I in Bursa (from the collection of İstanbul Türk Ocağı) (Ismayıl Hakkı, "Türk Sanatlarının Tedkikine Medhal," figure no. 4)

٥ ــ صالح طورقده ايكى عصرلق بر خانهنك ميرهسى . بو خانه اخيرأ هدم ايتدبرلشدر .
(آثار عتيقه انجمنى قولكسيونندن)

FIGURE 14. Facade of a two-century-old house in Salma Tomruk [Fatih]. This house was demolished later (from the collection of Asar-ı Atika Encümeni [Commission on Antiquities]) (Ismayıl Hakkı, "Türk Sanatlarının Tedkikine Medhal," figure no. 5)

To demonstrate how superficial these claims are, it will suffice to examine, for example, ancient Greek art from the perspective of its relations with other nations and civilizations. In accordance with [Karl Otfried] Müller's theory, this ancient art used to be viewed as wholly autonomous, with no past outside itself. However, as archaeological studies have shown, the ancient Greeks, like all societies, did not live outside the realm of human interaction, that their earliest works were adapted from the Assyrians, the Egyptians and the Phoenicians, and that, in truth, the ancient Greek civilization—on the European continent—had built on the traditions of the past. Similarly, the pointed arch, which is the very distinctive element of Gothic art, itself considered as one of the world's most original, is claimed by some European scholars to have been brought from Egypt and adopted from Arab arts. According to Gustave Le Bon's account, the arch had been used by the Arabs in Egypt, Sicily, and Italy since the twelfth century. If Turkish art were impure and unoriginal by virtue of its relation to the Arab, Persian, and Byzantine arts, then by the same reasoning, ancient Greek and Gothic art should be deemed as equally impure and unoriginal!

The truth is that no such thing as self creation exists in the history of art, or in the history of life, and therefore no artistic tradition can be censured for adopting elements from other traditions. Such cultural exchange between civilizations is highly beneficial, and, furthermore, it does not put the autonomy and authenticity of national art in question, for, after all, the distinctiveness of an artistic tradition depends not on the elements it has borrowed from other traditions, but on the new synthesis it achieves among those elements. What determines originality or unoriginality is the very character of this synthesis. So long as this synthesis engenders distinct value and meaning, then the art deserves distinct consideration, and is original. Whatever its basic components may be, it is still original. Given that art is meaning, the object that expresses this meaning consists of not the sum of its parts, but rather the living synthesis resulting from all the parts coming together in uniquely harmonious fashion. Thus, rather than considering art as if it were an object of scientific study and attempting to understand it analytically and quantitatively by reducing it to its parts, if it is perceived as an organic whole, a living system, then it will be possible to determine its specific place in the history of civilization and to discover whence it comes and whither it is headed. It is in this respect that Turkish art, in my view, is one of the most exceptional traditions of art known to history and humanity. For, despite its parts—its domes, arches, ceramic tiles, and calligraphy—that take their inspiration from this or that source, it possesses, in its totality, an authentic and extraordinary presence. This quality of Turkishness, this character that is unique to Turkish art is absent in Arab, Persian or Byzantine arts. Accordingly, in considering the Turkish art of the periods following the construction of the Mosque of Sultan Bayezid II, it is perhaps more accurate to compare it to ancient Greek art rather that the arts of its immediate neighbors. No matter how far one may wish to reduce Turkish art to other regional traditions with respect to certain of its elements, it evokes, in equal part, the genius of the ancient Greeks with respect to its forms, and the transcendent values and meanings embodied in these forms. The works during the period extending from the conquest of Istanbul to the construction of the Yeni Valide Mosque are akin to those of ancient Greece, faithful to the principles of reason and logic and the qualities of simplicity and clarity; they are universal in character and belong to humanity. [Henri-Louis] Bergson described the ancient Greeks as the inventors of stylistic clarity in the history of humankind. In my opinion, the classical period of Turkish art [mid-fifteenth to early seventeenth centuries] presents an irrefutable experience of this clarity, carried to perfection in its most unusual manifestations.

For people who have severed their ties with past traditions that merit no preservation, but who possess such timeless attributes as language, intellect and willpower in order to engender a fresh and vibrant way of life, the investigation of their national art should be a matter of the highest priority. What else but the positive use of reason and resolve would ensure the soundness of such an investigation? Rather than brimming with religious and political sentiments, the investigation should follow the principles of reason and scientific disposition. If so, the question we must pose is: "What is the scientific method to study the history of Turkish arts?"

The first requirement of a scientific approach is to free the mind of all prior assumptions. To sow a new seed in the intellect, it is first necessary to root out the weeds grown of all the false seeds sown in the past. This principle is especially important for Turkish intellectuals because Turkish arts also belong to the present history in which we live and whose fortunes we share, at least in part. Especially when studying sacred Islamic buildings, the danger of distortions due to religious or national sentiments is substantial. Moreover, most of the ideas we commonly espouse in the name of science and history are not objective judgments deriving from scientific sources. Rather, they are notions spread by word of mouth that usually gain credence either during a particular era or because of the public renown of a particular artist. The subjective judgments are reinforced even further by the fact that the works of Turkish artists have not yet been subjected to methodical research and evaluation. Especially the history of an architectural style or that of a literary school is a delicate matter requiring very close and scrupulous investigations. Because it is possible to end up with mistakes or misattributions, we ought to begin our work first by freeing our mind from unverified ideas concerning the inventory and its worth. To illustrate, Hafız Osman's worldwide renown makes him appear to us as an innovator unmatched in the history of calligraphy. However, we render this judgment before we consider his past. We must examine his association with Sheikh Hamdullah from a scientific perspective. The same applies to Mimar Sinan, whom we revere as a revolutionary figure in Turkish art history. Perhaps, our perspective regarding Sinan will change significantly after an extensive study is completed about his predecessors. Considering the working methods of today's architects, one might assume that Sinan built his structures—say, the Mosque of Sultan Bayezid II and the Mosque of Süleyman I—after making two-dimensional architectural drawings and sectional sketches. However, in my opinion, it is not so easy to dismiss the possibility that he and other architects used previous buildings as actual models, and modified parts or invented new ones, thereby creating their art concretely and physically, with the power of their imagination. Consequently, unless we ascertain their method of invention and construction, it would be wrong to make assumptions about the past simply through the lens of contemporary practices. [...] Art history concerns itself not with words, idioms or analogies but physical objects. Art history is the history of mosques, fountains, inscriptions, tombstones, tiles and muqarnas. [...] To approach art history independent of objects, as if it were a catalogue of words and pronouncements, is the most defective approach. In art research, truth and reality must replace conjecture.

Having called attention to the impressionistic character of commentaries to date, our first task ought to be the discovery of Turkish artworks. I say, "discovery" because the national history of art is replete with subjects yet undiscovered.[4] We have nearly no scientific information about our artworks, the genres and the artists that constitute this history. It is wrong to assume that Turkish architecture consists of only mosque architecture. True, it is almost impossible to find old wood-structure buildings in a city like Istanbul that has seen so many fires and undergone countless changes and reconstructions. However, in Anatolian cities such as Niğde, Nevşehir, and Avanos, there are many examples of stone structures built by Turkish masons, and they bear distinctly Turkish characteristics. These are prime examples of residential architecture. Moreover, there are several timber cities like Çankırı that epitomize Turkish art of woodworking. Anatolian architecture is not merely a subject of scientific investigation but also a source of inspiration for the artists. No one is aware that the city cemeteries, excellent repositories of technique and elegance, are like open-air museums. Not everyone has seen the jeli script on the facade of the mausoleum of Mustafa Rakım, one of the masters of Turkish calligraphy. What do we know about the tombstones in Konya cemeteries, which period they were built in, what materials they were made of? Has anyone researched the history of those porticoed courts of Greek houses in the vicinity of Niğde or Fertek, structures that recall madrasa architecture? What sort of parallelism can be drawn between an old room in Hacı Bektaş Veli Mausoleum and the rooms of a typical Turkish house? We have no information of this sort. All in all, so many unknowns. To study them, we need to search for them, discover them first.

The search should not be limited to a certain artwork or genre, rather it should expand to include the full range of evidence pertaining to the entirety of Turkish art. Sanctuaries, houses, sarcophagi, bridges, hammams, public fountains, dikes, castles, calligraphy, bookbinding, illustrated manuscripts, papermaking, embroidery, carpets, textiles and garments—all should be included in our investigation.

A READER

---

4   I use the word undiscovered to mean that it has not been discovered or examined by scientific inquiry.—Ismayıl Hakkı.

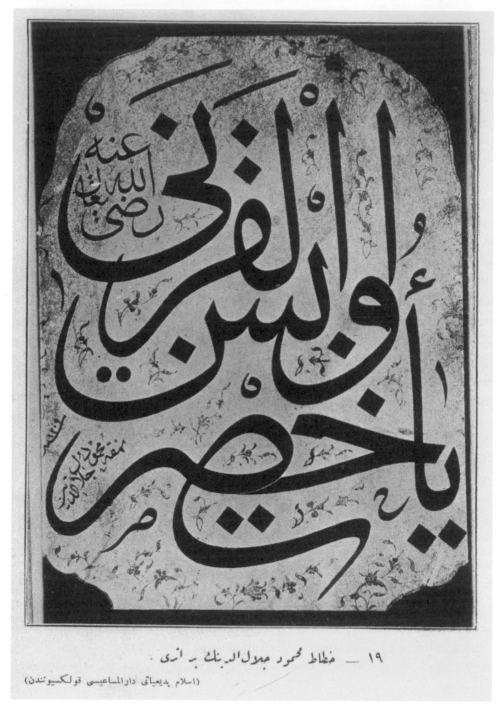

FIGURE 15. A work by calligrapher Mahmud Celaleddin (from the collection of İslam Bediyatı Darülmesaisi [Workshop for Islamic Aesthetics]) (Ismayıl Hakkı, "Türk Sanatlarının Tedkikine Medhal," figure no. 19)

FIGURE 16. Sarcophagi in the Mausoleum of Alaaddin in Konya (from the collection of Mebâni-i Diniye İdaresi [Administration of Religious Buildings]) (Ismayıl Hakkı, "Türk Sanatlarının Tedkikine Medhal," figure no. 6)

Furthermore, we should not be influenced by the prevalent opinion. Art history is not solely the "history of masterpieces," it is the history of all works that possess aesthetic significance. The history of sanctuaries, for instance, should not be confined to the largest or the best-known sanctuaries, but it should include from the most elevated to the most modest, from the most embellished to the plainest, from the most intricate to the simplest, from the most renowned to the entirely unknown. For the aim is to find not new sources of pleasure but material for evaluation and insight based on reason. Yet it is almost universal to represent Turkish art in terms of its most popular and renowned examples. This mentality shared by certain art historians is quite dangerous. When studying the evolution of a complex art tradition, it is not right to assume that the masterworks are the most essential. True, the Mosque of Şehzade Mehmed, the Mosque of Süleyman I, the ablution fountain of the Yeni Valide Mosque, the codex of Hafız Osman's calligraphic art, these are by all means outstanding works that deserve extensive study. Yet, who can claim that they contain everything we need to know about the life and the evolution of our arts? Alongside these majestic and inexhaustible artworks, there are less essential works, those of secondary importance and mixed genres or styles. Yet, an unpretentious tomb, an ordinary shrine, an ordinary drawing well, or a plain headstone is indeed an ingenuous work of art that expresses the ethos of the era and its character most appositely and even more faithfully.

Fantasy, originality, or individual imagination is not the foremost concern in these works. Each of the parts in these simple and ordinary objects mirrors its period in most essential and authentic ways. So much so that neither their artless-

١٠ ــ استانبولده بايرام پاشا نربه‌سی حولیسنده قر قدیم بر قوبو دولابی
(آثار عتیقه انجمنی قولکسیوندن)

FIGURE 17. An old-style well pulley in the courtyard of Bayrampaşa Mausoleum in Istanbul (from the collection of Asar-ı Atika Encümeni) (Ismayıl Hakkı, "Türk Sanatlarının Tedkikine Medhal," figure no. 10)

۲۳ ــ داود پاشا جامعی قبرستاننده هجرتك اون ایکنجی عصرنه عائد بر طاشه.
«تاریخی ۲۱۵۳ در»
(آثار عتیقه انجمنی قولکسیونندن)

FIGURE 18. A stone dating from the twelfth century of Hegira [the seventeenth to eighteenth centuries] in the cemetery of the Mosque of Davud Pasha (from the collection of Asar-ı Atika Encümeni) (Ismayıl Hakkı, "Türk Sanatlarının Tedkikine Medhal," figure no. 23)

ness nor their lack of worth outweighs their singularity. Consequently, if we want to see the characteristics specific to the genre of these works, we ought to focus our attention on these modest creations to delve deeply all the way into the very cells of the period's architecture. Just as a single-cell organism is as important in biological research as the life of an animal, the study of ordinary objects is as indispensable to the history of architecture as the study of grand and complex structures. Accordingly, while we study the Mosque of Sultan Bayezid II as a consummate example of its period's architecture, there is much to gain also from studying lesser examples such as the Mosque of Atik Ali Pasha or the Mosque of Firuz Ağa, or the simple mausoleum[5] built to honor the chief carpenter of Fatih Sultan Mehmed, for each belongs to the same period. When going from the Mosque of Sultan Bayezid II to the plain mausoleum of the chief carpenter, we observe that much of the edifice of the latter could not outlast the modesty of its construction, yet we also notice that the dome, the diamond patterned column heads, and fragments of the arcades have survived... For the same reason, the Haseki Sultan complex, a lesser work by Mimar Sinan, merits scientific investigation as much as the Mosque of Süleyman I, his masterwork since both can inform us about the norms and characteristics of the period.

These objects of study should be not only discovered and publicized but also dated for the sake of history. There are two reasons for this urgency. First, these objects are in danger of decay, and they should at least be recorded in the collective memory. Second, the work is necessary for scientific study. The comparative evaluation of artworks is possible only once they are dated and identified. True, the best instrument for such comparative evaluation is the human memory. However, considering the extremely wide range of characteristics that also closely resemble one another, the only instrument that can aid in the functions of a powerful memory is the historical record.

[...] Once the records are complete, the historian's work is not over. The next task is classification. History must also identify the discrete artistic periods. How can this be accomplished? How will these artistic periods take shape? The principal task is the investigation of consequential characteristics that demarcate periods. How or where are these consequential characteristics to be found? Undoubtedly, the most dangerous method is to resort to subjective judgements: classifying artworks as "magnificent," "dignified," "serene" and by any other abstract attribute

---

5   It is located in the district of Hırka-i Şerif, in Hüsrev Pasha neighborhood in Fatih.—
     Ismayıl Hakkı.

carries significant risk. Such generalizations might be possible only after the research is completed. We ought to begin first by identifying certain objective characteristics. They need to be concrete and observable distinctions that can be found in architectural plans, column heads, animate and inanimate motifs and so on. One may ask: "But what is the relationship between these observable distinctions and the intangible values that an artwork expresses?" As a matter of fact, the physical characteristics of every art object correspond to its intangible values. As in living creatures, material distinctions go hand in hand with spiritual distinctions. Moreover, similar to the evolution of living creatures, the emergent differences in the evolution of art are not accidental. For instance, in Arab art, jeli inscriptions in Kufic and Thuluth styles were mostly written on panels ornamented with floral motifs. However, on Turkish buildings, especially those constructed after the period following the conquest of Istanbul, jeli inscriptions begin to appear on flat and blank surfaces without ornamentation. Turkish jeli script and floral motifs become incongruous and irreconcilable elements. This difference in material form arises from a fundamental shift in perspective that suffuses the spirit of the artworks in this new period. Indeed, although the jeli script remained stylistically unchanged in Arab and Turkish arts, it was, as a subject of art, governed by different perspectives in each culture. In Arab arts, calligraphy was treated as a primary or complementary element of decorative arts, an opportunity for ornamentation. The Turkish perspective concerning calligraphy is entirely different: The letters of the jeli script in Turkish art have nothing to do with decoration; rather, they are the very subject of art themselves, singular in form and rendered beautifully as such. The Turkish artists did not embellish calligraphy, because they were satisfied with its intrinsic beauty.

[...] The principal criteria mentioned so far pertain to the investigation of artworks, and they are almost incontestable givens. However, besides examining artworks in and of themselves, it is also possible to examine them dynamically. What is necessary is not merely to observe these physical works of art but to understand their emergence, formation, and evolution. Art history should answer both "What is art?" and also "How has it come to be?" The latter concerns the dynamic dimension of art history. To analyze Turkish art dynamically, we need to approach it from the following three angles:

1. Studying Turkish art in relation to its past: Here, the "past" refers not only to the recent past but to all antecedent periods, all the stages of its maturation. It is a mistake to conceptualize Turkish art as merely Ottoman art or Seljuk art. The

origins of Turkish art are being discovered in periods well before the emergence of Islam. If possible, it is necessary to go even farther back to uncover the earliest artifacts of Turkic agriculture. For art as life has been an uninterrupted progression. The future is always hidden in the present. And the present is a living organism impregnated by the past. To imagine that the most sacred motifs may have the most secular origins, and that the most secular forms may result from the metamorphosis of a sacred object or belief from the past, are legitimate hypotheses consistent with the internal logic of art history. Because every event in this history can be understood only in relation to its antecedents, the most effective method of scientific investigation ought to begin by considering the simplest events and advance towards the most complex. In this sense, Turkish art history is the continuation of Turkish archaeology. What I asserted earlier concerning the dispassionate analysis of form applies equally to that of the emergence of new forms which requires that we free ourselves of sentimentalism. For instance, the idea that evolution is a "measurable and plausible" process, and that its manifestations in art history transpire through certain small and unnoticeable changes is an a priori notion. Rather than limiting ourselves to a strictly rational approach, we might think that the history of Turkish art, like the history of plant and animal life, entails a process of creative evolution that also includes sudden changes.

2. Studying Turkish art in relation to the other artistic traditions with which it interacted historically: The influence between artistic traditions is a particular manifestation of the influence between civilizations. No artistic tradition exists by itself. In art history, we have seen influences at play not only between neighboring traditions but even between those that are distant from each other. The collective power of imagination is not as conservative or uncompromising as it is generally assumed. This power, whenever it found elements and techniques that it could incorporate and internalize, has done so, regardless of differences in nationality, religion, sect, proximity or distance. This ebb and flow between artistic civilizations is known to have produced strange results at times, even unexpected departures. The carved Chinese or Indian dragons dating back to the twelfth century in the Bayeux Cathedral exemplify such departures.[6] Although such interventions are attributed to individual artists, it is also possible to observe distinct and sustained currents that have influenced diverse schools of arts in a particular period, producing their strongest impact near the center. One of the strangest examples of this can be seen between the fifth and eighth centuries, when European art, under

---

6   Bréhier, "Les methods dans l'histoire de l'art," *Revue international de l'enseignement,* 1906.—Ismayıl Hakkı.

the influence of Oriental art, adopted a decorative style, stripping itself of human subjects.[7] According to the same scholar, the reason for the similarity between the Assyrian or Copt engravings and the Merovingian tombs of the southwest during the same period is not the inaptitude of the laborers who belonged to two separate civilizations; rather, it is the saturation of the Gaul land with Oriental artifacts and the Gaul artists copying the ivory, textile and vase motifs that arrived from the Orient.[8] When the medieval Italian monuments are perceived as the products of a certain school of art, a complication arises. According to [Emile-Auguste-Joseph] Bertaux's analysis, these monuments are extremely complex, comprising a mixture of influences from Roman art, Byzantine art, the art of northern tribes and even Arab art of the twelfth century. Even concerning the tombstone adornments in Istanbul cemeteries, the late style of employing nature motifs instead of the older abstract shapes can only be explained by the influence of foreign and distant civilizations. For in the periods preceding this century, neither this subject matter nor this particular style was familiar to Turkish artists. Once these monuments of our art history are analyzed, we will see that the tombstones have undergone a wholesale transformation, with even the most conventional adornments having assumed a naturalistic and realistic character. This change first witnessed in the sixteenth century becomes most commonplace while approaching the eighteenth century.

[3. Studying Turkish art in terms of its original contributions:][9] An art style is not merely the admixture of recurrent practices far and near. It also includes original elements independent of centuries of antecedent models. In this respect, art styles do not repeat themselves; rather, they counteract each other. Art history, then, is not the history of imitation and repetition, rather it is the history of departures and innovation. When art is defined as a miracle of heritage, what needs the most explanation is not what it has inherited from the past, but the part that bears no resemblance to the past. What makes an artwork an artwork, what gives it its character and originality, if not this innovation? Therefore, we have an obligation to examine those very elements of Turkish art history that bear no resemblance to its past. What elements have Turkish arts carried along its riverbed? The answer to this question is undoubtedly important. However, what elements has this same riverbed rejected or abandoned? The answer to this question is even more important. Concerning such selection and evolution, I cannot help but recognize—as in Neo Lamarckian and Bergsonian perspectives—the role of a transcendent power.

---

7   Ibid.—Ismayıl Hakkı.

8   Ibid. *İlahiyat Mecmuası*, no. 2.—Ismayıl Hakkı.

9   Number 3 is missing in the original text.—Ed.

So long as we refuse to perceive art as a discrete phenomenon, it is impossible to explain these dynamic transformations. The arts are like systems of philosophy. Just as the empirical reality of a system is made of certain ideas and logical relationships, the empirical reality of an artwork is made of forms, materials, and details. And just as a system is not these empirical elements themselves but the dynamic totality created with them in a particular manner, the artwork, too, is the meaning it expresses by means of its empirical materiality. This is why the various Islamic arts, while they share common attributes, do not express the same meaning or perspective. The most original, distinctive, and individual life of an artwork lies in this immaterial, transcendent region of meaning. We need to grasp this meaning not by relying exclusively on the eye or the intellect and breaking the artwork into its parts, as if it were a scientific work or an objective totality; rather, we need to experience the artwork as a subject of the senses and of inspiration in order to grasp its meaning with heart and intuition.

In this respect, the important rule in art analysis is to approach the work as an organism and understand it as a system. Neither a column head, nor a gate, not

١٤ — صوقوللی محمد پاشا جامعی : مقطع رسمی .
(رسمك آصلی معمار سداد بك طرفندن وجوده كتيرلمشدر)

FIGURE 19. The Mosque of Sokullu Mehmed Pasha: Section (The original drawing is by Mimar Sedad Bey) (Ismayıl Hakkı, "Türk Sanatlarının Tedkikine Medhal," figure no. 14)

even a dome expresses meaning by itself or reveals the full nature of the artwork. What we call meaning and nature are holistic and composite notions that become actualized organically, with life and intention. Therefore, when Turkish art is studied with purely analytic intelligence rather than holistic intelligence, it ends up being reduced to sundry objects or simplistic elements borrowed from the Arabs, Persians or Byzantines, and the resulting history of Turkish arts is nothing more than a history of imitation and repetition. But when approached with holistic intelligence, Turkish art emerges as one of the world's most original arts.

The overly ornamented interiors commonly seen in Arabic art signified nothing for Turkish architecture during certain periods of its history. As seen in Seljuk art, the Turks' approach to interior ornamentation is different. Especially after the conquest of Istanbul, the Turks did not employ floral patterns on the column heads. And yet, the example of Byzantine art was in plain sight for them. Or in the case of Kufic calligraphy, they could have continued to follow the example of the Arabs and accept Kufic calligraphy as a decorative element in ornamentation, given how the geometric shapes of the letters made it especially suitable for those stylistic elongations and lockets and swirls. Yet, the Turks gradually abandoned this tradition that they had been faithfully practicing in the period when Bursa was the Ottoman capital; rare exceptions notwithstanding, they almost never thought of using it following the conquest of Istanbul. Their reticence in this instance—unlike their eagerness in other instances—can only be explained in terms of artistic perspectives and the meaning and character the artists wished to give to their artwork. Once we approach the history of Turkish arts in this manner, we will be able to perceive it as a light stream of certain predilections, perspectives and ideals that, taken together, will constitute the life and philosophy of the history of Turkish art. We will then see Turkish art as an organism that is born, that has evolved as much by necessity as by achievement, an art that has been alive as much as lifegiving. Undoubtedly, this part of the research will be the most difficult to accomplish and therefore the last to be undertaken. What I call "the life and philosophy" of our art history is entirely different from the opinions of a critic who, after being awed and mesmerized by a couple of artworks, applies his impressions inspired by those experiences to the entirety of art history. For, in my opinion, such philosophical elucidation will be possible after all the analytic investigation is completed. Only after the comprehensive analysis and classification of artistic practices, objects and movements that life has made manifest in the shape of a column head, a gate, a dome, tiles or calligraphy that we can develop a philosophical perspective on the nature and ideals of that very same life.

[...] As I conclude my essay, I ask myself, "What are the benefits of researching Turkish arts?" and I can provide the following answers:

1. We will discover how Turkish culture has expressed itself in forms, objects, and styles.

2. We will discover how Turkish culture has absorbed and internalized foreign elements, as well as its capacity of representation.

3. We will discover the influence of Turkish culture on other cultures, and how it has served the aims of humanity.

4. We will remind contemporary culture of its own cultural past, and we will infuse contemporary Turkish culture with the blood that matches its type.

5. It is through retrospection that the creative functions of our collective imagination will obtain greater celerity and vigor.

What a great difference there is between turning to the past in the name of history and memory, on the one hand, and retreating due to a moribund conservatism, on the other. Before every leap, there comes acceleration. This type of acceleration involves not turning one's face towards the past, but rather relying on it. It is through strength derived from the past that a new future in art becomes possible. Nothing in life comes from nothing, and the future is the extension of the past. Researching the history of Turkish arts does not suggest cultural regression, rather, it encourages us to reach back to our cultural sources, seize our own momentum and gather our senses.

Translated by Aron Aji and Nergis Perçinel

FIGURE 20. Family of Şakir [?] ibnü'l-Mustafa Asım. To my son Asım, the light of my eye, my darling, 12 Kânunuevvel 908 [December 12, 1908][1] (from the collection of Ömer M. Koç)

---

1   The caption is taken from the original photograph.—Ed.

AHMED MİDHAT

A Journey in Europe[1]

[...] Until now Europe has observed the countries of the Orient as though enjoying a lovely painting. This is because the diligent philosophers of Europe who conduct serious research have only recently begun to investigate the facts concerning the Orient, these matters having previously been exclusively reserved for fanciful depictions by novelists and poets, who are the embellishers of daydreams. According to their imaginings, the Oriental woman is a beloved casually lounging on a divan, one of her pearl-beaded slippers lying on the floor and the other dangling from the toes of one bare foot. Her garments are designed not so much for modesty as for adornment, so that her legs, which she has extended across the divan, are half-exposed, and her belly and bosom are only partially concealed by layers of tulle as flimsy and transparent as dreams. Her disheveled hair falls in ringlets over her bare shoulders and over her arm, which is draped carelessly from the edge of the divan. In her hand she holds the serpentine coil of the tube of the ornate nargile that sits several meters away, with the jewel-and-amber mouthpiece positioned near her lips. The room's decor consists of mother-of-pearl-inlay wardrobes, chairs, bookrests, and gauzy shades hung from the ceiling while a black jariya stands fanning her with varicolored peacock plumes. And there you have the Oriental woman as hitherto portrayed in Europe. Pleasing to the eye though this tableau may be, it is not reality, but a mere poetic conceit, and all notions and beliefs born of it are themselves pure fantasy. One would suppose that this entity is not the mistress of her own household, not the wife of her husband nor the mother of her children, but a plaything of the man of the house, with the sole purpose of giving him pleasure. What a terrible mistake! Such fantasies can hold no interest for the conscientious, truth-loving Europe of today, which seeks out genuine beauty in that which is real. For truth seeking Europe, this book by my friend Sheikh Hamza[2] is most

1   Ahmed Midhat, *Avrupa'da Bir Cevelan* (Istanbul: Tercüman-ı Hakikat Matbaası, 1307/1889–90), 164–67, 241–42, 504–05, 525–28.
2   Hamza Fathallah, *Bakurat al-kalam 'ala huquq al-nisa'fi Islam.* — Ed.

worthy of commendation, comprised as it is of serious works that lay the truth out plainly and eclipse those dazzling fantasies. If you read it, you will see the great difference between fantasy and reality of which I have given you a brief description. I can demonstrate the difference for you now in a few words. You should think that this country cannot be investigated solely in terms of its geographical character. The examination of countries goes hand in hand with the examination of the peoples who live therein. The investigation of peoples, in turn, is possible only by establishing the character of the great men whom it has produced. Given that the great men of the Ottomans are already known to Europe, one need not go to the trouble of introducing them anew. Great soldiers, great diplomats, great admirals, great economists, great scholars and writers and artists, all of them regarded as veritable pioneers in their occupations, have secured a place for Ottoman history, in all of its significance, among the ranks of the most glorious of histories. What is more, their distinction is not limited to a single category. Nay, various categories are combined. For example, the sultan of the Ottomans who subjugates warriors in his crushing grip yet has the delicate sensibilities of the poet when he surrenders himself to the gazelle-eyed beauty and describes her in measured verses, is also a sultan of the literati. Among the glorious members of the world-conquering Ottoman dynasty, there are as many as seven or eight men of letters renowned for their literary works. Likewise, among the viziers and emirs who were the greatest diplomats, economists, admirals, and commanders-in-chief of their times in the administration of the state, there are hundreds who are also distinguished by their scholarly merits. More noteworthy still, the scholarly pursuits of sultans, viziers, and emirs, which to outward appearance are incompatible with their stations, should be measured by the schools and libraries that they succeeded in establishing. Adding material achievements to these spiritual virtues, the Ottomans have turned the Mediterranean Sea into a unified Ottoman lake, sailed in ships that they built in the Red Sea to the shores of India to greet the European explorers, and, setting out to find the source of the Nile, explored Central Africa before any other nation, and they were also the ones who hoisted sails upon the cannons to pull them across terrains inhospitable to draft animals, who moved massive galleons over mountains to transport them from one sea to another, and who gained entry into a capital city by excavating a tunnel for the passage of the cavalry. These achievements were not possible through raw courage but required the power of sciences such as geometry and dynamics, upon which the seafaring, artillery, military and various other technologies are based. Now, would so many achievements not be deemed too much for children born to mothers who are, as Europe supposes, "concubines" whose sole purpose in life is to serve bodily pleasures? What could be expected from the children of such mothers? No, good sirs, no! They would be nothing more than the creatures that today's Europe calls "natural children," unfit to join the ranks of generals, admirals, scholars, writers, or artists. Children receive their first lessons in material and spiritual virtues in their mothers' embrace. Even more so, in times when the methods of instruction and education were not as they are today, it seems inevitable that children's primary teachers and educators must have been their mothers. If Oriental women were in fact the concubines seen in those paintings, and if the people of the Orient were born of such a class of creatures who are but the means of sating lustful urges, would the Orient, with all its material and spiritual virtues, be deemed worthy of examination by the truth-seeking Europeans today? Would there be conferences convened on Oriental literatures and philosophies, attended by hundreds of renowned scholars? If their seclusion may be the reason that Oriental women are not well understood, the sons whom they have raised have not been secluded. They have presented their glory, in all its magnificence, to the witness-bearing eye of the world, with a population of one hundred and fifty million souls of diverse communities across an expansive country bordered on the east by the Iranian provinces, on the west by the shore of the Atlantic Ocean, on the south by India, and on the north by one half of Europe. From the virtues of these sons, it is a simple matter for diligent philosophers to deduce the virtues of their mothers. My virtuous friend the honorable Sheikh has compiled in this book the characterizations and descriptions of these Oriental women as they appear in the Holy Quran, the truth and purpose of which are for us undeniably divine, as well as in the hadith of the Prophet and in the opinions of theologians and men of letters whose expertise are premised upon the aforementioned Holy Verses and hadith. It is my desire that this book be translated into the languages of Europe.

[...] Concerning the veiling and seclusion of Oriental women, the topic of our present discussion, the Europeans have, for whatever reason, attached great import to this matter, posing many questions on the Islamic decrees and ancient traditions about these practices.

In responses I offered to these questions, I would first establish the true nature of veiling according to canonical law, then, referring to an account attributed to the honorable Fatima in the books of the Prophet's biography, explain that chaste women who value their reputation for womanly virtue and who enjoy security do not object to their seclusion, but on the contrary, they themselves shun conversation or social relations with men as prohibited under sharia law, and that they have decided resolutely that "[it] is better that men not see women and that women not see men." On the matter of seeing and social relations, I would demonstrate that the issue does not, as might be presumed from its outward appearance, lie in simply seeing or, as circumstances may require, speaking, but rather it concerns the establishment of boundaries for when the intermingling of women and men is permissible, and I would state that it is certainly permissible for women to converse with men in affairs involving audience with personages such as emirs and judges, and even in matters relating to fellow citizens, and that, furthermore, there is no prohibition even against women engaging in commerce, in which they may be successful. In short, the Europeans' interest is so extreme as to think that our women were roses, fragrant flowers of carnal delights, and that all of our men longed to smell those flowers as much as our women themselves were willing and ready to let them smell, and that we have therefore imprisoned them in their households to keep foreigners from smelling them. After demonstrating that their views were purely products of their imagination, I would assert that in the Orient this form of veiling is not unique to Islam, but in places where the influence of *alafranga* behavior has not yet penetrated, Jewish and Christian women are secluded in the same manner, and that Mary, the mother of the Christian community, was veiled with a white cloth, as still depicted in images, which is evidence of this custom among Christians, in the very origins of Christianity, and that one may deduce from histories that even the revealing dress of the ancient Greeks and Romans did not reach the level of present-day European women.

[...] **Crossing the Pont des Invalides**, we entered the exposition through the gate of the same name. We first explored the section in the Esplanade des Invalides and the Algerian and Egyptian exhibits, then we rode the Decauville Railway to the Eiffel Tower and took in the exhibits there. After sitting down to rest in one of the beerhouses in front of the central garden, we strolled through the garden and around the Coutan[3] fountain. From there, we wended our way to the Rue du Caire. The Oriental wares here pleased Madame Gülnar[4] extremely, and we split our sides laughing at the clumsy posture and manner of the Europeans riding on donkeys. While shopping for small items such as beads, red sheepskin-leather slippers, cigarette cases, pastries and Turkish delight, I spoke with Turks, Arabs, Christians and Jews from Alexandria, Beirut, Damascus, Izmir and Istanbul, at times in Turkish

---

3   Jules-Félix Coutan was the sculptor of the fountain.—Ed.
4   For Gülnar Hanım, see Zeynep Çelik, "Europe Knows Nothing about the Orient," note 44.—Ed.

and at times in Arabic, as Madame Gülnar, who is fascinated with such things, was amused to no end by our dickering and haggling in the Oriental fashion. We even went to see the Arab dancing girls, who are the greatest occasion of festivity and gaiety on the Rue du Caire, and among them especially la Belle Fatima. What we witnessed in this regard over the course of that day shall be explained, and the observations made from these shall be elaborated upon, to the fullest extent possible.

[...] **The Street of Egypt (Rue du Caire) and la Belle Fatima**—The Rue du Caire at the Exposition Universelle obliged French moral philosophers to voice strong objections. This place was the most popular destination of the exposition's attendees, and the reason for its popularity was not the work of the craftsmen brought in from Egypt, and not the donkeys or donkey drivers, nor was it the architectural elegance of the buildings in the Egyptian style, but rather the women singers and belly dancers. Although nearly all of these had adopted Muslim names for themselves, it is certain that none are adherents of Islam. The majority are Jews from Tunisia and Egypt, along with some Egyptian Copts. The manner in which these dancers moved their bodies, performing a variety of contortions and gyrations, is not such as would meet with approval over here, and it is known that even in Tunisia or Egypt if one wishes to see dances of this nature, one must go to certain out-of-the-way locales especially designated for such entertainments, as they are a form of debauchery. This provocative form of dance is observed to excite Parisian men as well as women greatly, and in fact some women and girls even imitate these dances, so that writers with a great concern for public morals have brought down strong rebukes on this style of dance. Whether or not they are right is not my concern here. Their protestations and the responses given by some Orientals have been translated and published in newspapers and have therefore been seen by my readers. The dancing girls of the genre that the French call ballet appear on stage in costumes of flannel, tulle and crepe so tight-fitting that one would think them stark naked, executing positions and movements that include lifting each of their legs in turn above their heads. I leave to the reader's discretion whether these are more or less provocative than the Egyptian dancing girls. What I truly wish to emphasize is the matter of the Europeans' fondness and enthusiasm for these Egyptian and Tunisian dances. The places where they are performed are for the most part small venues accommodating no more than fifty or a hundred spectators, while each dance lasts for eight to ten minutes, whereupon the curtain closes, and two minutes later the same dance begins anew. Do you suppose it possible that the first audience can exit completely for an entirely new one to arrive in the space of two minutes? More than half do not so much as stir from their seats. There are even some audience members who devote three or four hours of their time to this spectacle alone. The sites hosting performances of this nature number around ten, and it is no simple matter to gain entry into one of these dance houses on account of the crowds, and also because those who have once entered do not wish to leave. It is the French who invite the women to those places. The callers, supposedly in an attempt to make themselves look like Arabs, wear shalwars, chepkens and fezzes with or without turbans, and when they speak in French with the intent of urging the crowd on, their perfect French accents reveal their true nationality, provoking guffaws from the attentive members of the crowd. Now the most famous of these dancing girls is a Tunisian Jew called la Belle Fatima. To be sure, her renown for beauty is neither exaggerated nor unjustly conferred. She is in truth a beautiful woman. Several years ago, a beauty contest was held in the town of Sfax, and she entered, confident in her attributes. There she was examined by great painters and sculptors, experts in beauty and elegance, and of all the women present, this same Fatima was judged first in beauty and proportion, and she won the gold medal appertaining to that rank. With the utmost of pride, she hung this medal, the size of a flat pastry, upon her breast. I cannot say whether la Belle Fatima's style of dress conforms to Tunisian fashion, but I do not suppose that anyone has ever seen such an outfit on Oriental women of any class. Fatima has swathed herself in an armful of fine taffeta and crepe, yet her bosom, nape and arms are exposed! She has bedecked and bejeweled her head, neck, ears and wrists with diamond brooches, earrings, armbands, and bracelets. Though her attitude and air are quite haughty, now and then she smiles sweetly, whether the pretext arises or not, displaying her lovely teeth to the audience. A smile or a stern glare suits her pretty face equally well. Her dance is not quite so lascivious as the other girls'. Her movements and artful pauses oblige one to concede her prodigious skill. Yet she is not young but is a Jew who has passed thirty-five and is fast approaching forty. Rumor has it that the dissolute of Paris are mad about this woman. The money she earns has no limit. When la Belle Fatima rises to dance, tambourine-playing women shout *yahey!* and *aman aman!* Things take such a strange turn that even I, from the Orient, am dumbfounded. Nevertheless, the Exposition Universelle's area of debauchery and dissipation is not limited to the Rue du Caire or Fatima's theater. Various other examples of this will be presented to the reader's judicious eye in due course.

Translated by Gregory Key

FATMA ALİYE

The Women of Islam[1]

From the Introduction

[...] Although the Europeans, who occupy themselves with investigating and examining all things, have begun to expend effort in discovering the particulars of
our circumstances, I have come to understand through my encounters and conversations with certain experienced lady travelers from Europe that their beliefs and
suppositions about us are yet astonishingly incorrect, and just as they marvel at
the false reports that they have received, I, too, was extraordinarily amazed to hear
them, supposing that some nation other than ours was being described.

[...] One cannot, by touring a country's streets and bazaars and visiting its famous
sites, properly grasp the ideas and customs of its people. In order to discover the
true state of affairs, one must speak with the country's men and women. Although
it is of course not possible for traveling men to converse with our women, the latter
being secluded, those experienced travelers include equally knowledgeable ladies
by means of whom the other travelers might easily learn of the true circumstances
of the women of Islam. Nevertheless, even such knowledgeable ladies will understand nothing by venturing into the midst of a family whose language they do not
know and can only stare at them as if mute.

[...] In order for these travelers to learn the true state of affairs, they need to meet
and speak with families who both know French, and also live according to the principles of Islam while preserving national traditions, customs and religious practices. It is difficult for foreigners to discern this. They head directly to their Beyoğlu
hotels and, eager to conduct their investigations, ask questions of their interpreters, who know nothing beyond the Beyoğlu milieu but, obliged to give an answer,
improvise with or without knowledge, making up fictitious stories of our affairs.

---

1   Fatma Aliye, *Nisvan-ı İslam* (Istanbul: Tercüman-ı Hakikat Matbaası, 1309/1891–2), 5,
7, 11–12, 15–44, 85–102, 115–17, 158–61, 208, 210–11, 236–51, 254–56.

As is commonly known, Europeans have nothing to say about our religious principles which are grounded in reason and wisdom; they only believe the women of Islam to be oppressed and unjustly treated, and they express their condemnation of this in the strongest of terms.

In my conversations with certain experienced lady travelers, I became aware of so many mistaken beliefs the Europeans hold about us that I was unable to conceal my astonishment in my heart and felt compelled to write down three of these interlocutions as follows. [...]

From The First Conversation

One day last year in the noble month of Ramadan, word came that Madame F..., of European aristocracy, and a *karabaş*, that is, a celibate nun, were coming to our household with the desire to observe an iftar meal.

[...] Madame F... told us that, while she had hoped to see a room appointed in the Turkish fashion, she marveled to see nothing but sofas and chairs in the salon, and that, if possible, she would be pleased if we would show her the other rooms of our dwelling. I replied that to please her would be the occasion of our own pleasure, and so we would attempt to fulfill her request. Just then, Madame F..., pointed at the chief stewardess who stood facing, and asked:

"I just offered this lady my hand, but she did not take it. She took my umbrella. Now she remains standing and does not sit with us. Why is this?"

"Because she is a jariya,[2] Madame," I said.

"And the girls beside her?" she asked.

"They are so as well, Madame."

"Very well, Madame, but she has earrings in her ears and rings on her fingers, and she has a lovely watch and chain as well. If she is a slave and not a lady as I supposed a moment ago, I now wonder why she has more in the way of valuable jewelry than the others. The young girl on this side has only earrings, and they are not so precious as hers, and nothing else. The one on the other side has only a watch and chain!"

"The jariya you mistook for a lady," I said, "is the chief stewardess of this household, which is to say she is something like the directress of the other jariyas. The others come under her stewardship as novices, and until they learn to perform tasks

---

2   Commonly translated into English as concubine or slave, this term refers to a social institution with specific rules and traditions, as explained by Fatma Aliye.—Ed.

such as sewing their dresses and combing their hair, the chief stewardess sees to them herself or has them seen to by the apprentices she has already trained. However many jariyas there are, she acts as mother to them all. The chief stewardess answers to the lady of the house for their cleanliness and purity. Hence, because her labor is much greater than the others', her master has given her those gifts as compensation.

FIGURE 21. Family photograph taken in a studio (from the collection of Ömer M. Koç)

"As for this youngest one, she was acquired at the age of four, and up to the present much effort has been spent on her. Now she is fourteen years old. She has not yet been charged with duties because she would not have had the strength. The previous chief stewardess had a capable apprentice take care of her, and this apprentice is the girl about whom you have enquired, the present chief stewardess. Similarly, service will henceforth be expected of this young one. She will repay the labor that has been spent on her thus far. The earrings she wears she bought with money she saved from her monthly wages. The other jariya you asked about is still new, and so has put in enough work to afford only a watch and chain."

F. said, "Madame, the words I hear astonish me. If it will not disturb you, I would like to ask about certain details."

"As you wish..." I said.

"You speak of the previous chief stewardess. What has become of her?"

"Having trained apprentices who can take her place, she completed her duty, and so was married off. She now has three children."

"Where is she?"

"In her husband's household, where she went as a bride."

"Does the position of chief stewardess fall to the most senior?"

"Why no! The lady of the house chooses the most intelligent and capable of several jariyas trained by the chief stewardess. The others receive gifts in accord with their labor. And even should they achieve rank and the status of seniority, they cannot become chief stewardess. However, the chief stewardess cannot peremptorily demand service of them as she does of the novices, but she treats them as friends, giving them gentle reminders."

"You spoke of monthly wages. Do you pay your jariyas?"

"Without a doubt! Even though in truth their master meets all of their material needs, such as clothing and the like, they have souls as well. And every soul has its own desires and inclinations. Perhaps they crave a fruit not found in the household. Perhaps they fancy a different style of dress from that which their master provides. These they purchase with their wages, and with their savings from their wages."

"In addition to this, you give them gifts as they grow more senior, do you not?"

"Not only gifts, Madame. When a jariya is taken on as an apprentice, we prepare her trousseau. If a jariya pleases her master greatly, and if her master has the wherewithal, he will even buy her a house."

"Do you not already pay to purchase the jariyas?"

"Yes! But the money we give goes to the seller and is of no benefit to the jariya. It benefits only her relatives or the master who sells her. In Islam, we are enjoined not to leave the jariya's due unpaid. Thus, each is given presents and money and a trousseau, as remuneration for her labor."

"In that case, they are a kind of servant?"

"Yes! They are like servants employed with a monthly or yearly salary. But with a servant, the pay and period of service are determined when she is hired. If either is undetermined, then it is a voidable contract. However, the amount of money to be spent on a jariya is unknown, just as the period of service is indeterminate. This is therefore an arrangement similar to a voidable contract. But custom and practice are in force in this regard. And the money to be spent on a jariya by her master is in proportion to the jariya's loyalty and her masters' wealth. And this is determined by usage and custom. And although the period of service is indeterminate, sharia law commands us, 'Release your jariya after nine years of service, and if you have not the means or wealth, then sell her to a person of munificence who will release her.' However, usage and custom go a degree further, and those who do not release their slave girls are rebuked. In pious and munificent households, they are not kept even this long. This is because there are many religious reasons to release a jariya. For instance, when one achieves an aim, he releases a jariya as an offering of gratitude. When one makes a vow saying, 'If such and such aim of mine comes to fruition, then I shall release a jariya,' it is incumbent on him to honor this vow. If the jariya is a nursemaid, then she is released on the day that the child begins school. Because children are generally sent to school at the age of four, a nursemaid's period of servitude is four years. And if a man intentionally fails to observe a fast, he is required to free a subject. If he does not have the means, then he must fast for sixty days. This means that releasing a subject is equivalent to sixty days of fasting. Thus there are various religious grounds and national customs that compel the people of Islam to release subjects."

"Very well, but a servant may leave a household she does not like. A jariya is obliged to submit even if her masters are cruel."

"But why! A jariya can leave a household where she is unhappy merely by saying, 'Sell me.' And she is then sold to a buyer whom she likes. She cannot forcibly be sold to a buyer whom she dislikes. This is the custom. And religious law forbids oppression or cruelty towards her under any circumstance. When she makes recourse to the court, the Islamic judge will administer justice."

"Then they are no different from servants."

"Not so, Madame! We do not owe nearly so much to servants. A servant merely receives her monthly wages. When we no longer want her, we let her go and that is that. If she marries, she assembles her own trousseau. If she does not get along with her husband and decides to separate, she must search for a new place for herself. But things are not so for a jariya! If after being married off she does not get along with her husband and wishes to separate, she returns directly to her master's household as though it were her own father's house. It is her master's duty to find an appropriate husband and re-marry her. The master assumes the support of the children that they raise. He assists in their training and education. If she experiences cruelty from her husband, she complains to her master, and he will defend her. If her husband should decease without leaving enough of an inheritance to support her, then Madame, look out this window, just like this freed jariya holding her little son's hand and walking down there, she will come to her master's house together with her child. This is because, by religious law, if she cannot support herself, it is incumbent on whoever had freed her to support her. If he shirks his duty, then the religious judge will compel him by force to support her. Conversely, if a jariya should pass away in a state of wealth and affluence but without progeny, then whoever freed her receives a share of her inheritance. In other words, they are considered as family members. We could never entrust our coffers or chests to a servant. Yet we hand our jariya the keys to all of them, for she would never deceive us. She finds such an affinity and bond between her and her master that betraying him would amount to betraying herself. A jariya can betray her master only if a child can betray her parents. Should their master take ill, then jariyas will, like children afraid of losing their parents, work with all of their heart and soul not to let their master slip through their fingers. If they should have a headache, then their master will have them taken care of in the same manner. Although they obtain the right to choose and can go wherever they wish once freed, none ever forfeits her master's protection, which lasts until death, and return to her father and relatives."

"Naturally, that is because they hate their father and mother and family and relations who sold them."

"Pardon Madame! If you will permit, I will explain how that is not so."

"Permission? Why, I implore it of you. Just as I now perceive slaves differently from what I had been told, I am hearing an account of servitude from you that is perhaps entirely different from what I have supposed. Even were you tired of explaining things to me, my desire would compel me to plead with you until you complied. I beg of you, Madame, do go on."

"In Europe, as you know, young boys are sung to sleep with, 'En attendant sur mes genoux / Beau maréchal endormez-vous'[3] lullabies that impress the ranks of field marshal and general on their young minds and instill in them an enthusiasm for the military; likewise, among the Circassians, when a beautiful girl is born, the Circassians sing their pretty young girls to sleep with lullabies of 'You will go to Istanbul! You will be a pasha's wife! Don't forget your relations here; aid them.' As soon as the child can understand the words, her ears are filled with her aunts' praises of the felicity and prosperity in Istanbul. Her zeal is so great that she begins to jump about excitedly saying, 'When will I go there?' Her parents look after her, tending to her with heart and soul, because their daughter is beautiful. They have no doubt that she will be their benefactor some day. Once the girl is old enough

---

3   As you wait upon my knees
     Sleep, beautiful field marshal.—Trans.

to know herself, she is now embarrassed to tell her parents, and so she talks with other girls of her age about the bright future that awaits her, and she begins to complain that she has not been sent already. So as you see, Madame, this mother and father are sending their daughter to her betrothed who waits in another province. And such a betrothed he is that he will accept their daughter without a trousseau or other payments. Better yet, he will shower her with jewelry. The girl leaves her parents and relatives in order to attain the felicity and prosperity waiting for her. And she leaves with such confidence, as though she were saying, 'I will not trouble you to find me a husband, I will find him myself, and you will see how kindly I shall repay the labor you have spent in raising me.' This is because her image in the mirror reassures her that in the new city she will find a husband and happiness exactly as she wishes. Clearly, Madame, if her family does not send her, then she will bear enmity towards them. As for girls who are not beautiful and lack the hope that the others have, for their mirrors have given them no such reassurance, they are sad to know that their lives will be spent tilling the soil and weaving cotton rope, while they receive letters from their girl cousins—who seem no more beautiful than them but who have still gone to Istanbul—and learn from these letters about their comfort at having escaped a life of tilling and hoeing. In letters that arrive later on, the girls learn that their cousins have completed their duties as jariyas and that their masters have rewarded their loyalty by giving them a house and marrying them off to a suitable husband, and when the girls notice on the edge of the letter the tiny fingerprint of the newborn who is too young to say hello, and when they hear of the masters' support and patronage even after marriage, then the houses that the Circassian girls have grown up in seem ugly and cold, the breads and pastries that they always eat quite unappetizing, and their customary chores a great burden to them. Because these girls' minds are occupied with daydreams, they have no enthusiasm to do their work. They grow a bit lazy. And they are scolded for that. Which is harder to take than doing their chores. They are disheartened by their parents' upbraiding—'No work, no bread'; 'How strange,' the girls think, 'here I must sow and reap and bake bread just to eat a morsel, when I could go to Istanbul, get myself a master, and enjoy baked bread and cooked meals served to me. In return, they would ask nothing more of me than household service. Even if I were a lady, would I not still see to the work of my own home? And what are the chances that I will be rewarded for the work I am doing here? If I worked for a master, I would get my reward. I would be freed. Set up in life. And then I would be a true lady.' Even though it is nothing praiseworthy for a girl to fall into such daydreams in her paternal home, seeing that she ought to feel love for her parents and gratitude for her blessings, I give you these explanations as news and information, and free of judgement; however, if you attribute such fantasies of a Circassian girl entirely to selfishness because you find them to be incompatible with love of country and family, then you would find me as one who concurs with your opinion!"

"But Madame, you have described slavery in such a way that everyone will want to become a slave."

"No, Madame! Let us not proliferate slaves so much, or else there would be too few guardians for them, and the strength of guardianship will decrease!"

We both laughed. The nun had thus far not joined in our conversation, and it was clear from her demeanor that she was not doing much in the way of listening, either. I, however, decided to take Madame's words in another direction and said:

"The information I have given you about jariyas is based on the fundamental religious laws and on the customs and practices of families who are respectful of these and of all other necessities of humankind. But of course, just as one may see the good side of everything in this world, one may also see the bad. In fact, the bad side of some things predominates. Human nature, predisposed to abuse, is bent on changing and altering even the best of things. Hence it cannot be denied that various evils do occur regarding the jariyas. There are even fathers who, merely to gain money, forcibly sell their daughters when they do not wish to leave the paternal nest. Nor is the master entirely absent who treats his purchased jariya for his own personal gain rather than the munificence of sharia law, selling her after three to five years of employ and rendering her subject to the terms of slavery afresh. Can people not pervert and misuse for their own selfish purposes even the most beneficial and wonderful laws and rules?

"But human that we are, we also find comfort in the fact that those who pervert and abuse the judgments of sharia and the practice and precepts of Islam are truly quite rare, and that general public censures them as transgressors who stand outside the bounds of righteousness and munificence."

Madame F... greeted these reflections seriously and conceded that in Europe as well what is called munificence sometimes, perhaps often, fails to be observed between parents and children, between husbands and wives, and between brothers and sisters.

"Madame!" she exclaimed. "Whatever one can say against slavery is valid. In Europe it has all been said and written and is known to everyone. The aspects unknown to us are these points which you have explained. I am pleased and grateful to have heard them from you. I would like to ask you another question. You have eloquently expressed the hopes and expectations of Circassian girls in their separation from their fathers and mothers. But how do you explain those Circassians who sell their tiny babes even before they are old enough to have full awareness of themselves?"

"Madame! Those are the ones who are not content with their girls merely becoming women, but desire that they also be endowed with the education and training which are the crowning glory of ladyhood. They are the ones who love their children to such an extent that they would not leave them to the treatment of stepmothers. For do you know who buys these little girls?"

"Their sale occasioned such horror in my heart that I was not eager to think about who buys them."

"Would that horror keep you from listening to the explanation that I would provide?"

"No, I am listening."

"One group of those who purchase them are barren, and they adopt them as their own children. Another group buys the little ones properly and prepares them to be ladies. They see to it that they learn to read and write. They give them the training of urban girls. Such a jariya can later be worth anywhere from five hundred up to one thousand liras; therefore, her master looks after her as well as he is able. These make up the greater part of jariyas who are purchased by genteel families as future brides. And some train these little girls for their sons in their own homes. When they reach a marriageable age, they are married to the sons. Some of these dear girls are bought by large families so that they might be companions to their children. Most daughters of the elite have their own little jariyas of similar age. She is schooled and trained together with her mistress. And she is freed on the day that her mistress becomes a bride. Given that she has received a lady's education, a good husband will be found for her. And so Madame, because the Circassians see all this, rather than allow their children who have lost their mothers to be treated roughly at the hands of stepmothers, they sell them so that they will live in comfort and make their families shareholders in their own prosperity."

F. said, "Based on the information I have received from you, I feel that I have come not to the Turkey I have heard of and thought I knew so well, but altogether to another country by mistake."

"It is because the Europeans, on arriving in Dersaadet, go directly to the hotels in Beyoğlu, live exclusively among the people of Beyoğlu, and learn of their circumstances to some degree. They merely see the streets and quays of Istanbul and

Üsküdar and Boğaziçi in passing. The lifestyles, the manners and customs of these places do not admit comparison to Beyoğlu. The interpreters that they take with them know nothing beyond the milieu of Beyoğlu but, being obliged to answer the questions they are asked, they invent and say whatever comes to their minds. The travelers, believing everything they hear from them, record them in their travelogues. We, too, on reading some of these, believe that some country unknown to us is being described." [...]

From The Second Conversation

[...] Madame R., ever since she arrived, had been looking at all of the ladies present with great attentiveness, moving her gaze from one to another. Not casually but looking at each individually with careful scrutiny.

[...] "I had been certain that I would discover something which I had long claimed that I would, but my efforts over the past half hour have proven fruitless and shown me that I have failed. As I am disappointed over this defeat, please be so kind as to offer me the consolation of answering a question."

"Of course, Madame, do go on."

"Which of the ladies in this room are co-wives?"

"Pardon Madame! With your permission, there is something I wish to ask before providing the information you request."

"Please, Madame."

"How had you imagined you would discover the matter?"

"By the glances exchanged between co-wives, Madame. I have spent the past half hour in trying to discern who regards whom with hostile looks. Yet I see nothing other than kindness and affection amongst them. In such a large group as this, I do not think it possible that there are no co-wives, for in Turkey a lone wife who enjoys her husband all by herself is exceedingly rare. Now it is plain that my eye is not as keen as I had thought, and I am disconsolate over this."

"Your eye as well as your discernment are as you have always believed them to be, Madame. However, the other matter is entirely the opposite of what you suppose, for truly it is co-wives whom you will find to be exceedingly rare."

"Dear me, what are you telling me, Madame!"

"The truth, Madame."

"So none of the ladies present here are co-wives!"

"Neither are they co-wives nor does any of them present have a co-wife!"

"Truly, such scarcity pleases me as a woman, because of the affection and love I have for all my fellow women. Still, some co-wives do exist, I should have been pleased if I might have seen some together."

"What you say is very true, Madame. Women, regardless of nationality, share the same understanding concerning this matter."

"Oh! You do not mean to tell me that, although you are Turkish, you are of the same mind as I?"

"I do not as yet know your mind. However, on the matter of pitying the woman whose husband marries another, you will find not only me, but all Turkish women, in agreement with you."

"Yet according to what I have heard, a woman whose husband marries again does not complain of this condition, but submits, for this is God's command."

"If it were absolutely God's command, then every man would be obligated to take additional wives. The lord God did not issue any command to marry more than one wife under all circumstances. He gave permission to do so in case of necessity. Had it been God's command, as you say, death, too, is God's command, but is it to be desired? Both you and I believe death to be God's command, but is there any among you who wishes it?"

"True! Yet I have heard that in Islam, God has commanded men to take four wives."

"That which you call a command is rather permission from God in the event of necessity. Under previous laws, polygyny was permitted without any definite limit. Under Islamic sharia, more than four is forbidden, and even then it is regulated through so many restrictions and conditions that its execution in accord with religious law is a matter of great difficulty. This is because a man who would take multiple wives is obligated to maintain each in a separate quarter, and to ensure that their rooms are identical, from the furnishings to the ornamentation and paint, and that there is no difference whatsoever between them in terms of their clothing and valuables. I do not need to explain how arduous this would be. And in our country, a man is fully obligated to feed and dress his wife, so given that in this civilized world it is difficult to support even one wife, polygyny is quite rare. If he does not feed and support his wife, she has the right to seek recourse in a court of law. And this court will order that he provide for his wife. The husband is obliged to comply with that order."

"But if a man is wealthy and has the means to support four wives, polygyny is not forbidden?"

"It is not. However, it is mandatory that he not discriminate amongst his lawfully wedded wives, give more gifts or show more affection to any one of them. And if he fears that he might not be just in any of these matters, then he is required by sharia to content himself with only one wife."

"Oh! So very many difficulties! But rather than complicating the matter with such conditions, would it not have been better to forbid it altogether?"

"But what if the woman is barren and the husband wants children? Or if the woman is sickly and the husband wants another wife?"

"Is there no divorce? Let him divorce her and marry another, and still have only one."

"Let us leave aside, for your sake, the fact that a barren woman will not easily find another husband and will suffer poverty. How, though, can we allow a sickly wife to be thrown into the street?"

"What you say is quite true, and very well. But what shall we say of a man who takes a second wife even though his first wife is beautiful and in perfect health?"

"Madame, a pigeon makes do with one mate, while a rooster rules over many hens. Is man not a species of polygynous animal?"

"Is it not better to be like the pigeons?"

"Yes, it is better! And the majority are so. As sharia law must expel all things objectionable and embrace all occasions for happiness for a civilized society with a population of millions, it must include the necessary decrees for all cases. I, too, share your judgement that women will suffer when the permission granted for polygyny is abused. However, laws for women have been further defined so that they may free themselves from that oppression. Yet even in civilized societies where polygyny is absolutely forbidden, much harm has come from this. In brief, many men in Europe are without wives, and many women without husbands, and the abominable practice of taking mistresses has come into vogue. With the intent of sparing two or three women the sorrow of sharing one husband, the opportunity has been created for greater harm. For example, they have led to the misery of many innocents born into the world against religious laws, and to the tragedy and shame experienced by so many throughout their lives. Here, as you have said, a beautiful young woman of strong constitution whose husband may show disloyalty and take another wife, has the power to divorce him, marry another husband as she wishes, and thus renew her felicity. But the pitiable children who as yet lack self-knowledge, do they have the option of not being born in a manner that will every day be their shame? A woman of Islam is not for one day deprived of human rights. Yet the hopeless, so called 'natural children' are denied all manner of rights. No matter how hard they may work, learn of the arts and sciences, and obtain wealth, still they cannot take pride in themselves, and are a source of embarrassment and shame to their parents. No family would wish to give their daughter's hand to such a man, seeing him as unworthy of joining another family when he does not have his own. And as you already know what becomes of the girls, I shall not mention it. They are deprived of loving and of being loved. The mark of 'bastard' is etched indelibly into their foreheads. And what is their crime, Madame? These unfortunates were not born in this manner of their own will, nor can they free themselves from this unbidden predicament. But a woman of Islam may live with a co-wife if she so wishes, or she may divorce and find another husband if she does not. The sharia of Islam categorically prohibits adultery and grants men permission for polygyny in order to prevent children from being born illegitimately; in turn, it also grants women who do not want a co-wife the recourse of divorce in order to find a different husband who will be content with one wife."

"I cannot say much else than that your points are again quite true. But since we are women, let us try and say one or two things more to defend the fellow members of our sex. Husband and wife are as one body, and they should live without doubting the love between them, yet what joy can a poor wife derive from living in fear and trepidation, wondering every hour of every day whether her husband will take another wife?"

"If any women who can boast of their husbands' love, they are women of Islam, Madame. Even though a Muslim husband can marry another wife, he has not done so. This is because he loves his wife. Can there be greater evidence of his love and loyalty than this? And unlike men in your country, men here are not under any obligation of gratitude toward their wives on account of money that might occasion their hesitation. On the contrary, here at the time of marriage, the husband-to-be gives money for his bride's trousseau, and also agrees to owe his wife an amount of money in the event of divorce; not only does the wife receive that which is her due, but her husband also supports her for three months and ten days. In this way, the woman suffers no financial distress until finding another husband."

"In truth, although we give money, we are highly esteemed by our husbands."

"As far as esteem is concerned, respect for women among us is no less than it is amongst yourselves. In a way, it is even greater. We are not moved by outward, feigned approval. We look at the rightfulness of the situation. In Islam, women are shown respect on the level of the Quran. In fact, it is not permissible to take along the Holy Quran or women when traveling in a small group that lacks security. But in a large military squadron whose safety is assured, just as the Holy Quran may be taken, so may a woman."

After some thought, Madame requested that I translate for her, then, turning to the ladies, she said, "Among the people of Islam, men can take additional wives if they so choose. Do you not have any fear in this regard?"

One of the women answered, "Oh, my husband loves me! Why would he marry again?"

Another said, "Just let him try and he'll see what he has coming. I'm not a day guest."

And another: "If he does not love me and marries another, why, is there a shortage of husbands for me?"

Another still: "If my husband wanted, he would be right to marry again. I am eight or nine years his senior. As he is now forty-five years old, he is still young, whereas I am fifty-four. I am ashamed to pass in front of the mirror together with him."

[...] "Have you no complaint about having to wear the veil and being forbidden to talk with men?"

"My response to your question will be in two parts, Madame. The first is that which is commanded by religious law, and the second is the matter of custom and usage in accordance with the necessities of the circumstances and the times. A woman's hair is her adornment and is extremely attractive to the eye. The display of this object of temptation is for this reason forbidden in Judaism, and so it is in Islam."

"In that case, would it not suffice to cover only your hair? The women of Islam whom I see in the street are completely covered."

"Yes, it is sufficient to cover only their hair. But a woman's garment must also protect every part of her and not reveal her figure. The Turkish women you see now dress like the ladies in Europe. These women in the present company dress for a wedding and feast in exactly the manner as you dress for balls and soirées, and so it is with attire for visits as well. And on top of their outfit, they also wear an unadorned, loose-fitting garment and cover their hair with a headscarf, so that they are covered in accordance with sharia. The *yaşmak*, the *ferace*, the *çarşaf*, and the veil are the customs of different countries that were adopted later. When villagers and nomad tribes wear modest clothing free of adornment, they make do with a head covering alone. And they sit, move about, and walk with men. Among the Mulatthamin,[4] who in times past formed a state in the Maghreb and who still roam the deserts of Africa, it is the women who go about with their faces exposed, while the men's faces are covered. And this is their custom. As long as Muslim women's hair is covered, an uncovered face is not considered sacrilegious. If their clothing is modest and their hair is covered with a headscarf, then it is not religiously forbidden for women to meet with men."

"Then why do they not meet with them?"

"Every country has its share of established customs and practices. This is the custom here."

"Then it is not a religious requirement?"

[...] "Yes, in truth, your religion accords with reason and philosophy, and can be embraced by many a learned man who has been left without religion by the trinity. Now, thanks to the explanations you have given, I have resolved something that has long perplexed me. While our missionaries spend a great amount of money and endanger themselves in calling people to Christianity in many parts of the world, they have not been entirely successful. Yet, your hadjis and traders have, with little effort, converted thousands to Islam in the places through which they travel. I have thought for a long time about the mystery and wisdom of this. I now understand that, because your religion is quite simple, beautiful, and rational, people accept it with ease. In truth, nothing can be said against the beauty of your religion. However, there is one thing that troubles all. What sets a barrier to your beautiful religion, namely, the covering of women. And it is very difficult for Christian men and women, who are accustomed to the world in which they live, to accept this. If not for this matter, a great number of people seeking religion would readily become Muslim."

"As I have explained to you, according to the essence of sharia, the rule of covering applies only to the hair."

"They do not want even that. Yet if they became Muslim, they would be obligated."

---

4   The Berber tribe of North Africa known as the Tuareg.—Trans.

A READER

"By not covering her hair, a woman does not turn away from her religion, but she is committing a sin. The core of Islam consists of the belief in the unity of God and the prophethood of Muhammad, peace be upon him. If someone of any religion or sect accepts these two premises, then she is unconditionally a Muslim. In truth, certain divine obligations pertain to one who is Muslim, and these are things which God has commanded, such as ritual prayer and fasting, and things which he has forbidden, such as suicide and other transgressions. Those who do not carry out his commands and avoid his prohibitions are sinners, and on the day of judgment they will be deserving of punishment. But they are still Muslims. In the end, they will attain the blessings of paradise. If the Lord God so chooses, he will forgive, and if he chooses otherwise, he will still grant the sinner entry into heaven after inflicting torment commensurate with the sin. None can come between God and his supplicant. Muslims, unlike Christians, do not require priests for their sins to be forgiven, and they are not obliged to go to mosque for worship regardless of circumstance, just as Christians are not obliged to go to church. When they want to ask forgiveness for their sins, they retreat to a corner and plead to the Lord. They are not obligated to reveal their secrets to anyone but God." [...]

From The Third Conversation

[...] We received the news yesterday. Foreign visitors are to arrive today. And they have requested that we welcome them in alaturka dress.

[...] N. Hanım, being already dressed alaturka, was not inconvenienced by this. S. Hanım needed a robe. Bringing out two alaturka robes, I gave one to S. Hanım, and donned the other myself. On our heads, we put *hotoz* that I had had specially made; these headdresses were adorned with pretty, large embroidery depicting varieties of flowers. When we stood before the mirror, I will not lie, S. Hanım's ensemble looked nicer than mine, and I confessed as much to her. The loose-fitting robe worn over a corset bound at the waist was a more attractive look than without a corset. Although with the *alafranga* bodice a corset was not strictly necessary, it did greatly help the alaturka ensemble to fit neatly. And the sprinkling of embroidered flowers in her curly hair afforded much grace to her visage.

S. said, "If you like it so well, then curl your hair and wear a corset..."

I said, "I will put on a corset, but the frizzing would take far too long. They will be calling us to dinner soon. And we do not know what time the guests will be arriving. It is best for us to be ready."

[...] Just then, to our surprise Madame said, "We had asked that you dress *à la Turque*. Could you not have honored our request?"

S. Hanım, out of alarm and discomposure, almost spoke in English, to make herself perfectly understood, "How might we have dressed more *à la Turque* than this?" However, I nudged her in secret, as she was beside me, and so, having pronounced only part of her statement, she attempted to translate it into French. Failing at this as well, she finished in Turkish, and no one understood this trilingual sentence. Thus, our guests did not sense that our friend knew English. To our understanding, we had done as requested.

"The outfits we are wearing are alaturka," I said.

"Oh dear, no," said Madame, "That is not so. We want authentic *à la Turque*."

"What other kind of alaturka is there?" asked S.

"There are silver-threaded garments, are there not?"

Addressing N. Hanım, I said, "Go on, sister, go put on the silver-threaded robe you said you liked so much." Then, to the Madame: "She will now put one on and return!"

"Oh, thank you, you are too kind."

A short while later N. Hanım, our talented friend, returned wearing the silver-threaded robe. But our guests were still not wholly satisfied.

"No, not like that," Madame said. "We want Turkish dress."

"Yes," said Mademoiselle. "*à la Turque, à la Turque,* it is so nice!"

"Might you explain to us this *à la Turque* that you like so much? How does it look?"

"A silver-threaded short jacket, a thin blouse, a silver-threaded shalwar," said Madame.

"And so shall you see now, Madame," I said.

"What are you saying?" S. asked me. "Where will you find such to show them?"

"You'll see," I said.

I went and brought an album. In the street we had seen and bought a picture of a woman in an embroidered vest and shalwar. I opened the album and showed it to the guests.

"Is this the outfit you refer to?" I asked.

"Yes, yes this is it," the three of them said. "This is how we would like to see you dressed."

"Where have you seen people dressed like this?" I asked.

"We have not seen anyone," said Madame. "We have seen pictures in Paris."

"In that case, you will not get to see more than that here either."

"But why?" asked Madame. "Are there no Turkish women who dress so?"

"No!" I said.

"What a pity," said Madamoiselle. "Such a lovely outfit. Then we shall not see anyone so dressed in Istanbul."

"Here, you can see them in pictures such as this," I said.

"Who is the artist?" asked Aunt.

"I don't know. We saw it at the bazaar and we bought it."

"She has the air of an actress," said Madame.

"Yes, she certainly must be so," Aunt said.

"Here, actresses are all Christian," I said. "In that case, this one is not a Turkish woman but a Christian woman."

"In Paris," said Madame, "how carefully we look at such pictures, at the attire and the faces, thinking them pictures of Turkish women. It turns out, just as their clothing is not Turkish clothing, those wearing it are not Turkish women!"

"Yes," I said. "Just as everyone can have their portraits made in any clothing they wish, some Christian women have commissioned theirs in such attire. But I do not know what manner of attire they intend this to be. For as you see, on her head is an Arabian kaffiyeh, on her back a vest of the sort worn by Albanian women, and on her legs a pair of shalwar. The mother-of-pearl inlay chair in front of her is from Damascus, the coffee cup on top of it is from India, and truth be told, I do not know what nation's women use a nargile such as the one she is holding. And just look at the *alafranga* way she wears her hair up, and the cut and comb of it!"

"Yes," said Madame, "entirely *alla franca*. So this is not a Turkish outfit, or the outfit of a particular nation but a composite of various ones!"

A dipper, a ewer and coffee with a cover were brought in the customary Turkish manner. Our guests were very pleased at this. Asking permission, they stood up and inspected the items one by one. They very much liked the coffee tray's silver-threaded cover. Wishing to buy the same silver coffee ewer, they asked where it was sold. We suggested the jewelers' bazaar. They also enquired where the best Turkish fabrics were to be found. We told them that our fabrics were of many varieties. We recommended the places for Arabian and Bursa fabrics. For a while, we passed the time talking like this. We learned that they were the daughters of a very wealthy merchant, their mother and father lived in Paris, the elder sister had been married for five years, and her husband was of the same profession as her father. Their aunt resided with their mother, and the young Madame lived in her husband's manor.

S. Hanım asked the Aunt, "Why did you not marry?"

"I suppose it wasn't meant to be," she replied.

"Was it you who did not wish to marry?" asked S.

"Marriage is rather difficult where we are from."

"Why?"

"Because of the dowry!"

"But failing to find a husband for want of a dowry is the lot of ugly women, is it not? I have heard that the beautiful ones are taken without dowries."

"There are such cases," said the Aunt, "but ugly ones with dowries have been the cause of many undowried beauties being left without a husband. While none of the former end up unmarried, it's exceedingly rare to find men who will take the latter as wives."

"But your sister married," said S.

Madame interjected, "My father took my mother for love. He would have taken her even without a dowry. But my grandfather provided a dowry of his own will. Six or seven years after my mother married, my grandfather went bankrupt. At that time my aunt was a young girl."

"Did no one ask for her hand after that?"

"One did. Not only did he ask, we also loved each other."

"In that case," said S., "the matter of the dowry should have no weight anymore. Why did you not marry him?"

"Allow me to explain from the beginning," said the Aunt. "After my father's bankruptcy, I abandoned all hope of marriage. Later I chanced upon a wealthy, well-mannered, handsome, hardworking young man. He had worked to earn his fortune. We loved each other with a pure and clean affection that would have ended in marriage. Because I did not have a dowry, at first, I tried to overcome and forego this love. But when I saw his sincere intention of marriage, I dared to hope. The matter was decided. He would accept me with no money, and my father happily accepted the good intention of this man whose fortune would suffice to provide for me a most comfortable life. Until that time, we knew this man to be a member of a family from the provinces. When our marriage was about to be decided, my father spoke with him at great length, inquiring about his circumstances and his family. It came out that he had no family and was an illegitimate child."

"Oh my!" said S. "And yet you loved him. Such a difficult thing!"

"I loved him," said the Aunt, "but could love matter anymore? His being illegitimate was motive enough to hate him. It took no further effort to lose my love for him."

"But was he able to change his feelings towards you so easily?" I asked.

"No, he pursued me at great length," said the Aunt. "He was very insistent, saying, 'If your family does not consent, then let us go to another country and marry. I will not allow you to need anyone's charity.' But how could I accept? Even if I didn't think of myself, I had to think of the children that were to come. I would suffer lifelong shame before them for having brought them into the world by a bastard father. Once I abandoned my own family name, what name and title did my prospective husband have that I could assume with pride? With such thoughts, I rejected his offer and, since I could not see a man I was not going to marry, I informed him that I would never speak to him again."

"The poor man," said S. "Did he marry another later?"

"I never saw him again," said the Aunt. "He left Paris. I don't know what became of him. And because I had no dowry, no one else wanted me. Are there no old maids here who never marry?"

"Even in a million," I said, "not one would be found. Here neither the ugly nor the poor become old maids."

"But it seems one thing here is a problem. I hear that the men treat the women like servants."

"Here," I said, "managing the household and providing for the wives is the men's duty. However wealthy a woman may be, management of the household is not her responsibility. If the man has the means, he hires servants and cooks. If his means suffice only to feed themselves, then the wife, of her own generosity, sees to the household chores. The husband does not by religious law have the power to compel her in this matter. One day in the time of the caliph Omar, His Holiness, one of the faithful came to the gate to complain about his wife when he saw Omar emerge from the harem, grumbling in a rage, and the man asked, 'What is the matter, o Commander of the Faithful?' Omar said, 'You know women, the harem has angered me.' Omar then asked, 'Why are you here?' The man said, 'For no reason anymore. I had come to you to complain about my own harem. Seeing you in this state, I no longer feel any need to complain.' Whereupon Omar said, 'Silence, let us say nothing. Our harems see to the management of our households though it is not their duty. They give milk to our children though they do not owe it. If we complain out in the open, we will be the ones to lose.' This parable should make clear to you whether or not women owe household service by religious law."

[...] Mademoiselle said, "We have heard that Turkish women are all very fat. It is rare to find one who is not."

"Why would this be so?" I said.

"Because they are confined to their homes and rarely go out to the street," said Mademoiselle. "But I have been observing since I came here, and I have seen very few heavy women among you. And when we walked from Beyoğlu to the ferry, we saw many veiled women in the street. Even on the ferry, there was a crowd of women in a curtained-off area."

"Women are not shut up in their homes here," I said. "They may go out whenever they wish. They go shopping in the bazaar."

"Turkish women are like slaves in the hands of their husbands," said Madame. "We have heard that they can go nowhere without permission from their husbands."

"In every nation, it is the duty of women to obey their husbands," I said. "Yet the obligations are heavier among Christians than among the Turks. Where you are from, it is written in the marriage contract that a wife is bound and beholden to her husband, come what may. If so, then a husband can forcibly take his wife with him wherever he goes, is that not so?"

"That is as it should be," said Madame. "It is certainly well to be always together."

"And what if the husband is a travel enthusiast, and he goes on a polar expedition? Or if he likes to travel by sea, to roam the wide-open seas in a cutter? Or if he wishes to become a balloonist and travel the air?"

"May the men here not force their wives to go with them?" asked Madame.

"They may take them to places nearby, but if they plan to travel afar, the woman may join voluntarily. And if she does not so desire, she does not go. And I have heard that in your country women cannot sell any of their property without their husbands' permission. Here a woman is free and independent in the matter of selling her property and spending its profit as she wishes."

Translated by Gregory Key

HALID ZIYA

Forbidden Love[1]

[...] Mademoiselle de Courton had a curious wish about Istanbul: to go inside a Turkish home, to live a Turkish life in this Turkish country... As she entered Adnan Bey's seaside mansion, her heart fluttered as if she were entering the temple of her fancy. Once inside, her excitement gave way to dismay. She had envisioned a grand entryway appointed with marble; a dome resting on stone columns; here and there cedar divans with mother-of-pearl details and covered with Oriental rugs; and perched on them pair by pair women with hennaed hands and bare feet, eyes lined with kohl, heads perpetually swathed in *yaşmak*s, who slept from morning to evening, dozing to the sound of hand drums played by negresses, or else who sat off to the side, never setting down the ruby and emerald-encrusted hoses of their crystal nargiles as amber smells wafted from a small silver brazier. And she had never considered that a Turkish home might be anything other than the distant impressions that remained in her memory from the myths and legends about the Orient produced by all those Western writers and painters. Finding herself in the smart little guest room of the house, she regarded her guide with questioning eyes:

"Honestly! Are you quite certain that you've brought me to a Turkish home?"

The aging maiden simply could not grasp that her fancy had deceived her. Although she had spent years in Turkish polite society, in her heart she still wished to believe that the Oriental life she had imagined did in fact exist.

Translated by Gregory Key

---

1   Halid Ziya, "Aşk-ı Memnu," *Servet-i Fünun*, no. 420 (March 18, 1314/1899): 63.

HALİD ZİYA

The Last Generation[1]

[...] İrfan now spoke in French, wishing to include Jeanette in the conversation; his mother would be in Istanbul in ten or fifteen days, they were to stay as guests in his nanny's house in Eyüp, and he would decide later what to do next.

Jeanette listened with a most serious expression on her tiny face.

When İrfan finished, she said, "Eyüp, isn't that where Azade lives?"

Oh, how nice that would be, little Jeanette would be a Turkish lady; she would come along and be a charming complement to Azade.

She then imagined for herself the life of a Turkish lady. Dressed in one of those embroidered, red or perhaps yellow gusseted *entari* robes often displayed at the antiques bazaars, wearing a headscarf with striped edges, and slippers with silver threading, she saw herself ensconced on a divan and smoking a nargile behind a latticed screen. İrfan was there as well, sitting with his legs crossed on a prayer rug, reading to her in a soporific voice from *The Tales of the Arabian Nights*. Enchanted with this fanciful Oriental life, she shut her eyes to enjoy the imagined world more fully, murmuring, "How lovely, how lovely!" as if raving in her sleep.

Translated by Gregory Key

1   Halid Ziya, "Nesl-i Ahir," *Sabah*, no. 6891 (18 Teşrinisani 1324/December 1, 1908); no. 6892, part 82–83 (19 Teşrinisani 1324/December 2, 1908): 2.

FIGURE 22. Turkish Women in Foreign Press[1]

---

1   The caption is taken from the original text.—Ed.

"Turkish Women in Foreign Press"[2]

These are pictures of Turkish women frequently featured in foreign newspapers and magazines. These pictures upset us, make us angry at people responsible for this counterpropaganda against us. Yet, it is our nation's photographers who send these pictures to those newspapers. These are the pictures of Rum and Armenian women dressed in costume that Sabah Photography had taken forty years ago and has been selling as images of Turkish women ever since. The activities of this photography studio, this center of counterpropaganda against us, can they not be stopped?

Translated by İlker Hepkaner

A READER

---

2   "Ecnebi Basında Türk Kadınları," *Resimli Ay* 1, no. 3 (April 1340/1924): 32.

FIGURE 23. Beauties of the Orient[1]

---

1   The caption is taken from the original text.—Ed.

Siz, şarkın muhtelif milletlerine mensup güzel kadın nümunelerini gösteren bu resimlerden hangisini beğendiniz? Bu beğenişinin sebepleri nedir?. Fikrinizi kısaca yazarak bize gönderiniz..

Ekseriyeti kazananlardan birinciden beşinciye kadar senelik abone

Şarklıların da fizyoloji itibarıyla Avrupalılar kadar mütekâmil olduklarına bu resimler şahittir.

HİNTLİ
GÜZELİ

Soldan
Sağa
Guzeller
ARAP
MISIR
Aşağıda
TÜRK

ÇİNLİ
GÜZELİ

"Beauties of the Orient"[2]

Which one did you like?
A Chinese woman can be more beautiful than an English woman.

Which of these pictures of beautiful women from various Oriental countries did you like the best? What are the reasons for your choice? Write your opinion briefly and send it to us.

Five winners of the most popular choice will each win one-year subscription.

These pictures are proof that, in terms of physiology, the Orientals are as advanced as Europeans.

*   *   *

First page, left column: Syria, Palestine, Siam; right column: Indian Beauty, Chinese Beauty.

Second page, top, from left to right: Arab, Egyptian; bottom: Turk.

Translated by İlker Hepkaner

2   "Şark Güzelleri," *Resimli Ay*, no. 7 (September 7, 1930): 12–13.

THE UNIQUE CASE OF PIERRE LOTI

A READER

FIGURE 24. Pierre Loti (from the collection of Ömer M. Koç)

TEVFİK FİKRET

"Aziyade"[1]

In reviewing our exchange of last week in the published pages of *Servet-i Fünun,* I noticed that I had kept my discussion rather short on the lies perpetrated by Monsieur Loti and the false air of expertise he assumes concerning Istanbul and Turkish life. Little by little, I began to recall certain oddities of the contents of *Aziyade* regarding our customs and mores that at times go beyond mere errors or falsehoods and rise to the level of slander.

This particular Aziyade is the fourth wife, or perhaps concubine, of one Abidin Efendi, a wealthy elderly gentleman. Because Abidin Efendi is frequently absent from his home owing to the requirements of his profession, his wives are generally left to their own devices. Twenty or twenty-five years later, Monsieur Loti finds himself on the shores of Salonika with the English fleet, goes into the city one day, and while wandering about, forms a bond of love with the dark-lashed green eyes of Aziyade through the latticed windows of a large house. At that time he also finds a Jewish ferryman by the name of Samuel. I do not know how it happens—how they managed to communicate or how the arrangement was made—but Aziyade goes out to sea one night with her aged Arab attendant and a servant armed from head to toe; Loti in Samuel's caïque approaches their boat; the attendant and the servant board the Jew's caïque, and Loti is left together with his beloved. The interior of the boat is appointed like a nuptial chamber... There, amidst the soothing sweet fragrances of a sultry July night, upon the calm ripples of a warm summer sea, before the sleepy gaze of the great city... And, it appears, despite all the people who filled that city...

As these nocturnal meetings follow in succession and with such passion, love and secrecy, one day this officer is assigned to the embassy's ship in Istanbul. What to do now? Obey the command... Yes, one must obey the command. And Aziyade? She will obey her heart and will not allow her lover to remain alone in Istanbul.

A READER

---

1   Tevfik Fikret, "Aziyade," *Servet-i Fünun,* no. 402 (12 Teşrinisani 1314/November 24, 1898): 180–84.

As it happens, Abidin Efendi has decided to leave Salonika in the autumn, taking his entire family with him to the capital; and even if he goes back on his decision, Aziyade Hanım resolves to make this journey alone for Loti's sake.

Now Monsieur Loti, living on the upper floor of a house in Beyoğlu overlooking the Golden Horn, is busy with the Turkish lessons given by an Armenian priest, as he gazes at the shimmering reflections on the sea of the opposite shore; the sea shines like a polished mirror, and the pink and lilac streaks of light, melting off of the setting sun, fall amongst these reflections; he gazes further afield at the moss-covered tombstones that appear to be sleeping beneath the protective wings of black cypresses; by night time, he notices on the horizon a pale crescent moon as it descends behind the Süleymaniye Mosque, he hears the ringing cries of owls in the dark quiet of the eerie cypress forest, and he thinks of Aziyade, still not having received any news of her arrival in Istanbul; he entertains elaborate fantasies of retiring to the middle of Eyüp with her and living the life of a Turk all the while working so assiduously and taking such pains to learn Turkish, the language of his beloved, that within two months he has mastered all of its finer points and speaks it like a Turk. Wonderful! Loti writes to a friend in England about this astonishing feat of comprehension:

> [...] The Orient still has its charm, having preserved more of its Oriental character than is generally presumed. I managed to learn the Turkish language in two months; now I wear a fez and a kaftan and, just as children play at being soldiers, I play at being an "efendi."

Indeed, a kaftan, and a brocaded one, isn't that right, Loti Efendi!

*   *   *

Aziyade is, in essence, a chronicle of events jotted down in the form of a diary; a few letters are also interspersed among the pages filled with daily records of things felt and observed. These letters are made up of sentimental missives written by the author to his sister or one or two of his close friends, along with the responses that he receives. In these letters most of all, we see Loti with his larger-than-life, exuberant personality, his destructive morals, his ideas and his conduct. In these pages more than anywhere else, he scrutinizes himself: his filthy, loathsome self.

> [...] I am going to open my heart to you and reveal my conscience: the principle governing my actions is always to do exactly as my fancy dictates, in disregard of all moral codes and social constraints. I am neither bound to anything nor love anyone; I nurse neither faith nor hope.

I have spent a full twenty-seven years to reach this state...

In truth, one does not achieve such a degree of degeneracy with ease!

To console a friend, Monsieur Loti writes:

> My poor friend, believe me, time and pleasant diversion are the two greatest medicines for sorrow; the heart beats itself numb and at long last grows senseless to the aches... That pure love which you envision is, exactly like friendship, incorporeal and void. Forget about the woman whom you love and love a harlot instead. So what if you fail to obtain the one whom you so aggrandize and sanctify in your imaginings? Then give your heart to a circus acrobat with a lovely body.
>
> There is no god, no morality, nothing that we are conditioned to respect truly exists. All we have is life, and that passes quickly; it cannot be irrational to seek as much pleasure and diversion as possible while we await the horrible conclusion that is death.

Loti is not one to dispense advice that he himself does not follow. On the contrary, he has long since put into practice the ideas that he seeks to instill in us. His goal is to find a friend, a partner-in-crime, to recruit a few more souls to his mindset, to delay the judgment of the conscience with endless precedents and witnesses, and, even if he cannot escape the guilty verdict at the end of this spiritual trial, then at least to share it with others.

Thus, true to his own counsels, he amuses himself with a Jewish girl named Rebekah in order to take his mind off of Aziyade, who for three months has still not managed to arrive in Istanbul; he roams the streets and cemeteries with the girl in tow; he even describes one of those nightly strolls through the cemetery, when an armed watchman—neighborhood watchman!—emerges from behind a cypress, there, ready to march Loti off to do his worst to him; as fortune would have it, their path meets a steep drop-off, whereupon Loti flings himself at the unsuspecting man, sending him toppling over the precipice, after which he runs home as fast as his feet would carry him. His intent in reporting this is to show that in Istanbul, even the night watchmen assault passersby.

*　*　*

The period concludes in the autumn. This Beyoğlu life has grown tiresome for Loti, and besides, has he not already learned to speak Turkish like a Turk? What keeps him from passing over to Istanbul? Cross the Golden Horn, move to Eyüp no less. There, get a small house, a Muslim house, a Muslim attire, a Muslim name, say, Arif Efendi, and a few neighbors who do not concern themselves with him or inquire about his identity, his nationality, or how he lives, these and the coffeehouse revelries, Arif Efendi here, Arif Efendi there... Before long, Arif Efendi is the spoiled child of the neighborhood. In fact, even the muezzin who climbs the tiny minaret next to his house greets his dear neighbor every evening before beginning the call to prayer: "*Selamün aleyküm*, Arif Efendi!"

Now all is prepared, everything is set in place. Except for Aziyade. Oh, if only she would come; if only the women's quarters of that humble home, now empty, desolate and bare, could be adorned, enlivened and warmed with her presence, if only that euphoric love life in Salonika could start afresh...

And if only this would continue forever, under the tacit, indirect approval of the neighborhood folk, is that not so, Monsieur Loti? Not a bad fantasy at all! If every European who came to Istanbul could gift his country with such an *Aziyade*, our Occidental friends would have no more need of translations of *Tales of the Arabian Nights*!

*   *   *

Eyüp, 4 Teşrinisani 1876[2]

"Aziyade is here!" they told me; for the past two days I have been living in the fever of anticipation.

I had been told so by Hatice, the aged negress who accompanied Aziyade during the nights in Salonika, putting her own life at risk for the sake of her mistress. "This evening," she had said, "the caïque will carry her to the pier in Eyüp in front of your house." Thus I had been waiting there for three hours.

The day had gone by filled with beauty and brilliance. Golden Horn was exceptionally busy. At sunset, thousands of caïques approached Eyüp Pier bringing back the people who had scattered to crowded destinations in Istanbul, such as Galata or the Grand Bazaar, for their work.

They had begun recognizing me in Eyüp. "Good evening, Arif. What is it that you're waiting for?" They knew quite well that my name was not Arif and that I was a Christian from the Occident, but my Orientalist aspirations aroused no one's suspicions, so they all addressed me by my chosen name.

Two hours since sunset when the last caïque that undocked Azar Kapı[3] made its solitary advance toward us. Samuel had taken the oars, and a

---

2   Tevfik Fikret deliberately confuses the date to suggest Loti's poor grasp of Turkish conventions. The month is given in Rumi but the year is Gregorian.—Ed.

3   This should be Azap Kapı!—Tevfik Fikret.

woman wearing a *yaşmak* was seated astern on pillows. I saw that it was her...

By the time they pulled up to the pier, no one remained on the mosque square, and the night was cool. Without saying a word, I took her by the hand and ran home with her...

These lines which I have translated from Monsieur Loti's book describe Aziyade's first arrival at his home. My purpose in translating it verbatim is to give an example of Loti's facility with altering the facts. The great seaman! How skillfully he steers the truth, like a sloop whose helm he has taken. Everyone and everything in his novel is dependent on him. Customs and morals change at his whim, the streets are empty or crowded, places and even buildings move as he deems fit: Azap Kapısı suddenly appears in front of Eyüp, and the mosque square springs up next to the pier. Two hours after sunset, during prayer time no less, the crowds desert the streets and shut themselves up inside so that Loti Efendi might take a woman in a *yaşmak* to his home, running hand in hand with her through the mosque square!

Every page of the novel is replete with such lies and errors. Some of them so brazen that a person cannot help but hurl the book from his hand, only to pick it up five minutes later and continue reading, for these erroneous, mendacious pages are as if written not with a pen, but with a feather plucked from the wing of a fairy. So pleasing, so elegant, so ethereal. There you have it: the enchanting narrative! the alluring style! Loti compels you to read a book that you neither want to read nor believe in, one that even makes you angry, yet he compels you to read it, and to enjoy it!

Undoubtedly, Loti's lies will continue to be read for some time to come, and this is the reason why I suggested in my previous column that those of us who are able to write in French should take the trouble to correct errors such as these.

A READER

*   *   *

After Aziyade comes to Istanbul, she never leaves the house in Eyüp. She is there every night. By day Loti goes to his ship and returns in the evening to find Aziyade waiting for him. This part of the story, too, is full of oddities, fantasies, fairy tales, episodes of lovemaking, tales of Behice Hanım, incidents with the owls, and adventures in footwear. Yes, footwear! It is no shame, Aziyade Hanım still wears yellow shoes. Because she frequently wears them out, new ones are purchased while the old ones have to be sacrificed. This "shoe sacrifice" is another sort of entertainment: The love-stricken pair climbs up to the wooden terrace by the light of the moon, and from there they cast the shoes one by one. At times the discarded footwear hits the sea, at times the mud, and at times the head of a stray cat wandering nearby. Oh how this amuses the gentleman and the lady so... And the terrace, such a wonderful place; once up there, Üsküdar, Galata, Beyoğlu, the city, all of it, is at their feet!

We see that Monsieur Loti gets most confused in correctly locating places. Having missed the mark once, he cannot set himself right for some time.

Equestrianism is among Loti's interests. On his return from the ship, he always comes to Eyüp through Kasımpaşa, riding a horse his servant Ahmed brings him. On one of these excursions on horseback, as he is heading towards Ortaköy, he encounters a carriage. Inside are three women, one of whom is possessed of a rare beauty. He follows them. The ladies, especially Seniha Hanım, the beauty of Eyüp, take notice of him... Will coincidences never cease? They pass through Tophane, the Salı Pazarı, the Bridge, finally reaching Eyüp. There, they stop before the door of an old mansion. As the young woman is going inside, she favors the bold horseman with one last smile!

After writing these lines, Monsieur Loti explains that womenfolk in the Orient are very well disposed towards foreigners and that a canny youth might easily take advantage of them.

> My position in Istanbul, my knowledge of Turkish language and customs, and the quiet turning of my door on its old iron hinges were all most conducive to such escapades; had I so wished, my house might have become a place for illicit meetings with these idle beauties.

Even if we might forgive the esteemed Monsieur Loti such excesses and follow his novel without pause to its conclusion, we shall see that, first, Aziyade is evicted from the house the next day for none other than Seniha Hanım, however, only to be summoned back the following evening when their erotic intimacy begins anew; then, with the impetuousness of love, Loti and Ahmed seek the services of an old Rum to have Aziyade's name tattooed over his heart (as is the Turkish custom!); later, together with a few Turkish friends, Loti travels through the snow as far as Ankara and, on his return from this compulsory journey, he and Aziyade resume their torrid affair, while from time to time, she trembles and weeps in secret with the fear of separation and pain; and finally, on 19 March 1877, the order for the English embassy's vessel to sail for Southampton arrives with a lightning-like horror, wrenching Loti from the reluctant arms of his beloved.

These scenes of parting are not typical fairytales. Nothing is beyond the pale: neither the fact that Loti wishes to sign up for the military in Istanbul and later changes his mind, nor that Aziyade plans an entertainment for the last day and holds a feast for some vagabonds with the permission of her lover, serving them rakı, mastıka, and coffee, while she makes amorous music with a *laterna* amidst them... But during all this wild frolic, both are grieved by a profound sadness. In the end, one day near the noon hour, the embassy ship carrying Monsieur Loti departs from Istanbul and recedes into the distance while the Marmara Sea trembles in blue ripples.

Now a moment of silence... At this point, Abidin Efendi knows everything, and has tormented Aziyade, shutting the poor girl up in her quarters. Loti receives this news in a letter from his servant Ahmed in Istanbul. When he returns two months later, driven by a vague presentiment, he meets Hatice, that loyal aged negress, and learns from her bitter-poison words that the object of his heart's worship, poor little Aziyade, has died of the pain of separation:

> "Dead! Dead! She is dead!"
>
> On hearing the words that strike suddenly, like a flash of lightning, one cannot grasp them immediately. It takes some time for the pain to seize and bite into the heart.
>
> I carried on without pause, troubled that I was so calm and unaffected...

*   *   *

As soon as he leaves Aziyade's grave, Monsieur Loti goes straight to enlist in the Ottoman military. A few days later, Captain Arif Hüsam Efendi, with his yatagan at his waist, joins the valiant soldiers summoned off to war. And one day in a special column of the newspaper *Ceride-i Havadis*, the following lines appear:

> Among the dead of the last battle, the corpse of a young English naval officer by the name of Arif Hüsam Efendi, who of late had joined the career of the exalted Ottoman military... (and so on until the end).

*   *   *

There you have Monsieur Loti's *Aziyade*. I am able to write this much, as it is beyond my power to squeeze this marvelous work with all of its details and with all due criticism into the limited space of an exchange [such as this], when every page has some or other falsehood in need of correction and rebuke. In any case, my intent was to show how the Europeans do not know the Turkish language or Turkishness, and that the things they say about us in their ignorance are for the most part errors and slander. I wished to single out *Aziyade* as a shining and proud example of this ignorance. Perhaps I have committed an error in this. So be it, let it be one among my errors!

Translated by Gregory Key

ÖMER LÜTFİ

"Les désenchantées"[1]

I read with great interest Monsieur Pierre Loti's book that he devoted to Turkish women, or rather, to the pains they have had to endure because of their seclusion in the harem.

Before writing anything else, I consider it my duty to thank Monsieur Pierre Loti for the nice things he so kindly said about my country. He is, alas, a rare author with a conscience who has not been influenced too much by the classic perspective common to previous scholars who saw in the Orient nothing other than atrocities and incompetence, a perspective that drives people in the Orient to revolt. His reasoned ideas on the noble character of the Turks, their egalitarian sentiment which makes them consider even their slaves as their own children, and their heroism concerning their homeland or their beliefs, are the proof of his impartiality. Given that we have never been flattered by Europe or that a European author rarely writes something about us without inserting malice between the lines, every Turk would be thankful to him.

Before I touch on the thorny theme of this beautiful book, I would like to express my admiration for its pages that portray the beauties that nature has bestowed upon our beautiful Istanbul—perhaps to make up for all the tragedies lived within the city's walls since its beginnings.

A summer night, the moon up in the sky illuminating with its mysterious light the Fatih Mosque's magnificent domes and "the graceful and slender minarets as if they were planted in the sky"—how beautiful those pages about the nightly prayer! That moving description of the gloomy Edirnekapı Cemetery with its centuries-old cypresses, abandoned graveyards, goats, dogs, and beggars waiting for another funeral, the same cemetery where dear Mecide sleeps her eternal sleep in her forgotten grave, among the broken gravestones strewn on the ground. And then, that Eyüpsultan neighborhood, the Golden Horn, Istanbul presenting all her marvels at dawn or dusk... we can read all these pages a hundred times, without boredom.

---

1   Ömer Lütfi, "Les désenchantées," *Idjtihad*, no. 3 (January 1907): 213–16.

Especially towards the end of the book, the description of the approaching winter on the Bosphorus, the howling wind blowing from the Black Sea, "those pink heaths turning rust color, slowly dying on the Asian hills," those empty, firmly locked houses which represent autumn, departures, the end, the marble docks "where leaves swirl about, dancing, whipped by the downpour." How well they are described, with such sincerity and heartfelt sorrow! Living as we are away from our lovely country, in these endless sandy deserts with nothing to lure the eye, in an African country with its changeless blue sky, it is impossible to read these vivid descriptions and not be seized with longing. We are both sad and pleased. Because we feel that our soul has brushed off the exhausting dust of this tropical country, and it is closer to reuniting with the ideal.

There is nothing unexpected in these beautiful depictions; nor are they surprising, written as they are by an author like Monsieur Loti. His talent as a poet and author is certainly known and recognized. Truly, the moment I found out that he was writing a new book on Istanbul, I had immediately anticipated the descriptions I would encounter, and I must admit that I have not been disappointed.

II.

After granting this honorable academic his due, let us proceed further and delve into the subject of this beautiful book which has created such a stir, especially in the Orient.

It is easy to summarize the subject in a few words:

The "disenchanted women," according to its protagonist André Lhery,[2] are:

> Turkish women who, under the protection of traditions and dogma, have been in a perfectly peaceful slumber! However, the breath of an evil magician, that is, of the West, suddenly blows over them, breaking the spell, and all of the women open their eyes at once, waking up to the disease of life, the pain of knowing...

Sure, why not! Yet, unfortunately, Turkish women are not the only ones seized with the pain of knowing! For several centuries, all human beings who can think have been tested and they have lost parts of their bloodied hearts in this fight. But what is unique about our women's pain is that, supposedly, they are living their life in seclusion, deprived of the air, the sun, and especially men's existence; hence their

---

2   André Lhery is the male hero of *Les désenchantées* and, like the author himself, is a sailor and a writer.—Trans.

pain is extremely acute! In other words, what our women are most tortured by is life in the harem. In the past, they were aware of nothing, it was impossible for them to realize the miserable conditions we had created for them. But now that they are enlightened and informed, they can see better; they can no longer accept being an object of pleasure in our hands; they are asking for their place in the salon, the theater, the ballroom; they are requesting the famed French novelist André Lhery to be their spokesman, to defend their needs, before the benevolent humanity!

Yet, needless to say, since we know our women, their level of education, and their needs better than someone outside our country, we can't help but doubt the veracity of their request! And just for this reason here, before we read the novel he promised to write for women, we kindly ask André Lhery to show proof for the pleas he received. The almost amorous adventure he lives with Djénane and her two cousins does not convince us. Because we cannot see our women in these women. These three women, we suspect, are French women disguised as Turkish women!

I know André Lhery will object, arguing that he is misunderstood. I am sure he will claim that these three poor women whom he befriended made no exaggerated requests as we maliciously claim, and he will remind us of a conversation among them:

> I observed that they adopted most of the Islamic traditions and never complained about their veil, but sometimes, while among certain select friends, I had the impression that they wanted to remove this veil. First among their requests was to be treated as free and responsible human beings who can think, and be allowed, while remaining covered if necessary, to have conversations with certain men, especially their fiancés.

Very well, but they already have all, or almost all, of these rights!

It is not true that there is an iron grate on every window of the harem. If you notice these especially on the ground level, it is not because our women are prisoners but because there are thieves! It is also not true that our women cannot leave their house after sundown. At night they visit each other more than men do! Nor is it true that our women are rarely, only once or twice, allowed on those popular Şehzadebaşı excursions. During the month of Ramadan, women are in Şehzadebaşı every day, whether on foot or in a carriage, and more frequently than men. Better yet, whenever there is a gathering, a market, or a stroll in Istanbul, along the Bosphorus or its surroundings, women outnumber men. Even André himself says he witnessed this in the beautiful Beykoz valley, and in Göksu. He even wrote that one morning he saw his three women friends rowing on the Bosphorus; this clearly does not accord with the so-called harshness of the harem life.

With your permission, I will object to Monsieur Loti who claims that our women are supervised to such an extent that they must dodge twenty harem masters and bribe another twenty just to go to a rendezvous. To begin with, we have almost no harem masters left in Istanbul anymore. Their numbers dwindle with each passing day. That fad is over. Besides, no one who wants to go to a rendezvous needs to devise clever plans or roam the streets of Istanbul's deserted neighborhoods. Affairs like these can be had in Pera every day, and more easily than anywhere else. Inside a house or a shop, for instance! Nor do you have to resort to a plan of the kind one reads in novels. All you need is self-confidence and maybe some excitement depending on your degree of interest in the person you are meeting, and all this happens here just like in every big city of Europe.

As for women receiving men of a certain status at their home—while we wait for evolution, the inevitable evolution, to make this also possible—for now they just settle for flirting with them in Kâğıthane, Göksu, or somewhere else.

In short, I do not claim that the life our women currently lead is ideal for them. However, if this is all that André's friends are asking, they can find the way to do as they please without any pain now while waiting for better days to come.

But no! Their demands are not this modest! These young women have in mind other thoughts which seem impossible to realize at least for a while longer. First and foremost, they yearn for the life of the salon and the ball—they are dying for it!

This is eminently clear in the letters they send to André: "In the hours when André is surrounded by women and flowers at a ball, they are crying in their dark and lukewarm, dimly lit harem." Another letter describes a winter day in the life of a Turkish woman. My God, there is nothing extraordinary about this life! It is no different from lives led by women from wealthy families anywhere in Europe, in cities with limited opportunity for entertainment. Yet, according to André's lady friends, Turkish women are oppressed all the more because of this:

> She retires to her chamber at night, and burying her head in her pillow made of silk with gold and silver embroidery, she sobs unconsolably, while European women attend the balls and theaters in Pera, their beauty glowing under the lights and adored.

This letter also contains a section which I, even as a man, cannot quote without blushing with embarrassment: the husband's return home at night. The letter goes:

Here, the husband enters the house, his arrival announced by the clinking of his sword as he climbs the stairs. The poor woman's soul completely freezes. Out of habit, she glances at herself in the mirror; her reflection looks beautiful to her, and the thought crosses her mind: *All this beauty only for him, what a pity!*

I think we are adequately informed about the claims and pleas of André's friends. And I am convinced, as I mentioned above, that these are not Turkish women. They carry a French, in fact, a Parisian soul: For these women, home has no meaning; what alone matters is life at the salons, the theaters, and the ballrooms!

No, I am not shocked by these quite typically feminine wishes because I am a Muslim. Quite the opposite, if I believed, like André does, that these beautiful women would forever "look through the screens of their covered windows and stare at those views that they had known as children, views that the gray drifts of aging will sweep away one by one," I, too, would be terribly affected, I admit. But I must say that these wishes, no matter how tolerable or even legitimate they may be, will never belong to a real Turkish woman, a reasonably educated Turkish woman. She has internalized the harem habits so deeply that she feels no such unhappiness about not being able to attend salons and balls. She carries these inherited habits in her blood. No, this is not possible for now nor for a long time.

Translated by İlker Hepkaner

A READER

İZZET MELİH

"Loti Sends His Regrets"[1]

(A letter from the famed Orientalist to an Istanbulite friend)

Monsieur Bey,

Thank you for the details you have provided concerning recent events in your country. "Now," you say, "we can expect all and demand all. Turkey will no longer remain a stranger to notions of progress and the advance of civilization." You are right to be hopeful, of course! You are, indeed... My newspaper provides me daily with overwhelming proofs of this. To use an oft-repeated phrase, you will evolve into an advanced society, and you are well pleased by this. But, o luckless man, are you aware that you are to lose all that is picturesque and charming, all the captivat ing originality that makes you a nation unique in all the world?— Oh, to live idly, free of care, ambition or ideals, to drink cup after cup of coffee, to smoke nargile, to dream longingly, endlessly, and to die in the end without any regrets... How wonderful! A life teeming with pleasures! As I think on how all this is to change, how you, too, will join the ranks of the civilized, that is to say, become restless and refined, I am saddened, seized with despair and regret, and I experience the sad- ness one feels beside the tomb of a deceased beloved... (The deceased beloved here is my radiant dream of the Orient.)

You understand me, do you not, for you are one of my faithful readers; you know my capricious and morbid soul, ever so thirsty for sensations and pleasures, a soul of the artist and the poet!

Already in *Les désenchantées*, I complained of the enlightened little *hanıms*, the poor dark phantoms like Djénane, Melek and Zeyneb. I mocked the young Turkish men who, wishing to become civilized, created for themselves sources of suffering, and I admired the wise and naive ones immersed in a slumber guarded by faith and dogma. The new buildings, the worldly agitation of Pera and Boğaziçi filled me with revulsion...

1   İzzet Melih, "Les regrets de Pierre Loti," *Kalem*, no. 2 (September 10, 1908): 10–11.

A READER

Now the disaster is to spread at a relentless, dizzying speed. You are to have senators and deputies. This is a sacrilege, a banality unbecoming of the Turks. You are to have the comforts of civilization: broad, well-paved streets, electric streetcars, electric lights, and myriad similar idiocies.

In the name of God the Just and Merciful, what will you do to my Istanbul, whose magnificent silhouette with its countless minarets cutting into the azure horizon I can never forget? What will you turn it into, this incomparable city of narrow, serpentine streets and mysterious, forbidden harems?

You will alter and spoil all of these beautiful things. If I return to your country some day, I shall find nothing of what once charmed and dazzled me. I shall be unable to show myself in Kâğıthane and Göksu in a superb caïque, dressed up and adorned like a *hanımefendi*: that beloved waterway shall have transformed into a chic excursion spot.

And dear Aziyadé-Nejibé, perhaps I shall no longer have the strength even to take seriously the naive tale of our illusory love or to leave flowers at your grave site teeming with fantasies. Forgive me, my distant lover... Your image was so sweet that in the end even I believed you truly existed.

My beautiful dreams fleeing from me, facing this dreary and fatal end, I want to weep, to sob like a child.

O Istanbul, o enchanted, proud city! In answer to my desperate pleas, may the mercy of God leave your naive and pure soul, your innocent and sublime soul, untouched for a few more years...

Pierre Loti
[İzzet Melih]

Translated by Gregory Key

İZZET MELİH

"Reply to Loti"[1]

[Djénane's[2] letter to the author of *Les désenchantées*]

Venerable Master,

You may be surprised to read these lines. "How can this be?" you may ask. "Djénane lives! So she did not die for the beautiful eyes of André Lhery, the hero of my most recent and—if I may say so—greatly successful novel." No, sir, she did not die... To be honest, I was not at all devastated by that well-groomed physique of the celebrated author. I hope I do not offend you, Loti Efendi, and that you receive with your characteristic courtesy these words that come to you not from the world beyond but from Istanbul, your inexhaustible wellspring of inspiration to which you owe the greater part of your literary fortune and which you *of course* do not wish to see altered into a prosaic banality.

Your regrets were most touching; some of your lady admirers read them with tears in their eyes. A witty lady among them whispers in my ear: "True, our eyes were filled with tears... of laughter." But pay her no mind, and rather listen to one who responds to you in all seriousness.

Your faithful readers, greatly moved by your complaints, gathered recently, presided over by our greatest poetess and, following quite lively deliberations, resolved to present a joint request to the relevant authorities:

"So as to avoid trampling the hallowed rights of Art, of Great Art, and wounding the heart of Pierre Loti, Julien Viaud, the chief admirer of Oriental decrepitude, we appeal to your magnanimity and sense of justice, and humbly request that you

1 İzzet Melih, "Réponse à Loti," *Kalem*, no. 3 (September 18, 1908): 12.

2 Djénane (Canan) is the heroine of Pierre Loti's novel *Les désenchantées* (translated into Turkish variously as *Meyûseler* [Despairing Women], *Bezgin Kadınlar* [Disheartened Women], and *Mutsuz Kadınlar* [Unhappy Women]). This young Turkish woman who, like her friends Zeyneb and Melek, has received an excellent Western education, writes a letter to the famous French writer André Lhery, of whom she is a fan, complaining of the harem life and of being forcibly married. Djénane dies at the end of the novel.—Trans.

combat by every means necessary this scourge called civilization and stop change and progress in Turkey."

We had just adopted this measure by an overwhelming majority when the afore-mentioned lady of wit said with a mocking laugh, "I doubt that our statesmen are possessed of such morbid sensibilities as to take our request seriously. True, peti-tions are no longer swept under the rug as they once were, but ours has excellent chances of proving an exception. In which case, who knows what calamity awaits our dear poet? What manner of book can he possibly write about our country af-ter this? Certainly not *Les enchantées*—*The Happy Women*! He has need of melan-choly, tears, death, grief..."

Translated by Gregory Key

NÂZIM HİKMET

"Pierre Loti"[1]

Hashish!
Obedience!
Kismet!
Cage, khan, caravan,
    shadirvan!
Sultan dancing on silver trays!
Maharaja, padishah,
a thousand-and-one-year-old shah.
Dangling from minarets
clogs with mother-of-pearl inlays
Women with hennaed noses,
their feet weaving at the loom.
Green-turbaned imams singing prayers in the wind!

There you have it, the French poet's Orient!
There,
   the Orient in books
      printed a million a minute!
Yet
not yesterday,
  not today,
   not tomorrow,
there was, there is or ever will be
such an Orient!

The Orient:
Fields on which
    bare naked slaves
      die hungry!
Countries owned by everyone
but the children of the Orient!
Land where hunger dies of famine
while the granaries burst with wheat—

---

1   Nâzım Hikmet, "Piyer Loti," *Bütün Şiirleri*, 18th ed. (Istanbul: Yapı Kredi Yayınları, 2020), 34.

Europe's granaries.

Asia.
American dreadnoughts. On their steel masts,
        your Chinese
                hang themselves
from their long hairs like yellow candles.
The Himalayas.
On the highest,
        the steepest,
                the snowiest peak,
British officers listen to jazz bands.
They dip their grimy black toenails
in the Ganges,
        where the pariah cast their white-toothed dead.
Anatolia from end to end,
        Armstrong's training ground.

Asia's bosom is swollen.
The Orient
        will take
        no more.
Enough is enough!
Even if one of them
were to give his life
        for our famished cattle,
let him die unseen, far from our sight,
if he is a bourgeois.
You, above all,
        you, *Pierre Loti!*
The typhoid lice that travels among us
biting into our yellow oilcloth skin
is dearer to us than you,
                French cadet!
French cadet, how you've forgotten
        the olive-eyed Azade
faster than you would
                a harlot.
You had set Azade's headstone in our hearts
but you took it for a wooden slab
        and used it for target practice.

Those not in the know
        ought to know:
You are nothing but a charlatan.
Charlatan!

Peddler to the Orient
of worthless French fabrics
at five-hundred-percent profit:
                    Pierre Loti!
You were, it turns out, a bourgeois swine.
If I believed in souls rather than matter,
I swear, on the day the Orient is liberated,
            I would hang your soul on a cross
            at the head of a bridge
and smoke a cigarette!

Europe's sans-culottes,
I gave you my hand,
we gave you our hands.
            Embrace us!
Let us ride our red horses, side by side.
The aim is near.
Look:
            Liberation is just days away.
The Orient's year of liberation
Is waving at us its bloodied handkerchief.
Let us gallop our red horses across the belly of imperialism.

1925

Translated by Aron Aji

FIGURE 25. Yusuf Franko, Mr. Jarosojinski, The Secretary of the French Embassy in his Oriental salon[1] (*Youssouf, Types et charges 1884* [facsimile of the original caricature album from the collection of Ömer M. Koç, published by the Vehbi Koç Foundation, 2016])

---

1   The caption is taken from the album.—Ed.

"Tourists"[1]

How many melancholy days
Have we been seized by fits of laughter
At the sight of tourists dragged about
From Pera down to Galata

They stack them in phaetons,
Like salted mackerel,
Then queue them up to show
The markets, squares, and coffeehouses.

Wharfs, bridges, and shops,
Time-worn walls where serpents nest,
Old-time villages and ancient towers,
Every bazaar, every hole-in-the-wall.

They drive these hapless folk
From hill to stream and back,
To show them everything except mercy.
Armies would perish in such campaigns.

They walk first, then they climb
All about the city and the outskirts,
Even Yüksek Kaldırım Street
Bending around the old tower.

Braving the arduous descent,
They reach the bottom of the slope.
A curse on Belisarius
For the ruins he left behind.

They take them in just one day,
From Samatya to Büyükada,
A mad race that leaves even
the hardiest gasping for breath

---

1   "Les Touristes," *Kalem* 1, no. 28 (26 Şubat 1324/March 11, 1909): 14–15.

Never mind the risk
Of doing them in
They tear them from Dikilitaş
And hurl them to Feriköy.

Doubled over, panting
At breakneck limp,
March, march onward to Kavak
Then gallop to Maltepe

Tongues hanging out, throats parched,
With no hope of safe return
Suddenly they find themselves
Crawling from Eyüp to Üsküdar.

Then they run and run
From Kuzguncuk to Hippodrome
They squirm with aching heads
And leaden legs.

Lest they be lost along the way
Like sheep that leave the herd,
The guide, with outstretched finger,
Counts them all, time and time again.

At the end of the wild race,
They pay the price with interest.
And we are plenty entertained
Without even reaching for our purse.

God bless the tourists
For the gifts they bring:
Stories for the journalists,
Pastime for the gossips.

[...]

Vesuvius, the famed soup spoon,
The Parthenon, opera backdrop,
The Pyramids, scones made of stone,
The tourist has seen it all—yet in Pera

The most magical thing he may see
The greatest foe of the commonplace,
The most archaeological of all,

The most wondrous of wonders
Is not, though you will scarce believe,
The ancient monuments,
Nor the historic ruins,
Not our customs or costumes,

Not our handsome porters in felt coats,
Nor our much-beloved dogs,
And not our nimble fire brigade
In their knee-length trousers,

Not our picturesque vistas,
Nor our city's beggars and ne'er-do-wells
Who weep and moan and weep some more
On the vagrant district bridge,

Not the matchless and elegant art
Of our markets, great and small,
Nor Yeniçarşı teeming
With games of love and chance,

And not the Oriental Belles,
Few in number, still they catch our eye,
Swaying with childlike grace
Among the flowers on balconies,

Not the dreadful or playful sea,
Nor the regal or lethal sky,
Nay, what the tourist truly seeks
Is the unexpected and monumental,

The tourist, fond of distant realms
Is on the hunt, but what he truly ought
To see while passing through is this:
The Oriental who thumbs his nose at him.

Translated by Gregory Key

A READER

ÖMER SEYFEDDİN

"Secret Sanctuary"[1]

To Müfide Hanımefendi:

The other day in Tokatlıyan, Sermed introduced me to a European man. His friend from Sorbonne, no less! A well-mannered, trim, handsome fellow with brown hair and dewy blue eyes. An ardent lover of "the Orient." These were his first words:

"My dear sir, you don't know yourselves. You overestimate Europe and fail to see the beauties around you or experience your own mysteries..."

Unsure if it was fair or not, I received the chiding with a faint smile:

"How do you know what we don't see or experience?"

"I have seen it with my own eyes," he said excitedly. "I have been at Sermed's place for three nights now. Everything is *alla franca*—the food, the living room, the bedroom, the way his wife or his brothers dress, even the way they move, think, their points of view... all fondly European. Ah, where is Loti's Turkey?"

"Loti's Turkey is on the other side!" I said.

"Yes, that's what they tell me. An impenetrable world, however! Too bad that you don't like this picturesque world."

"Some among us like it!" I said.

"Are you one of those?"

"O yes..." I nodded with exaggerated enthusiasm.

How innocent these Frenks[2] who can't get past their stereotypes! This young European, too. We started talking about Turkey. He insisted we didn't know ourselves; we called our most beautiful, richest, most unique streets dirty; now we valued European buildings bereft of beauty, ostentatious boulevards, geometric monstrosities murdering nature... His anger towards Rums went beyond mere grudge. He hated Beyoğlu so much, he almost turned yellow with disgust, "What a re-

1   Ömer Seyfeddin, "Gizli Mabed," *İfham*, no. 100 (10 Teşrinisani 1335/November 10, 1919): 3–4.

2   A common reference to Europeans, including the Levantines. —Trans.

pulsive caricature of the West, oh God!" His mind was filled with Loti's flights of fancy. What we called squalid, savage, ignorant in our wretched surroundings, he called, "fascinating!" amazed that the endless trash heaps, the owl-infested run-down shacks stirred no aesthetic excitement in us. Finally, he kindly asked if he could visit a Turkish house that had not been Europeanized. I thought of my old wet nurse who lived in Karagümrük. A quite pious, quite stoic, quite conservative woman. She lived with her old Arab maid and had a comfortable life with the small income she inherited from her husband.

"In that case, I will take you to the house of an old widow who has not become Europeanized at all!" I said.

He thanked me; he was happy. "When?" he asked.

"Today, even now if you like."

"Is that possible?"

"It is. But we need a fez for your head," I said.

Suddenly showing up unannounced at this alaturka house would leave no time for courtesies or extravagance; it would show everything natural and picturesque to this Orient-lover. Noticing the poor guy's excitement, Sermed couldn't stop laughing. We said goodbye to him and took a carriage. We descended to Beyazıd. We bought a fez for the little Frenk, and got it fitted for his head. He didn't want to take the tram.

"All the way down here, is it all Turkish neighborhood?" he said.

"Yes, all Turkish neighborhood."

"In that case, I would appreciate it if we walked."

"Certainly!" I said.

We passed by burnt-down houses. The fog, a cloudy, dark sky seemed to cast a painful sorrow over the run-down houses and quiet ruins. I warned him on the way there that I would introduce him as a Circassian to my wet nurse.

She was not the jittery type who would run away from a rooster. However, maybe she wouldn't want to present herself to a Christian. This simple trick inflamed his imagination even worse. He kept stopping in front of crooked, black, rotten, wooden houses, wall ruins, caved roofs, saying, "What a view! What a view!" unable to turn his gaze away. It took us two hours to reach her home. This was a three-story, wooden, small, dilapidated building. I knocked. The old maid opened the door:

"Is my wet nurse here?" I asked.

"She is visiting a neighbor. Please come in..."

"Hurry, Karanfil Dadı,[3] please run and tell her I am here. I brought a guest, too. We'll stay the night," I said.

We entered the house. Past the clean but dark hallway, we climbed a big staircase. In the parlor, the Frenk was awestruck. On the floor was an Ajem carpet. The walls were decorated with calligraphy plates and panels that my wet nurse's *hattat* husband had left behind.

Fez-colored drapes flowed down to touch the cushions on the divans that were covered with thick red blankets. We sat across from each other. He adored the privacy grills on the windows.

"I feel like I am in a dream!" he said. When my wet nurse arrived, he kissed her hand, just as I did. Sometimes he forgot about the fez on his head; he inadvertently curtsied and bowed. My wet nurse did not notice much but,

"Your words don't sound Circassian," she said.

"Dear mother, this is not the Circassian you know," I said, "it is a new Circassian that showed up after migration, a mix of Russian and Chechnian!"

As I made it up, this Circassian guest had come to Istanbul to go on hajj. When my wet nurse noted that it was not the hajj season, I covered it up with another lie. He came a little early to learn some Turkish.

"Oh, being a hajji this young, what an honor, what an honor, I wish the same upon you!" she said.

"Amin, amin!"

The Frenk all of a sudden recognized the word, and repeated it with his own accent, intent on showing familiarity:

"Amen, amen!"

My wet nurse insisted that I go on hajj with this Circassian. In short, we talked about hajj, hodjas and such until dinner time. Word for word, I quickly translated my wet nurse's advice into Circassian. When we sat down to eat, the Frenk was plenty dizzy with his aesthetic excitement. The silver tray, used only for stranger guests, almost drove the poor man crazy. He abandoned the fork and tried eating with his hands, mimicking my wet nurse. I made him stop. I told him eating with hands is exclusively for old women. As he was starting to declare that sitting cross-legged on the floor was the most comfortable position, we were done with dinner. We had our coffee. I showed him some family heirlooms, old calligraphy manuscripts from my wet nurse's husband's library. He absolutely adored the or-

---

3   Nanny.—Trans.

nate illuminations, the leather covers and the miniatures. When it was bedtime, Karanfil and I took him to the top floor. A bed was made for him in the room above the garden. I showed him the bathroom and the like. "Bonsoir," I said, and retired into the room on the middle floor.

There was a storm that night. Heavy rain. The skies cleared by morning. I found him awake and dressed up. He was sitting on the bed, writing something.

"Bonjour..."

"Bonjour, mon ami!"

"What are you writing?"

"Oh, my emotions!"

"You had many emotions?"

"Can't describe, I can't describe to you..."

"..."

We went downstairs and had our morning coffee. We kissed the hands of my wet nurse. I took the Frenk to Fatih district on foot to drown him in picturesque Oriental vistas. We sat at the coffeehouse facing the mosque and ordered a nargile for each. To keep him from blowing into it, I taught him the labor of carefully inhaling it. We started feeling heady. To get him excited, ecstatic, I said:

"My dear sir, look at this sanctuary," I said. "How exquisite, how grandiose, isn't it?"

"..."

The Frenk smiled but didn't seem particularly excited. His indifference didn't sit well with me, especially after he shook with admiration in the presence of rundown public fountains and crooked walls.

"I wonder if you didn't like this sanctuary," I said.

"This, this sanctuary is nothing..." he smirked, squinting his blue eyes.

"What do you mean nothing? This is the most magnificent monument in Istanbul."

"This is nothing... This sanctuary, nothing..."

"What do you mean?"

"I saw an even more magnificent one than this."

"But that's impossible," I said, "when did you see it?"

"Last night..."

"In your dream?"

"No..."

"Where then?"

"In the house."

"Which house?"

"The house we slept in..."

I was perplexed.

"What then did you see?"

"Something Pierre Loti himself didn't get to see! A secret no European has ever known!"

"..."

I smiled.

"Yes, I saw your secret sanctuary," he said.

"Dear sir, what sort of secret sanctuary?"

"You've been hiding it in vain. I saw it alright! Last night I saw your secret sanctuary that you have been hiding from Europeans for centuries, your private sanctuary."

"..."

"You can of course rest assured that I will keep this secret. I won't write about it when I return to Paris. It will stay like a sacred memory in my notebook."

"I understand nothing of your words," I said.

"Don't insist, I saw what I saw."

"What, pray tell?"

"Your secret sanctuary!"

"We have no secret sanctuary whatsoever."

"Please, no need to deny, I saw it."

"Strange, very strange!" I was shaking my head. The little Frenk couldn't resist. He pulled out of his pocket a notebook bound with Moroccan leather.

"See it for yourself then," he said. And he started reading the last pages:

> [...] Morning! I am writing these lines with exhilaration. A Turkishman whom Sermed introduced me to yesterday took me to the most secret place in Istanbul. Jacques Casanova, Pierre Loti and so on would like to think that they've seen the Orient by drinking a cup or two of coffee at the parlors of villas and waterside mansions. The real Orient lies hidden in layers unseen...

And I saw something no European had seen before. I'm in the house of an old widow. A very pious woman. The interior, the dinner settings, traditions, customs, in short, everything unspoiled. Entirely *alaturka*. They put me up in a room on the top floor. I woke up very early morning. Left my bed. An odd, curious feeling was gnawing at me. I tiptoed out of the room. There was a room across the hall. Door ajar. I pushed slightly. And what stood before me? A secret family sanctuary!

White curtains drawn shut. Faint light seeping through them. Big plaques hanging on the walls. In the corners of the room, heavy, walnut coffins with iron rings. Undoubtedly, they contain the mummies of their loved ones. I tried prying one open. Impossible. Locked shut. Then, on the floor, vessels big and small. Some made of copper, some porcelain! Some of them very precious, for example, the one by the door, gold-rimmed, right in front of the first coffin. At the corner, a green vase... God knows what kind of clay it was made of. Spanning the sanctuary from corner to corner, several rope lines forming geometric shapes I cannot decipher. Hanging on these occult lines, no doubt, relics of their dead. Holy water in the vessels. Some contain a little, others almost overflowing. I tasted this mysterious, holy water, brought from who knows which secret, which sacred corner of Mecca, Medina. It tasted a little tart... Sediments on the bottom, light, but very light, sand. I drank from each vessel. Each tasted the same. My heart started pounding. I got out, excited like a blackguard, a traitor, an infidel who had trespassed a forbidden sanctuary. I felt like the coffins would suddenly open and out would come centuries-long dead Turks in quilted turbans, brandishing their yatagans, charging toward me. The plaques on the walls almost trembled. Liquids inside the sacred vessels began to swirl. As if gathering up a tempest, only to drown me right then and there. I could almost sense inside me the rage, the silence, the sublimity of these holy waters...

A vague and mysterious languor, fire coursing through my veins. I hear the deep reverberations of a strange, dark dome inside my brain. I feel such inexplicable excitement...

I couldn't hold myself any longer. I laughed so hard that the Frenk dropped his nargile hose. The nargile itself almost toppled. I disturbed the drowsy calm of all the customers who had come to enjoy their morning. They all stared at me.

The Frenk asked: "What are you laughing at?"

"Oh god, you were in no secret sanctuary!" I said.

"Where was I then?"

"My wet nurse's trunk room."

"What is a trunk room?"

"We don't have dressers, or mirrored wardrobes. Our stuff is in trunks, and trunks are in a room. The walnut chests with rings on them, what you thought were coffins, are our garment trunks."

"But the plaques on the wall?"

"My foster father's artwork! My wet nurse is not selling them because they are heirlooms."

The Frenk was in disbelief. I was still laughing.

"What about those ropes, the geometric shapes? Those 'relics'?"

"The ropes we hang clothes on when it rains. Lines, triangles are all coincidence, and what you think as relics, they are unused clothes."

The Frenk still wouldn't believe me. His blue eyes suddenly clouded, he shook his head, as if he caught my lie.

"And those vessels with holy waters? How do you explain those, dear sir?" he said.

"It rained all night. That room at my wet nurse's house has forever had a leaky roof. Karanfil must have put those pots and pans to keep the floor from getting wet with rainwater," I said.

The Frenk sat still, like his famous compatriot who thought our "Maşallah" amulets hanging on our walls were the emblems of a national insurance company, or the slippers stitched with nazar beads, those little good-luck charms swinging on the eaves of our houses, were shoes that belonged to thieves who dropped them while leaping from roof to roof. The Frenk thought some more. He inhaled his nargile deeply, then gulped. His notebook was spread open in his hand; closing it, he put it back in his pocket. I kept chuckling every so often.

"Don't laugh, my dear sir, even your trunk rooms have something mysterious, something incomprehensible, a sacred air about them."

"How so?"

"Such a thing it is... You are blind to it... Obviously you can't see..." he said. However, he could not tell for the life of him what it was, that thing he could see and we couldn't.

You know it already: Turks are extremely polite when they judge others! "If we are blind, then you are mute," was at the tip of my tongue, but I kept it to myself. I didn't make a sound.

Translated by İlker Hepkaner and Aron Aji

A READER

ERCÜMEND EKREM

Around the World with Meşhedi[1]

[...] Occidentalist is the exact opposite of the term Orientalist. Just as you perceive the Orient as a land of strange wonders and you consider researching and learning about it as a field of inquiry so that you pass for an expert in this field, we invented a new profession, Occidentalism, as opposed to Orientalism, to research you. And I, the most expert Occidentalist, can state that the strange wonders I have seen among you outshine ours. For example, compare some of our tongue twisters you have been collecting recently with the speeches Lloyd George has given in the parliament, and you will see no difference between them. They are entirely identical in meaning, beauty, and inspiration. And they were born out of the human need to talk nonsense every so often. I am about to conclude my research. When I return to Istanbul, I will send you a copy of the report I will present at my university. I have collected many pieces of Political Nonsense in the Occident. It is shaping to be a curious essay.

Mister Professor was listening to me, mouth agape. I took another sip from my glass, and continued:

"Yes sir, that's how it is! We, the Orientals, do not want to fall behind you in any respect. We will even go further than you in some matters. You have played us for a fool until now, ridiculed us as you please. You have dispatched committees to research us like we were strange animals. You have observed an occasional incident and added a thousand lies to it, to present the Turks to your countrymen as freaks of nature. So much so that when one of us mentions our nationality in Paris, London, or New York, a herd of curious bystanders gathers around us. They study us one by one as if we are Alaskan foxes or Siberian wolves. When we open our mouth and utter a word, some of them are astonished, saying 'Oh, this one speaks like a human being!' Thank god we have come to our senses fast. Your insults have opened our eyes. We have understood that we are also human, and even more talented than you. Now, we want to tell you this: If any difference still exists between us and the civilized nations, rest assured, it is in our favor."

Translated by İlker Hepkaner

1   Ercümend Ekrem, *Meşhedi ile Devriâlem* (Istanbul: Suhulet Kütüphanesi, 1927), 118–19.

AHMED HAŞİM

The Hospice for Storks[1] *[Gurebahane-i Laklakan]*

Ten or fifteen years ago I had traveled to Bursa for a week's vacation. Following a three- or four-hour ferry ride that was sad, dirty, and unenjoyable, a small train— dragging itself along like a giant caterpillar on the plains—had dropped me off that same night in a lush city at the foot of Keşiş Mountain, which rose to the heavens like a dark wall.

Around the time, an "architectural" nationalism had taken hold among the learned youth in Istanbul. Everyone boasted of coming across the name of an old architect heretofore unheard of; articles discussed the significance and nobility of aged marble; poems praised the beauty of arches and pillars. Literary language teemed with the idiom of stonemasonry and carpentry. Architecture became the exclusive measure of Turkish civilization. Debates on architecture at times gave way to friendships, at times to enmities. The inner forces aroused by the national- ist consciousness had not yet been subdued by great disasters nor had they reached the level of sophistication they enjoy today. These forces were like fireworks; after drawing fluid lines in colorful bursts, they would fizzle out in the nighttime of life.

It was of course quite obvious what I would also be doing in Bursa around that time: visiting places of worship, studying ornamentation and tileworks, asking questions, thinking, taking notes, and in the end, returning to Istanbul endowed with a more or less fabricated yet new discovery about the history and matchless qualities of our architecture, bringing with me powerful documents gathered on site, for use in future debates. So that is in fact what I did...

In Çekirge, I visited Hüdavendigâr's tomb. I admired the illuminated Quranic calligraphy that the caretaker said was some three-hundred years old. In awe, I forced my hands to touch the prayer rug made of gazelle hide, an armored shirt and a helmet, the warrior-worthy artifacts that belonged to the Sultan, the tomb's hallowed dweller. Then I went to Muradiye. I sat thinking for a long time in the

1   Ahmed Haşim, "Gurebahane-i Laklakan," *Gurebahane-i Laklakan* (Istanbul: İlhami Fevzi Matbaası, 1928), 4–20.

tomb's multicolored tiled garden, breathing the air of red tulips and molten ruby carnations. Another day, I went to the Green Mosque. The green tiles that covered the walls of this place of worship gave off a mysterious underwater light. Bathing in that light, I sat face-to-face speaking with the mosque's caretaker for quite some time about ornamentation and engraving. "A strange thing," the caretaker said, "for a while now, visitors from Istanbul have been asking me the same questions as you." Like most of the turbaned custodians at the mosques visited by foreigners, this one, too, was smart, talkative, and clever. He spoke to me about the ceramic tiles unearthed then stolen when the mosque was being renovated under the supervision of a French architect named Parvillée, during Vefik Pasha's time. And if I really wanted to know more about this, he advised me to meet with *"Greguvar Bay,"* a friend of the Turks and a lover of Turkish art who had settled in Bursa fifty-six years ago. This was not the first time I had heard the name Gregoire Baille. He comes up in the writings of several French authors and littérateurs as a strange art-fanatic who chose to sequester himself in Bursa and to live and die among the roses and the tiles. I wrote to him requesting a visit and received his reply the same day. The next afternoon he would be waiting for me at his home in Setbaşı.

Baille received me in the shade of sycamore and mulberry trees. We lit our cigarettes, drank cups of coffee. A bit later, we were served raspberry sherbet on a silver tray. Drinking from crystal glasses that sparkled in the light, we cooled our throats with the iced, red and delightfully fragrant refreshments, and wiped our lips afterwards with brocaded silk napkins. While we spoke, now a veiled woman now a little girl in red pants carrying a tray full of berries would emerge from the garden's green depths ringing with nightingale songs and sparrow chirps. Madame Baille would say to each of them in fine Turkish, "Farewell... Come again whenever you like... Our garden is yours, too!"

I told Monsieur Baille that I came to meet him and to see his mansion which so many authors and poets had described in their books, immortalizing it in history and literature. The poor old man was pleased. I gathered from our conversation that Gregoire Baille was a kind of Pierre Loti, though without his genius. His estate was his only accomplishment. He was deeply pleased to hear that his good taste had a charm about it that aroused his guests' curiosity.

First, he showed me around the mansion. I noticed nothing worthy of consideration other than the colorful wall-piece made in Kütahya which imitated the tilework in Muradiye. Besides, Gregoire Baille didn't put too much value in his mansion. His life's masterpiece was *Gurebahane-i Laklakan,*[2] located in a remote corner of his garden. Gregoire Baille would later tell me the story behind the comical name. We left the mansion and strolled around every stretch of the garden, stopping while we talked. At every step, he provided details about a particular feature of his garden:

"You find the garden to be neglected, no? I wanted it to look unkempt and abandoned. I waited for years for the vines to grow like spiderwebs and cover all the trees. You must know how hard I worked to make the pines intimate human silhouettes, to give the tree branches this savage look, in short, to make the garden look like an untamed forest. My love of Turkish art has also taught me a love of 'nature.' To see nature in its pristine state takes a lot of hard work. A garden resembling a forest, is it possible to imagine a better form of beauty? The French 'Le Nôtre' style landscaping now seems hideous and meaningless to me."

Later, he explained to me the secret to his method of selecting each individual tree in the garden.

"Maybe you noticed—most of the trees surrounding us are willows and cypresses. I chose these types of trees so that my garden is suffused with the scents of death and the afterlife. This graveyard smell that you get is because of the leaves. No other nation understands cemeteries as beautifully as you do. Frenk cemeteries destroy death's sweet and severe beauty. In France, an icy air wanders about the tombstones, making them seem taller, their outlines sharper, as if the dead are waiting behind the doors of their ornate and indomitable tombs, eager with self-satisfied rage to attack the intrusive visitor. What one senses in the weighty silence of the Christian cemetery is this air of hostility almost. Yet in your cemeteries, a gentle smile lingers in the air, free and untroubled by the pressures of any worldly anxiety. In Muslim cemeteries, a person wants to stop and weep for all the dead—so endearing and close they are to life. You are right to build your cemeteries in the middle of the city. These are gardens where the trees produce the very fruits of pathos and reason that the living must taste. In my garden, I wanted to tame spring with autumn and give every season the bitter taste of reason by planting trees that exude the fragrances of a cemetery."

Stopping before one of the six short, cone shaped pine trees scattered across the garden, he said:

"I didn't plant these pines for no reason. Sadly, I don't know the name of their variety in Turkish, but I love them because they remind me of whirling Mevlevi

---

2   A type of hospice or aviary for birds (storks) that have been abandoned.—Trans.

dervishes. Look, doesn't this pine resemble the open robe of a dervish caught in his whirling? As I look at these pine trees, I imagine my garden as a large *sema-hane*[3] and the trees are Mevlevis—heedless, ecstatic—whirling from end to end, to the melodious songs of the nightingale."

We arrived in front of a small, dilapidated building with a few rooms lined side by side. Monsieur Gregoire Baille said:

"And here it is: Gurebahane-i Laklakan, my hospice for storks! You need to know that this corner of my garden is my own imagination turned reality. Inside these three run-down rooms surrounded by this garden corner, the waning days of my life are spent in dreams and tranquility. Whenever I can, I take refuge here. Even my wife does not accompany me. In this hermitage, my only friends are a few old and infirm storks. I don't know if you've seen them while visiting Bursa. In the middle of the Haffaflar Bazaar where they sell shoes, there is a public square. This square is a safe haven for wounded and sick animals. Storks with broken legs or wings, senile crows, blind or deaf owls, all are fed there, thanks to people's charity. There is an elderly person who is paid monthly by the merchants; he is possibly a hundred years old, as infirm as the storks he looks after, and every day he collects alms, buys tripe, cleans it and divides it among these wretched birds who have sought refuge in human mercy. I brought a few of the storks here from the Haffaflar Bazaar. At my age, am I any different from these old storks? This corner is a sanctuary for them as well as for myself. Here, we will live out our last days together and pass on; so, for this reason, I named this place Gurebahane-i Laklakan."

In fact, a stork with broken wings was dolefully wandering at a distance among the trees like a sick person in white hospital gowns; every so often it would stop and stare through the leaves and branches, fixing its red beady eyes at the blue patches of open sky.

Up three wooden steps, and we entered the first room. It was called, the "Sadi Room" and looked not unlike those vintage shops that sold Turkish artifacts. The wall facing the door was covered from floor to ceiling with tiles that featured in beautiful *talik* calligraphy a lost poem by Sadi that had been discovered by a British man in India. The tiles were also adorned with interlaced roses, leaves, and nightingales. The room almost seemed like a small, still life of a rose garden, a "Gülistan"[4] filled with the scents, songs, and shadows from the garden outside.

---

3   The room where dervishes perform their ceremonies in a Mevlevi lodge.—Trans.

4   Gülistan means "rose garden" or "flower garden," but it is also the name of Sadi's most famous work written in Persian in 1258. For more information see Franklin

Gregoire Baille spoke excitedly:

"I copied these from the most famous tiles. I had the calligrapher Hafız...[*][5] inscribe this poem by Sadi. This man is the last master calligrapher and illuminator living in Bursa. He works in a small shop at the market, creating his final masterpieces amidst the indifference of a generation that no longer understands beauty. He is old and hungry. He won't live long, you should go and meet him, console him."

Next, we moved to the "Rose and Nightingale Room." This room's walls, like the other, were also covered in ceramic tiles. Gregoire Baille explained to me why he named this room the "Rose and Nightingale Room":

"Ten or fifteen years ago, I had a discussion with a European visitor concerning the richness of Oriental languages. I had told this man that hundreds of Turkish adjectives and nouns derive from or include this single word, 'gül' for rose. As proof of my claim, I made the calligrapher add to this wall all the female names with the word 'gül' in them: Gülizar, Gülbû, Gülruh, and so forth..."

The names were inscribed elegantly inside colorful circles and interspersed among the motifs adorning the tiles. Like the "Sadi Room," the "Rose and Nightingale Room," too, was filled with handcrafted objects by Turkish artisans from the past: coral and ivory spoons, arrows, pitchers and bowls, silver mirrors, wood-burning grills, nargiles, sections of rugs, embroidered coverings, leatherbound books and more.

Gregoire Baille would pick each object with great care, hold it to the light, and offer myriad details, aesthetic and historical, about every one of its features. Each room took us an hour to visit. We eventually came to the third and last room: the "Vefik Pasha Room."

"The late Vefik Pasha was my friend. He left us so many mementos in Bursa. This is why people who love Turkish art and Bursa will cherish this vizier's memory. The Green Mosque which he helped reunite with the sunlight, is his gift to this city. Before the restoration, the mosque was in ruins, a trash heap. Inside, the floors were covered with dirt and rubble, and its dome was cracked everywhere, on the verge of collapse. Repairing it would be difficult. Vefik Pasha summoned the famous French architect Parvillée to Bursa for this job. Parvillée started by cleaning up the interior halls. It was after this first stage of the project that our eyes beheld the mosque's treasure—its green tilework. We were mesmerized. Next, iron

---

Lewis, "GOLESTĀN-E SAʿDI," *Encyclopaedia Iranica*, vol. XI, fasc. 1 (2001): 79–86, available online at http://www.iranicaonline.org/articles/golestan-e-sadi.—Trans.

5   Unfortunately, I don't remember his name.—Ahmed Haşim.

fasteners were used to stabilize the dome, and the cracks were fixed with cement. Quite an ancient place of worship, the Green Mosque looks as if new because of these repairs. Parvillée wrote a valuable work on Turkish architecture based on his research while restoring the Green Mosque. Copies of this work are quite rare. He gave me one as a gift, I protect it inside an old Turkish leatherbound volume. I believe there is also a copy in the Müzehane Library[6] in Istanbul. I purchased this room's ceiling from the ruins of an old Turkish mansion, and, oh, if you knew the trouble I went through, the sacrifices I had to make, to transport and reinstall it without dismantling it. Look... Despite the centuries, a flawless ceiling with its authentic colors, golden inlays, and etchings still intact! Isn't this, just by itself, the proof of civilization?"

Anticipating how tired his visitors would be by the time they arrived at Vefik Pasha's Room after touring and stopping around so many objects and architectural effects, Gregoire Baille had deep, soft sofas placed in front of the Turkish-style iron-grate windows that overlooked the garden and Nilüfer Plane in the distance. I threw myself onto one of these sofas and, closing my eyes, listened to the rustling leaves and rippling creek outside. Gregoire Baille's understanding of Turkish art, his love for it, like so many other Europeans, did not please me. I expressed my thoughts to him openly:

"Monsieur Baille, I don't know why, but the way you foreigners appreciate Turkish art and, more generally, Oriental art, has something injurious about it. When we were in the 'Rose and Nightingale Room,' you showed me an old washbasin cover, the small decorative indentations on the copper surface, and you seemed amazed, and, I must say, to an extent rather beyond excessive. In fact, more amazed than admiring. And your amazement at our works of art, it seems to us, is because you underestimate our intelligence. Not that we made something beautiful that is worthy of astonishment, but that it is astonishing that we made something beautiful! Three or four thousand years ago the pyramids were built, the columns of the Luxor Temple were erected, and all of these, made by people like us with two arms and two legs, but with knowledge and experience infinitely more primitive than our own... So what could possibly be so worthy of astonishment about a person making a fancy lace design on that copper lid today or three hundred years ago? Miracles used to happen in times when tools were primitive. But today it's not even a miracle that humans can fly! Something weighing a thousand kilos can be flown across a distance in one second that in the past a caravan couldn't even

_____

6   The Library of the Imperial Museum of Antiquities.—Ed.

travel in ten days. Perhaps the beaver's teeth shaving down a tree is worthy of astonishment, but certainly not people decorating copper panels!"

After reflecting on what I said for a while, my host responded to my objections in a manner so gentle that I wasn't sure was sincere.

"What you have enumerated as reasons not to be amazed, on the contrary, drives us to amazement. In this day and age when the human hand has abandoned its work to machines, it has also lost the skill to create beauty. Man-made machines have debased the human hand. Seeing the beautiful objects created by hands of bygone times, it is impossible not to marvel at what today's devalued human hand was once capable of doing. Ancient Egyptian, Babylonian, Chaldean, Greek, and Phoenician works, ancient Arab and Iranian artifacts—all of these amaze us. Our astonishment is because of the inaptitude of the human hand today. For this reason, our imagination remains unmoved, say, by the Panama Canal which we know was easily opened by giant machines, while we are excited and amazed by a simple lace embroidery made by the hands of a young woman two hundred years ago in Bursa, Konya, or Izmir."

After exchanging a few more thoughts on the matter, we left the Vefik Pasha Room. Night had fallen. Outside, on a covered terrace overlooking the garden, a large vintage tray rested on a low stool, waiting for us. Arranged in a circle on the tray were wooden spoons, and on the floor, surrounding the tray, were a few small cushions. Engraved on a marble plaque almost buried among the leaves was the date of the evening that Pierre Loti had joined the iftar, breaking fast with the imams of the Green Mosque at this exact table. Madam Baille had tea prepared for us under a pergola surrounded in all sides with rose bushes near Gurebahane-i Laklakan. Reclined on old thatched chairs, we remained silent, sipping the delicious Chinese tea, yielding to the evening hues deepening around us and the blue green sky in a corner of which a delicate crescent moon had taken shape.

In the distance we could hear water from a stream and the call to prayer; the air was filled with familial smells carried by the evening smoke. Bats fluttered so close they could almost touch us. Now, everywhere around the garden, steeped in its otherworldly and overpowering scents, the green Mevlevis whirled all the more freely and ecstatically.

After leaving Bursa, I didn't hear Gregoire Baille mentioned in conversation again. I learned much later that he passed away in Bursa.

Translated by Micah A. Hughes and Aron Aji

A READER

Authors' Biographies

Ahmed Haşim (1884–1933)

Ahmed Haşim was a poet, essayist, and satirist whose major writings were published in *Servet-i Fünun*, as well as other leading literary periodicals of the time. Acknowledged as a symbolist and individualist, he advocated against political and didactic approaches to literature and art.

Ahmed Midhat (1844–1912)

Highly prolific and popular novelist and publisher of several important periodicals, Ahmed Midhat is also known for his 1889 travelogue, *Avrupa'da Bir Cevelan* (A Journey in Europe), which is a documentary and a commentary of European culture and society of the time.

Celal Esad [Arseven] (1875–1971)

One the first art historians of Turkey, Celal Esad Arseven played an instrumental role in defining "Turkish" art and architecture. His extensive writings span from Byzantine to late Ottoman art and architecture, to music. He was a publisher of the satire journal *Kalem*.

Ebüzziya Mehmed Tevfik (1848–1913)

Prominent editor and journalist, Ebüzziya Mehmed Tevfik wrote in the leading periodicals of the time. He published *İbret* with Namık Kemal and founded the journal *Mecmua-ı Ebüzziya*. He also compiled *Numune-i Edebiyyat-ı Osmaniyye*, an anthology of Ottoman literature, and a dictionary, *Lügat-ı Ebüzziya*.

Ercümend Ekrem [Talu] (1888–1956)

Satirist, novelist, and journalist, Ercümend Ekrem made his reputation by accounts of Istanbul in the style of seventeenth-century Ottoman traveler Evliya Çelebi. He published a series of popular adventure books around two characters, Meşhedi Cafer and Torik Necmi.

Fatma Aliye [Topuz] (1832–1936)

One of the first woman novelists of Turkish literature, Fatma Aliye began her literary career with translations and essays, which she signed as "A Woman." She wrote her first novel, *Hayal ve Hakikat* (Imagination and Reality), in collaboration with her tutor Ahmed Midhat.

Halid Ziya [Uşaklıgil] (1866–1945)

The novelist *par excellence* of his time, Halid Ziya started his literary career by translating novels, plays, and poems from French. He published his *Mai ve Siyah* (Blue and Black) as a serial in *Servet-i Fünun* during Tevfik Fikret's tenure. *Aşk-ı Memnu* (Forbidden Love) is widely recognized as an Ottoman classic.

Halide Edib [Adıvar] (1884–1964)

Eminent novelist Halide Edib also wrote essays, travelogues, and memoirs. A strong political voice, she joined the Kemalist forces and served in different capacities during the War of Independence. This war became the focus and the background of her many novels. Her now classic *The Clown and His Daughter (Sinekli Bakkal)* was first published in English.

Ismayıl Hakkı [İsmail Hakkı Baltacıoğlu] (1886–1978)

Essayist and pedagogue Ismayıl Hakkı Baltacıoğlu's wide repertory of interests included sociology, literature, history, and art. He founded and edited the highly influential *Yeni Adam*, a critical weekly that focused on culture, literature, and arts.

İzzet Melih [Devrim] (1887–1966)

Poet, novelist, essayist, and playwright. He is best known for his novel *Sermed*, which was translated into French with a foreword by Pierre Loti.

Namık Kemal (1840–1888)

Novelist, poet, playwright, essayist, and critic, renown for his oppositional politics expressed through a fiery style and for his long-lasting influence on Turkish intelligentsia. Namık Kemal is credited for being the author of the first modern novel in Turkish, titled *İntibah* (Rebirth). He served as one of the editors of the dissentious periodical *İbret* (1870–73).

Nâzım Hikmet [Ran] (1902–1963)

Nâzım Hikmet is globally the best known Turkish poet, whose poems have been translated into more than fifty languages. Due to his Marxist beliefs, he spent many years in prison in Turkey and was forced to live in exile in the Soviet Union after 1951. Among his best known long epic poems are *Human Landscapes* and *The Epic of Sheikh Bedreddin*.

Ömer Lütfi (1871–1939)

Novelist, short story writer, and essayist, Ömer Lütfi published his work in the well-circulated periodicals of his time, among them *İkdam* and *Servet-i Fünun*.

Ömer Seyfeddin (1884–1920)

Short story writer Ömer Seyfeddin argued for the purification of the Turkish language in support of his Turkist ideology and in order to make literature accessible to a wide readership. He was an advocate for national values and social cricism.

Sabiha Sertel (1895–1968)

Sabiha Sertel was among the early Turkish women journalists. Her career developed in collaboration with that of her husband, Zekeriya Sertel. Together, they published *Resimli Ay* and later *Tan,* both of which featured her articles on the condition of women, social inequalities, and working class struggles. In addition to her studies on Tevfik Fikret, she is best known for *The Struggle for Modern Turkey* (*Roman Gibi*), her posthumously published memoirs. She died in Baku in exile.

Şevket Süreyya [Aydemir] (1897–1976)

Biographer, non-fiction writer, novelist, and economist. Şevket Süreyya Aydemir was one of the publishers of *Kadro*, a journal charged to shape the ideology of the Turkish Republic. He is the author of several biographies of leading political figures, among them Ataturk and Enver Pasha. His autobiographical *Suyu Arayan Adam* (A Man in Seach of Water) is a lucid account of historically turbulent times.

Tevfik Fikret (1867–1915)

Poet and essayist, Tevfik Fikret became the editor-in-chief of *Servet-i Fünun* in 1896. During his tenure, *Servet-i Fünun* became the center of an avant-garde literary movement, known as Edebiyat-ı Cedide (The New Literature). Tevfik Fikret raised a unique political voice opposing the late Ottoman regime, under both Abdülhamid II and the Young Turks.

Zekeriya Sertel (1890–1980)

Parallel to his collaborative publishing career with his wife Sabiha Sertel, Zekeriya Sertel worked on *Hayat Ansiklopedisi,* a ten-volume encyclopedia. He has written two books on the life of Nâzım Hikmet and one on the anti-fascist and oppositional stand of *Tan* to the one-party regime. Due to their political activism, Zekeriya and Sabiha Sertel lived many years in exile.

Historical Periodicals

İbret (1870–1873, intermittently)

Published during Sultan Abdülaziz's autocratic regime, the political journal served as the organ of New Ottomans, who advocated a constitutional monarchy. Ebüzziya Tevfik and Namık Kemal as its contributing editors and principal writers, *İbret* maintained a relentless voice of opposition for 132 issues, until its closure by the government and and the exiling of its writers.

Mecmua-i Ebüzziya (1880–1912)

Mecmua-i Ebüzziya was published by Ebüzziya Mehmed Tevfik during the years of strict censorship under Abdülhamid II. With a special permit stipulating that it would not cover current politics, the journal issued articles on literature, arts, and sciences. Among its notable authors, Namık Kemal and Ahmed Midhat stand out. The journal also published translations of Voltaire, J.J. Rousseau, and Émile Zola.

Servet-i Fünun (1891–1944)

Especially after Tevfik Fikret was appointed as its literature editor, *Servet-i Fünun* became an influential journal of a series of literary movements, starting with Edebiyat-ı Cedide (The New Literature), and including Milli Edebiyat (National Literature), and Yeni Meşaleciler (The New Torchbearers). Most notably, it published poems, short stories, and serialized novels by leading writers.

Sabah (1876–1922, 1919–22 as Peyam-i Sabah)

With one of the longest publication histories among the periodicals of its time, *Sabah* was committed to wide accessibility. Among its authors were Ahmed Midhat, Fatma Aliye, and Halid Ziya. It covered a wide range of subjects, including politics, literary movements, medicine, maritime history, as well as current affairs such as wars, epidemics, and public uprisals. Its end was marked by the lynching of Ali Kemal, its editor-in-chief at the time, known for his criticism of the Kemalist movement.

Tarîk (1919)

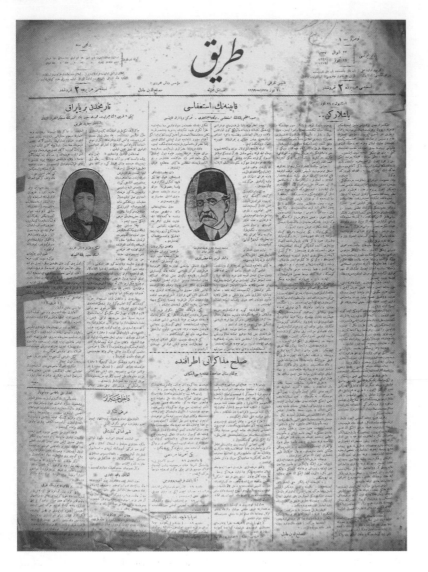

A short-lived daily newspaper.

İkdam (1894–1961)

Acknowledged as the newspaper with the longest history in Turkey, its name shifted from *İkdam* to *Yeni İkdam*, *İktihâm*, *İkdam*, *Halk Gazetesi*, *İkdam*, *Sabah Postası*, *İkdam*, and *Gece Postası*. It is credited for using correspondent reporters in different cities during the Hamidian regime. A pioneer in war reporting, *İkdam* is known for its coverage of the Turkish War of Independence. It followed a consistent Turkic ideology. Ahmed Midhat, Fatma Aliye, Halid Ziya, and Abdurrahman Şeref were among its contributors.

Resimli Ay (1924–1931, intermittently)

Edited by the husband and wife team, Sabiha Sertel and Zekeriya Sertel, *Resimli Ay* was a literary journal with a socialist bent which also delved into popular culture. Nâzım Hikmet joined its cadres in 1929 and edited a notable special issue, titled, "Putları Yıkıyoruz" (We Are Destroying the Idols) aiming to discredit authors he labeled as old-guard idols, including Yakup Kadri and Ahmed Haşim.

Kadro (1932–1935)

Dedicated to crystallize the principles of the Turkish Republican ideology, this semi-offical journal published on a wide spectrum of topics, ranging from economic policy to literary criticism by such writers as Şevket Süreyya, Falih Rıfkı, and Yakup Kadri.

Darülfünun İlahiyat Fakültesi Mecmuası (1925–1933)

Published by the School of Theology of Istanbul University, this academic journal focused on religious, social, historical, philosophical, and cultural topics. It maintained a distance from current politics.

İçtihad (1904–1932)

Toute œuvre de pensée
est reçue
et insérée volontiers

Abonnement annuel: 13 Fr.

L'abonnement
u un An
COMPREND 12 NUMÉROS

IDJTIHAD

LIBRE EXAMEN

Revue sociale et littéraire de l'Orient et de l'Occident

(Paraissant mensuellement)

RÉDACTION
et
DIRECTION
Rue MOUSKy, Caire

TÉLÉPHONE

Adresse télégraphique :
IDJTIHAD, CAIRE

IIme ANNÉE — N° 5 — Janvier 1907

Lettres sur L'ISlam

II

La cité islamique.-- Le Gouvernemeut.

J'ai indiqué dans ma première lettre une raison importante pour laquelle l'Islam avait laissé péricliter son pouvoir temporel : parce qu'il n'a pas su l'asseoir sur les bases du respect des nationalités conquises.

S'il a agi de la sorte, c,est qu'il avait évidemment un idéal où le concept de nationalités distinctes, quoique professant une même religion, n'existait pas. Voyons donc dans ses grandes ligus ce qu'cot cet idéal qu'on a essayé de réaliser: comment se conçoit en un mot la Cité islamique.

L'Islam, dans la pensée de ses fondateurs, est plus qu'une religion: c'est une Cité nouvelle, avec ses lois cultuelles -plus que religieuses-, sociales -plus qu'indivi-duelles-, théocratiques-plus que politiques.

Dieu a donné la vérité à son Envoyé. L'obéissance la plus absolue est d'obligation envers Dieu, envers son Envoyé et envers ses successeurs,les Califes. Obéissance non seulement dans le domaine individuel des prescriptions religieuses, mais aussi dans le domaine des prescriptions sociales et politiques , inséparables des premières . Le Calife ne peut rien changer à la loi, mais il a autorité pour l'interpréter et pour l'appliquer en dernier ressort . La Vérité apportée par Mahomet est la Vérité absolue et comme telle,tout le monde doit -ou devrait- s'y soumettre .

Ceux qui s'y sonmettent sont dans l'Islam (C'est le sens même du mot)'. Ceux qui ne s'y soumettent pas sont invités à le faire et la guerre doit leur être déclarée " jusqu'à ce que tout le monde soit devenu musulman " dit le texte.

Ce texte ajoute " on paye la Capitation". Ce fut la première atténuation à la rigueur de l'idée musulmane . On aurait pu tuer ou expulser les non musulmans comme furent tués ou expulsés les Juifs du Hedjàz; mais c'eût été difficile de mettre à mort ou chasser la population presque

---

İçtihad, a journal specializing in science, politics, and literature, was published in Geneva, Cairo, and Istanbul. Tevfik Fikret, Ömer Seyfeddin, Ahmed Haşim, and Halide Edib were among its contributors. Because of its support of Westernization, the journal was a frequent target of attack by both Islamists and Turkists.

Kalem (1908–1911)

Recognized as a pioneer of modern Turkish caricature and political satire journalism, *Kalem* targeted issues ranging from Westernization to gender equality, daily life, and politics. Art historian Celal Esad was one of its founders.

İfham (1912–13, 1919–20)

Turanist ideology dominated the first period of *İfham*, while the second period was charaterized by its support of the National Struggle that led to the foundation of the Turkish Republic. Ömer Seyfeddin, Halide Edib, Ismayıl Hakkı, Sabiha Sertel and Zekeriya Sertel were among its contributors.

Index